JUNK

Digging Through America's
Love Affair with Stuff

ALISON STEWART

CHICAGO
REVIEW
PRESS

First edition
Published by Chicago Review Press Incorporated
814 North Franklin Street
Chicago, Illinois 60610
ISBN 978-1-61373-055-3

Library of Congress Cataloging-in-Publication Data
Is available from the Library of Congress.

Interior design: Nord Compo

Printed in the United States of America
5 4 3 2 1

CONTENTS

———————

INTRODUCTION

"Put it in the basement."

EVERYONE IN OUR FAMILY said those words at least two or three times a year. Maybe more. OK, definitely more. And that was over a period of nearly fifty years.

For me, it started with high school textbooks. Just weeks after I graduated, my parents moved. They packed up twenty-seven years of their life, and *my* books, and sent it all about six exits down the New Jersey Turnpike and into a spacious brick home in a leafy small town. I went off to Brown and my stuff went to Princeton. That was 1984.

When I made return trips home from college my folks would ask me if I wanted to take any of my texts with me. I'd always told my parents, *Not right now*, but I assured them I would get the books out of the basement soon.

I am not sure why I wanted to keep those books. Somewhere in my mind I assumed I'd need to refer to Milton's *Paradise Lost* at some point in my post-collegiate life. I also stashed away, among other things, some faux Wedgewood embossed low-ball glasses that belonged to my grandmother. She used them for sweet tea. I planned on using them for cocktails.

Over the course of the next ten years I used my parents' basement as a personal storage space. I was living in an apartment the size of a goldfish aquarium, so Mom and Dad kept my books and the newly anointed barware in the basement alongside my Michael Jackson *Bad* LP—as in long-playing record, for those readers born after the O. J. Simpson car chase. Of course that twelve-inch plastic disc would be valuable one day. I am not sure to whom I thought I might sell it, but hey, you never know. I really had planned to learn how to hawk things on eBay rather than just bidding.

My sister had plenty of stuff in my parents' basement, too. She left behind a few yearbooks and a wedding dress. Her old dollhouse was saved for her daughters to enjoy one day. They both now have graduate degrees. Mostly, the basement was a place to stuff our stuff. We, everyone in my family, would put things down there that we believed we would get to one day, possibly need one day, or possibly give away one day.

One day.

One day came and went a thousand times over while everything in the basement stayed put until 2012. That was the year my sister and I had to clean out our late parents' home to sell it. I knew it would be difficult to sift through their things and relive so many memories while being confronted with the fact that they were no longer around to remember with us. After the flower arrangements and funerals, the thank-you notes and the tears, there was a practical matter at hand: the house. Which meant, *the basement.*

The first days of the clean out were fairly easy. Mom and Dad both had great taste in clothes, so bags and bags of suits, shoes, purses, and ties went to charitable groups like Dress for Success and The Clothes Closet for college seniors who can't afford new interview suits. Most of the sheets and towels went to shelters set up after Hurricane Sandy. Boxes of books were donated, all except for my great grandfather's Harvard Classics; I'd had my eye on those since I was eleven.

After the initial flurry of activity, my sister and I finally acknowledged the elephant in the room—or rather, the elephant that was the basement. It had been an unspoken issue from day one. Maybe we thought it would go away if we didn't talk about it. When getting a face full of the reality of your parents' death, on some level these kinds of unreasonable thoughts seem plausible.

Walking through the house you'd never know about the subterranean level. The first two floors were wide-open spaces, walls painted a soft white with eggshell finish. There weren't a lot of decorations or tchotchkes, just a few simple things like a hand-carved sailboat. On the walls there were paintings by R. C. Gorman depicting serene Native American women, seated and wrapped in colorful blankets. The kitchen was white. Completely white: Counters. Appliances. Floors. White floors in a kitchen that my mother mopped herself well into her eighties. The couches in the living room and family room were white too. It was all so very tasteful and orderly. A stranger would never know what lurked below.

I didn't like going into the basement. Even walking by the door gave me the creeps. For some reason I began to equate it with the attic crawl space in the scene in *The Sixth Sense* when the little kid who sees dead people gets pulled in and roughed up by a pissed-off ghost. When I walked past the basement on the way to the powder room, I kept my eyes focused straight ahead.

This was a fairly recent phobia for me. When I was younger, I loved going down there to see if my Nancy Drew books were still stacked in a corner or to sift through old photos of the family in Mexico circa 1971. But over time the basement stopped being a family museum and became a family mausoleum. It wasn't a hoarding situation. Or a garbage situation. It was a junk situation.

———————

Day one. Game face on. I'd psyched myself up. It was going to be a long slog. I would eat the previously mentioned elephant one bite at a time. I flicked on the light switch just inside the door and walked down the curved stairwell and arrived at the final landing and looked around. And then I ran back up.

My second approach was more successful. I created a new paradigm: this was my job. I was an executor of an estate, being paid to deal with all matters. I had a time frame to get this done, so I better get to it. But first I'd need tools and backup.

I went to one of those giant home improvement barns and walked the aisles looking for supplies. I wasn't exactly sure what I would need so I went with my gut. I bought bags—Ziploc, contractor, and recycling. Rope. Labels. Storage bins. More bags. Duct tape. Plastic gloves. Flashlights. I am surprised I wasn't stopped and questioned at checkout about my motives given that my shopping cart would have fulfilled the punch list of a first-time abductor.

Once I assembled all my "tools" I felt I was ready. All I needed was a support team. My sister and my friend Silvia were on board. My sister lived out of state, so we agreed to meet once a month for a long weekend of cleaning out until the basement was barren. In between our intensive weekend sessions Silvia and I would work on our own.

All three of us were at the first session. Our spirits were good for the first eight hours. There were some big laughs. I found my mother's charge card for the now defunct Bambergers department store, only it wasn't any old credit card: across the top it said HOME-MAKER'S CARD. Try giving out one of those in 2015. There were other finds worthy of a time capsule. A billfold with francs and lira. A toy bank that looked like a one-foot crayon. A *Life* magazine from the year I was born. In one day we filled ten bags full of giveaways and another ten full of trash, and had made a few piles that weren't quite identifiable yet. After day one, full of warm fuzzies, tears, and a few "Oh, wow" moments, we walked back up the stairs satisfied. We went out to dinner, had some wine, and felt like we were on our way.

The next morning we returned, flicked on the lights, walked energetically down the stairs, and stopped cold. The place looked the same. The *same.* Was this a cruel joke? Had someone put back everything we removed? Were we starring in the sequel to the movie *Groundhog Day*? We'd imagined a dramatic before and after reveal. It was still a before and before scene. How was it possible that the area looked like it had twenty-four hours earlier given that three grown women hyped-up on caffeine and adrenaline had purged or stored anything we'd put our hands on? How?

Though at that first glance it appeared we had not made a single dent, we had. A teeny, tiny little dent. A ping, really. It was then that I realized I was at the first stage of the Kübler-Ross DABDA grief model. It was the big *D*. I was in denial. Somehow I'd decided that this project wasn't so bad and that it wouldn't take long to, you know, tidy up. Given what was in front of me, stage one was over almost as soon as it began. It didn't take me long to move right through the denial to the next phase, that *A*.

Anger. Why was there all this stuff? What the hell were we going to do? Why did they have to die anyway? How were we going to do this? My sister expressed it best when she pulled out an enormous bag of used Christmas bows and proceeded to shout, "Really, Mother? *Really?*" But for my mom, a child of the Great Depression, a shiny Christmas bow was an enormous luxury and not something to toss in the trash. I think she physically could not throw one away. And so, she didn't. The bows made sense to me—however, the cheap water glass from my prom with a blue stamp that read "G.R.H.S, 'We've Got Tonight' May 27, 1983," did not. The theme was the name of a soft-rock Bob Seger song. As an adult I realized it was a wholly inappropriate theme song for hormonal teenagers, given the lyrics spelled out the rationale for a one-night stand. *(We've got tonight, who needs tomorrow? We've got tonight babe, why don't you stay?)*

My anger subsided quickly when I realized so much of this junk was the history of our family. We found my sister's report cards from fifth grade. In 1966 she was a very good student and "was learning to become gracious about winning." Both are still true for her at age fifty-nine. I found boxes and boxes of VHS tapes my parents had recorded of my newscasts. We found an autographed book of poetry by Langston Hughes that my mother received when she was a teenager. We found a button from the 1963 March on Washington when Dr. King gave his "I Have a Dream" speech. We recovered the letter my grandfather wrote to our great-grandfather asking for my grandmother's hand in marriage. All this junk was the unfortunate byproduct of a lot of love.

The anger melted into the next stage, bargaining, and we started a set of boxes called "Family Hold" to put in a storage unit. Family Hold ranged from clothing to dishware, anything that brought up the emotions tied to family. There was one rule about Family Hold to insure things ran smoothly and relatively tear-free: do not look at pictures. Pictures could derail a whole day. Pictures could send you into an emotional spiral that resulted in the fetal position and worse, in my eyes as the taskmaster, ineffectiveness. As long as photos were avoided and put somewhere safe, we would be able to forge ahead.

And we did. Days turned into weeks that turned into months. No amount of bargaining was going to get the job done, and that was when the second *D*—depression—set in. Cleaning out the basement felt like a Sisyphean task.

When we walked into the house for the umpteenth time, I realized that the leaves had begun to fall. We'd been at this for so long our shorts and T-shirts had been replaced by sweaters and down vests. We were into a whole new weather pattern and the basement was still, well, the basement. Acceptance, that final *A*, arrived around the same time as the first blast of cold, crisp air. I knew it in my bones. This task was beyond me, Silvia, my sister, or any configuration of us. We needed professional help.

——————

"How may we help you have a stress-free day?" greeted the booker for College Hunks Hauling Junk. I clamped my lips together to keep myself from blurting out something cynical or rude and simply told them I'd like to make an appointment. Hey, stress-free? I'm in. I'd never even heard of this company that employs strong college boys to move stuff. Then one day while driving back from yet another hardware store supply run, I saw one of the company's big orange trucks painted with a cartoon of a superhero-like college boy carrying brimming boxes. I memorized the 1-888 number.

"What is it you'd like to haul away?"

It was a simple question, but at the moment I wasn't sure whether or not to tell the truth. I was reminded of the time I was at a little airport with very small planes. I watched as women getting their boarding passes twitched when the counter agent asked their weight so that the planes could be evenly balanced. Their facial expressions were easy to read: lie and go down in a death spiral because the plane was lopsided or tell the truth and have their significant other give them the eye the next time they ordered dessert. I could have lied about the size of my haul and said it wasn't so much, just some knickknacks and old furniture.

Instead, I opted for the truth. "About fifty years of life."

And so began a short but intense relationship with John and his college hunks hauling junk. The first visit was all business. He explained the pricing policy to me: "We price according to how much of the truck we fill."

"It is going to be the whole truck," I said.

"OK then."

John was a tall, thin, sandy-haired fellow who spoke with the energetic gusto of a Dale Carnegie graduate. Over time I learned he had been a political science major in college but grew disillusioned with our government. He just wanted to do work that made a difference. He explained how a portion of the company's profits go toward college scholarships. He proudly told me one College Hunks tale: "There's a great story about one of our trucks pulling up to a shelter with two beds, a chair, and a table just as a family whose home had been flooded arrived. They had someplace they could move into but no furniture. Our guys didn't even take it off the truck. It went straight to the people in need." I don't know if it was apocryphal or a happy accident, but John sure believed it.

His two helpers introduced themselves, offering firm handshakes and big smiles. They wore khaki pants and orange-and-green polo shirts. I offered nervous warnings as we approached the basement.

"There's a lot of weird stuff down here." They just smiled.

"I marked it off in zones. We can just tackle zone one today."

More smiles.

"A lot of it is my stuff, too . . ."

As we walked downstairs they didn't flinch. All John said was, "Yes, this is definitely the whole truck." He looked over his shoulder to his junior hunks and shouted, "We need boxes and bags!" much like the way a TV surgeon asks a nurse for the scalpel, stat!

I marveled at the good nature of these buff young bros. No matter how many times I threw out little apologetic qualifiers, "Sorry about that pile" or "Bet you've never seen that many nonworking pens," the fellas just smiled and kept working. Their boss must teach them not to crack. I would not want to play poker with any of those guys. Only once did I get a whiff of *What the fuck?* from any of the workers. He asked shyly, "Ma'am, what is this exactly?" He quickly followed up with, "I'm just trying to figure out where to put it on the truck." He was truly stumped, as was I for a moment. In his hands he held a two-piece, foot-tall ceramic black cat with an electrical cord coming out the back. The head came off at the neck and inside was a mesh disc sectioned into six pie-shaped pieces. The bottom half was empty. It was heavy. I had to do a little mental detective work searching my memory for clues. I could visualize it in my childhood home and I was reminded of two smells: cat box smell and trying to cover cat box smell. And I also recalled our cat Midnight not liking the thing very much. She was black, too, and would paw at the ceramic version of herself. It hit me: it was some sort of air freshener that looked like an Egyptian cat statue.

After I figured all of this out, I answered the guy. "I don't know."

He accepted this and put it in a box, I guess for later inspection. It was one of many white lies I would tell during this process. There are white lies you tell to deceive and there are white lies you tell to survive. I was in survival mode.

Old dishes were wrapped and boxed. Good furniture was put to the side to go into the truck last. They were so good and so fast I had to retrieve a working cordless phone that had been swooped up in the process. It wasn't their fault. It was in the zone, so it was fair game.

I watched as John and company backed down the driveway in a truck filled with furniture stacked so high you could see one lone chair leg sticking up like a flagpole. I took a deep breath and went back to the basement, hoping to see a difference, unlike my earlier amateur attempts. I exhaled with relief when I could see roughly a quarter of the basement floor. I was sold on using pros. I booked them four more times in the next few months. After their last visit I sent my twenty-five-year-old niece a picture of a nearly empty basement and she texted me back, "A Christmas miracle!"

There was one wrinkle. College Hunks could not take anything remotely regarded as hazardous and that included paint cans that had been hiding in a closet in the basement. For that I had to find someone who liked cash and would carry out anything.

Let's call him Zephyr, which means strong wind. It isn't really that far off his real name, or at least the name he gave me. Big, burly, and bald, Zephyr was as polite and straightforward as the corporate guys, but a lot more talkative.

"Bet you can't guess what my favorite channel is? Lifetime. *Lifetime!* I just love those movies." He laughed at the ridiculousness of a two-hundred-plus-pound man curled up on a couch taking in the plucky damsel in distress movie of the week starring a three-named former child star. He looked a bit like the genie from *Aladdin* and he promised to grant my wish that this would all finally go away. I'd been told he was a character and he did not disappoint. As he walked around the property preparing an estimate in his head, he dispensed advice.

"Hold out for the best offer you can—houses fly out of this neighborhood."

"You don't have to paint that whole back, just touch it up!"

"New roof? Aw, bad move. It ain't your house much longer."

"These people looking for houses want the inside clean. Crazy clean."

For the most part the house was empty except for the few Family Hold boxes headed for storage. The garage somehow had become a bit of a dumping ground for those one or two things we just couldn't seem to throw or give away because they could be useful to someone, somewhere. One or two things had grown to one or two piles.

Zephyr surveyed what was left, which was mostly a garage full of tools and small electrical equipment. I could tell he was calculating in his mind whether to charge us to take the things away or give us a little cash for the items he thought he could still sell. With all the head shaking going on, I could tell it was going to be the former. He wanted me to know he was fair.

"I met an old man. He loved his chair. Wanted to move it into his retirement home. Someone wanted to charge him five hundred dollars to move it. That ain't right. I did it for seventy-five dollars; drove it into NYC and when I got there, he was so grateful he made me lunch." When he went into the garage for a final look-see, I turned to my sister and asked what she thought about him. "I stopped listening after a while." The she deadpanned, "I do remember that he held the secret to life."

I learned a lot about his life by the end of the meeting. He was originally from Louisiana. We discovered we both like Steve Harvey and we both had small children. He said he learned his lesson from his first marriage and lets his wife be the boss. He believed in putting people to work and he assembled small crews for each job. "Don't ask me for money. I won't give it to you. I will give you a job and help you earn something. Anyone can work hard, but a lot of guys who want to work hard can't get anyone to hire them. I will, if they promise to work hard." That explained the somewhat dodgy-looking smoke-soaked men who arrived to clean out the garage the next day. They definitely weren't pros, as evidenced by the busted molding at the base of one doorway. And they were very curious.

"Yo, lady, you live here?"

"No. My parents did."

"How much you gonna sell for?"

"I'm not sure."

"A lot, I bet."

"Yeah, ah, could you watch the door frame?"

Zephyr separated out the items that could be of use to someone else. He said he donates what he can, and he seemed to have specific people in mind, not charities. In some ways he was a refreshing alternative to the superslick experts. He was keeping it real. This was junk. It wasn't pretty to remove. The corporate chains let you know what they do with your items. Zephyr seemed to operate with a "don't ask, don't tell" policy. I never asked what became of the paint cans, and he never told me. Eight hundred dollars later, the place was spotless.

The day we packed up the few remaining family hold boxes to go to storage, it was snowing.

Sitting on a shelf was a box neatly labeled "Pieces of string too short to tie things with." Inside the box? Many short pieces of strings much too short to tie up anything. Then there was a bazooka, as in the gun, not gum, found in the pantry, the baggie full of dusty silk flowers, and half of a plastic Easter egg found on the basement floor. I heard these tales from average people, not hoarders or collectors, but regular folks who, when pressed, would fess up to owning many discarded articles of little use. You know, junk.

What qualifies as junk is subjective. One of the first uses of a now famous phrase equating something useless to something spectacular dates back to 1860. In *Popular Tales of the West Highlands* John Francis Campbell makes the case for collecting stories and fairy tales even though others might think it silly.

> Practical men may despise the tales, earnest men condemn them as lies, some even consider them wicked; one refused to write any more for a whole estate; my best friend says they are all "blethers." But one man's rubbish may be another's treasure; and what is the standard of value in such a pursuit as this?

"One man's trash is another man's treasure" is the battle cry for the true junk warrior.

Each generation has a different relationship with the items that find their way into a life. Just try to convince a child of the Depression that using a department store bag once is the right thing to do. Their children, the Baby Boomers (seventy-six million of them), were taught to buy, buy, buy and that something new is almost always better. Practically speaking, during their lifetime it did become cheaper to buy new than to fix the old. Their children, the Millennials (eighty million of them), live in a world where a new mp3 player, smartphone, or e-reader is released biannually. There are homes in America where you can find three generations of families with four different generations of iPad under one roof. George Carlin said it best when he joked, "That's all your house is: a place to keep your stuff. . . . A house is just a pile of stuff with a cover on it. . . . That's what your house is, a place to keep your stuff while you go out and get more stuff."

Economist Thorstein Veblen first presented the idea of conspicuous consumption in the 1890s, and a century later a few resourceful entrepreneurs tackled the problem of what to do with all that has been conspicuously consumed. After the "go-go greedy" 1980s, the next decade became the "What the hell do we do with all this stuff?" '90s. The answer: Self storage is now a $24 billion industry. Junk removal became a viable, respectable, corporate enterprise. National franchises—The Junk Kings,

College Hunks Hauling Junk, and the seminal 1-800-Got-Junk—popped up across the country. The growth of this industry has been swift. 1-800-Got-Junk started with a $700 pickup truck. In 1999, it made $1 million. In 2011, the company earned $91.5 million.

Three of the highest rated cable television shows today are about storing junk (*Storage Wars*), selling junk (*Pawn Stars*), and finding junk (*American Pickers*). There's a genre of women's magazine devoted entirely to dealing with stuff. *Getting Organized* magazine's tagline is "Treat yourself to some sanity." *Better Homes and Gardens*, with a readership of thirty-five million, publishes an extra edition twice a year simply called *Storage*. And ironically, when looking for magazines about clutter, I Googled "magazine clutter" and got 50,600,000 results, and most dealt with how to avoid drowning in periodicals—even the ones about how to de-junk your life.

Someone wrote that only in America do we leave cars worth thousands of dollars in the driveway and put our useless junk in the garage. Other countries do treat their junk differently, but some developed nations like Japan are seeing the problem, too. Where you can buy stuff, people do. However, in a place like Cuba, junk doesn't often become an issue because new things rarely make it into the country—everything must be reused. While visiting Havana, I was amazed at how our host cooked dinner for us. He pulled out a beat-up, wrought iron chair missing a seat. In its place sat a loosely woven metal basket full of charcoal. It was his version of a Weber Kettle Grill, and it worked great!

He upcycled out of necessity, but these days many people are starting to do so out of a concern for the environment. The books *The Story of Stuff: The Impact of Overconsumption on the Planet, Our Communities, and Our Health—and How We Can Make It Better* and *Garbage Land* offer earnest and frightening looks at the dangers of too many material goods.

For me, junk became a very personal issue—one that led to this book. Looking back, if I could have poured a truckload of cement into that basement, filled the room to the ceiling, and claimed I had no idea what happened, I would have done so. It took me eight months to clean out that house. Junk removal took over my life.

This clean-out process left me with so many questions. Why do people hold on to junk? Are we hardwired for it like some animals? And how did removing junk, storing it, and organizing it become million-dollar industries? And what qualifies as junk anyway? These questions led me to spend nearly two years on the junk research trail, from yard sales to McMansions to deserts. The result is a who, what, where, when, and why of junk—not necessarily in that order, because, as I discovered, junk knows no order.

A couple of notes. Because stuff is personal and many nice people let me invade their space, some of the names have been changed out of respect for their privacy. I've noted the changes with an asterisk. But they are all real—boy, are they real—and they have the junk to prove it. All the junk removal ride alongs and interviews were conducted during the busy spring-cleaning season, from May 2014 to August 2014. The Q&As are edited for clarity and to stay on topic because, frankly, I can be chatty during an interview.

And, yes, you will see the word *junk* a lot in this book. A lot. And as tempting as it may be, I do not suggest you make a game out of taking a drink every time you read the word. It would be very bad for your liver.

I

WHAT IS IT?

1

THE 411 ON JUNK

JUNK. CHAFF. DROSS. Trash. Stuff. Garbage. Rubbish. Debris. Para-
phernalia. Throwaways. Collectibles. Gimcrack. Gear. Trappings.
Knickknacks. Thingamabobs and thingamajigs. Junk seems to share
the quality of indefinability with another famously (or infamously)
difficult object to identify. As Supreme Court Justice Potter Stewart said, not about junk but about obscene hard-core pornography,
"I shall not today attempt to further define the kinds of material
I understand to be embraced by that shorthand description; and
perhaps I could never succeed in intelligibly doing so. But I know
it when I see it."

Well, a great place to see it—and get the 411 on it—is the 411.

US Route 411 runs just over three hundred miles, heading from
central Alabama, passing diagonally through Georgia's west border,
and winding up in Tennessee. While it doesn't intersect with any major
metropolitan areas, it does skirt close to Birmingham on its south end
and Knoxville on the north. The towns connected by Route 411 are
small and home to folks who have a healthy love of family and football.

Most days driving along the 411 you will see an occasional cow
and smell some awesome BBQ, especially in Rainbow City, Alabama,

where you can get a whole BBQ butt for thirty dollars at a roadside joint. Travel writer Ronda Robinson describes the drive as "a vacation in itself, a respite from computers, e-mail, deadlines, and a sense of busyness and urgency in general. Unlike the interstate, where speed seems to be the ultimate objective, 411 provides a meditative retreat."[1] This is probably true, except for four days every fall when US Route 411 becomes a giant 250-mile-long junk-a-palooza known as the Highway 411 Yard Sale.

Day One: Alabama

"Hold on to my chicken," commanded Sherry as she futzed with the items for sale on a folding card table set up in her carport. She reconsidered for a moment. "My daughter says I don't need another chicken."

"Your daughter don't know what you need," was how Betty Jo felt about it.

Sherry, the original owner of the chicken-shaped table lamp, was having second thoughts. Should she sell it, or shouldn't she? Letting go is a common problem for people who have attachments to things they know they no longer need but secretly still like or even love. Ultimately she put it back on the card table with the rest of the things she hoped would be gone by the end of the weekend. She saw the 411 as a good opportunity for a little fall clean out. "I got a whole mantel full of stuff, and then I just decided it is time to get rid of it."

Sherry and Betty Jo, along with Alice, Patty, Shirley, and their mom, Imogene, spent the bright fall morning cajoling and encouraging shoppers to take home any number of gently used items. They posted a sign out on Highway 411 that pointed toward Sherry's house on Happy Hollow Road. It was part of a modern middle-class subdivision plopped in the midst of what was once a wooded area. The trees seem to exact their revenge by dropping, almost launching, giant chestnuts onto unsuspecting yard sale goers. The street name was fitting for these Golden Girls of Jefferson County, Alabama. The ladies of Happy Hollow were laughing, teasing, and trading inside jokes in a way that suggested that maybe there was something stronger in their cups than coffee. While the yard sale was a way to clean out their homes, Sherry pointed out it was also an opportunity for a good time. "You meet a lot of different people from different walks of life." A petite lady in her forties, Sherry's primly matched floral shorts-and-shirt outfit did not jibe with her bawdy laugh and tales of girls' weekends in the city. "I told my pastor, if everyone come to church I invited, you'll have to build a new church. That's the Friendship Baptist Church." She made sure I wrote it down.

These ladies spent a lot of time on the presentation of their goods. They had arranged the tables into rows so that shoppers would have enough space to walk up and down. The offerings included a walker, a tiger costume, an avocado-green Crock-Pot, and many VHS tapes, including *The Secrets of Hunting Whitetail Deer*. There was a hot dog statue, which was a little ceramic dachshund inside a bun, with a bright yellow mustard squiggle down its back. Betty Jo, big, loud and hilarious, was doing the hard sell on a fish fryer, a black metal cylinder that was about the size of a toddler. It was marked at twenty-five dollars. In her heart she really wanted someone to take the box of hymnals from the Pentecostal Church of God where her late husband was a minister.

Every inch of every table was covered with household goods, candles, and knickknacks. They had been neatly arranged and tagged with prices. However, a little neighborly yard work was the source of a bit of tension. "I had cleaned and then the man next door mowed the yard and the dust just settled. But I mean, you can tell it's clean, not stuff that's been packed up." These ladies had made a true distinction between what they had to offer and a bunch of junk. "That's right. I won't put out anything you can't use," Sherry explained.

Betty Jo agreed. "Stuff you buy, you like it. Junk needs to go into the garbage." She put it simply: "Junk has gots to go!"

The next stop on this mega-long yard sale was down the road
a bit. After a turn into a wide dirt driveway there were four rows
of low-slung, single-level, metal storage units. They were gray, or

possibly white with a layer of grime and dust kicked up from the cars. The owners seemed as eerily similar as the units themselves. They were mostly couples in their mid fifties to early sixties, men in baseball caps and women in white sneakers. They were all pulling boxes and boxes of oldness out of the units. A grandmotherly woman was scurrying about nervously arranging and rearranging her things. She was trying to make an attractive marketplace for potential buyers. She could rearrange the old records and used snow boots for hours and it wouldn't really make a difference. It was a clear fall day, with leaves whipping around the edges of the property, but the stale smell of the lockers seemed to overpower the crispness in the air. Nothing seemed very crisp or fresh. It all seemed kind of squishy and moldy.

"Can't move dishes . . . no one wants dishes," said an older gentleman who had, well, a lot of dishes for sale. He was very chatty and never stopped moving things out of his unit and onto the gravel. He was trying to create a little goat path inside the unit for potential buyers to wander into the ten-by-fifteen-by-eight metal box. He shared that he and his wife were caretakers for their grown son, who was an amputee. He wasn't looking for sympathy. This was just his truth. Selling stuff out of the locker helped them get by.

A neighboring unit owner was considering what to charge for a bag of corks. A dollar was the final decision. This may have been her lucky day. There was a middle-aged gal, about a week overdue for getting her dark roots touched up, who was pawing her way through every storage unit—even the ones that seemed claustrophobic from a distance of ten feet away.

"I'm a collector," she said.

Of what?

"Everything."

Well then. There's a bag of corks waiting for you.

"They are just looking for junk." Hugh Stump has seen it year after year since the event started back in 2003. He is the executive director of the Greater Gadsden (Alabama) Tourism Board, and he welcomes all those folks who want to sell their random stuff because it brings bodies to town, and those bodies stay in Gadsden's hotels and eat in its restaurants. "The purpose of the yard sales are to get people off the interstate and back into the country roads. A bunch of chambers of commerce got together and said, 'Let's put on a yard sale and advertise among our communities and get people to come buy some stuff in the communities.'"

Because of its location, close to the gorgeous Noccalula Falls Park and a doable drive from two fair-sized airports, Gadsden is part of several annual come-one-come-all sales. Stump is partial to the much bigger summer event, the 127 Corridor Sale, marketed as "The World's Largest Yard Sale." It runs 690 miles from Addison, Michigan, to Gadsden, Alabama, or vice versa. It has been covered on HGTV and has its own website with a countdown clock. Antique dealers come from all over the country to that one. Stump loves it and describes it as a huge weekend for his county.

In comparison, the 411 is just a tiny little old thing, although it does have its own T-shirt—homemade of course. "This sale is more of a county sale," according to Stump. "It is the uniqueness of the road. Highway 411 is a state highway. Etowah County come across to St. Clair County and into Rainbow City, across the Coosa River and creek." The road narrows at one point and, as Stump explained, the pickings would be slim. "Heading toward Leesburg and Centre, the road widens out. You will see a lot more yard sales."

The way it works is you just get on 411 and drive. That's it. You slow down a bit when you see a tent, RV, or sign, eyeball the sale you are passing, and then make the split-second decision whether or not to pull off on the shoulder. Stump says it can get crowded, but mostly on the last day. "It is just regular people who are looking to buy stuff. You can get a lot of antique dealers, but the majority are just people, regular people."

The advice to just keep driving until the road widens was welcome because there's very little official information about the sale. There's not an official sponsor. There's no official set of rules. There's no official anything. The closest thing to an organizer is Parker Tinsley, one of the original supporters of the event, who has been quoted in the local paper every year for the annual story. There aren't any maps. No permits; no security. People just plunk down and set up shop right there on the roadside. There can be twenty-five set-ups back to back to back. People who live along the route sell space on their front lawns to folks who come in from out of town. Some slots go for five dollars a day. One family with a prime location divided its large front lawn into fifteen even slots, rented each for twenty dollars, and provided a port-o-john on the property.

Stump finds the whole thing kind of amusing. "I look at it as a bunch of people coming in buying a bunch of junk they don't need. They put it in their garage and they come back next year and sell it."

A well-preserved African American couple in their mid-sixties who I'll call the Mister and the Missus were very focused buyers. Watching their approach to the 411 sale was like watching a cheetah stalk its prey. They were deliberate, stealthy, and determined. The negotiation was swift and the cash transaction was a quiet strike at the end. For the entire day we'd pull up to sales at the same time and give a nod of the head but there wasn't much else in terms of communication. In a part of the world where I'd been called various forms of some sweet by total strangers (Hi, honey!, What can I get you, sugar?, Would you like another water, sweet pea?) their silence was noticeable.

It was the same pattern all day long. We would arrive at a sale at the same time; they would zero in on something of value, and then move on. At one point, we all came upon a large red hand-painted sign that screamed HIGHWAY 411 SALE propped up in front of a nondescript block of a building with literally a kitchen sink for sale by the front door. We found ourselves inside this packed space and it was hard to avoid each other, although the Missus did her best.

The lady running the sale warned us all about the poison ivy growing through the broken windows on the left. The building was once the Union Grove Baptist Church and her parents had bought it to use as a storage facility. "Throw it away? Noooo," said the church lady of her late parents' philosophy, and it was clearly the reason she had a church full of old oddities. Things were piled nearly to the ceiling. It was hard to tell what was what. The place required some junk spelunking. If you wanted to find a treasure, you best be prepared to dig.

The church lady was a very attractive woman in her forties who clearly spent some cash on her new age crystal jewelry. She showed off a bit of her husband's art that was placed in the one semi-organized corner of the building. They hoped to turn the church into a faith-based creative art studio, community center, and gallery, and they wanted to call it the Art of Worship. They believed in a type of artistic worship that was, in their words, "giving praise to God through spirit-led creative expression." She had a higher purpose associated with getting rid of everything in the building, including the 1960s era Aloha napkins in my friend's hand. My lifelong pal Scooter, who was doubling as my navigator on this trip, offered her a dollar for them. The church lady did not haggle one bit. "If it brings someone pleasure then I am happy," she said. It became clear that there were gems sprinkled between the old dictionaries and straw boater hats.

Suddenly the very quiet Mister and Missus piped up. They had been clearing things off two pieces of furniture that were barely noticeable to the untrained eye.

"How much for the table?" asked the Mister.

"Oh, it's not for sale," replied the church lady.

"And for the desk?" asked the Mister again.

"It's not for sale," the church lady said again quietly. The Mister would not be deterred. He tried chatting up her son a bit and explained that he and his wife were not from too far away. They lived in Talladega. It was then that he asked her son to help move a bench. The Mister saw something else and wanted a closer look. He was trying not to arouse others but clearly he thought he spied the mother lode. Underneath a couple old beat-up transistor radios and behind a distressed bench was a beautiful old dark wood-paneled radio, the kind you see in pictures from the 1930s in which Norman Rockwellian families are gathered around staring at the box with the voices coming out of it.

"Does it work?" The Mister looked directly at the church lady. She looked off and then looked back with a pained smile. "Yes . . . but I did promise it to the man up the street who is helping me clean out this place." She went on to explain how he was a local Civil War reenactor, but that revelation didn't seem to have the weight that she intended, given she was talking to two black people of a certain age. However, the Mister did not skip a beat. "But I'm here now." He was in full charm mode. The church lady hemmed. She hawed. She invoked the strength of her word. After a couple more tries, the Mister gave the woman his number and said if the man didn't come back this week to claim the radio, to give him a call. The Missus just gave the church lady the death stare. They had the good cop/bad cop routine down.

We ran into the couple again at the next stop, which was a bust except for the pure spectacle of a cool old-fashioned washing machine and a rusted Camaro hood for fifty bucks. I smiled at them again. This time, no response. None.

By the fifth stop Scooter couldn't take it anymore. He marched over and said, "Hey, you have a good eye, what are you all looking for?" The Mister started to answer but was cut off by the Missus. "We know what we are looking for." And she got in their car. End of conversation.

Then, finally, at one of the last stops, the Mister finally broke the silence. He whispered to us, "I got such a deal," as he carted off some chairs. It was also clear by the end of the day that we were not antiques dealers or any sort of buying competition. Yes, we—and by we I mean my friend Scooter—had picked up some really nice Fiestaware, some comic book glasses, and the ceramic dachshund hot dog from our first stop at Happy Hollow Road. We were hardly a threat. Finally it came out that they were retirees, she a former school principal (of course—who else has that kind of death stare), who wanted to open a little vintage store in Talladega. That's all we got. And we never saw them again.

There were so many people who lived in the area and were simply cleaning out their garages and taking advantage of the increased traffic on highway 411. Dottie B. had a prime spot, right on a corner with her front lawn facing the highway. It was terrifying to watch her seventy-something-year-old husband teetering on the top of a ladder hauling down things from the garage rafters. On the hood of their car they had about twenty brand-new T-shirts, most of them XXXL, with the state of Alabama on the front and the phrase "Alabama Is Praying for America," which made sense. However, the tiny, tiny blue sweater with a Star of David on the chest was a bit of a mystery. "It is for a dog," Dottie told us. A Jewish Chihuahua, maybe? Scooter bought it.

Others yard sale vendors were pros who had their patter down—
"If you see anything you want, must have, or desire, please inquire!"
one tattooed, mustached fellow shouted out, not unlike a carnival
barker. The crowds were thinning by 5:00 PM and he wanted to
move some of his military memorabilia. As the sun set, the prices
dropped as well. The tarps came out, buyers headed home, and sellers hunkered down in their campers and tents to get ready for early
birds who would show up the next day.

Day Two: Georgia

"Well, we killed it. Had to get rid of the rooster. He was attacking
the grandbabies."

Day two started with another fowl. This time it was on a farm
not too far from Cave Spring, Georgia. The sellers, a younger couple,
were filling in an older couple on the events of the past year. Clearly
these retirees had visited this particular yard sale last year, which
is why they got the update on the now-dead bird. The sellers still
had quite a few head of cattle that did not seem at all interested in
the people parading up the driveway of their farm. The wife told
me she and her man just fill the barn with stuff all year long. "You
all interested in any knives, guns? I can take you in the back." Her
husband offered us a chance to check out his weapon selection. No
thanks. No permit. No thanks.

The return visitor/buyer, Linda, was an emergency room nurse
who works near the Talladega Super Speedway. As she picked up
teacups and floral dessert plates, she told funny stories about taking
care of people who find themselves over-served at NASCAR events.
"Some people pay all that money for seats and never see the race
because they are SO drunk." Her husband kept an eye on her as
she considered this and considered that. They were headed up to
the Smoky Mountain Woodcarving Festival in Tennessee and he
seemed eager to get going before his wife loaded up the car. She

enjoyed taking this route each year because she was a self-described "piddler" who likes a knick or a knack. "My kids call it junk. I call it treasures." Her accent was so sweet and lilting it made me side with her. "My children said they are going to set fire to it—the house—full of stuff." The teacups went home with her.

I'd made a deal with myself that this was a research trip, not a shopping trip. Then I saw a red camouflage baseball hat with Budweiser across the front and Dale Earnhardt Jr.'s number eight embroidered on the side. Bud and Dale. Two of my husband's great loves. He is from St. Louis, home of the King of Beers, and he loves NASCAR. Did it matter that he owns at least six hats with Bud stitched somewhere on the lid or brim? Not really, I reasoned, because this one is red camo *and* Dale's number *and* Bud.

And this is how it starts. At that moment I saw the lure of things you don't need but could trick yourself into believing you do. One, the item had some usefulness. It was a hat after all. Two, it had some special meaning. My husband loves his hometown so much and his mother worked for Bud for years. It didn't matter that you can see Budweiser advertised pretty much everywhere except Babies"R"Us; somehow this Bud hat was special. Did he need it? No. Would he likely wear it in Greenwich Village, NYC, where we live? Unlikely. Did it come home with us and was my husband thrilled? Yes. Was it junk? I am not sure.

"Junk? Junk is garbage. Junk is stuff you just can't use anymore. Stuff is around that you can't use but someone else might," is what a veteran yard sale vendor named Sheryl told me. And it applied to my purchase. And it would seem to be the case again and again as we went from sale to sale to sale. Although on one table I saw, side by side, a stray rearview mirror inches away from a pair of big, white ladies underpants and a small Ziggy statue. Out of that trio, I'm not sure what was garbage, junk, or just stuff.

———————

Day Three: Tennessee

The rest of the trip was a series of déjà vu moments on repeat. Slow down. Pull over. Walk around. Debate about an item. Marvel that someone tries to sell, say, a half-eaten pack of those peanut butter cheese crackers you find in a vending machine (real item for sale), and get back in the car. The crowd got younger and thicker by the last day of the sale, and people were more willing to bargain.

People sold a lot of collections—lighthouses, bells, and thimbles to name a few. The amount of half-used items—perfume and cleaning products—was really odd. Nothing was quite as weird as the family selling printed wedding shower invitations for a woman named Mary Kay in Cleveland.

It was clear from my three-day-long polling that the key element of true junk is worthlessness. Stuff seems to be a thing that you don't want to use anymore but that someone else might, while treasures are any stuff or junk that appeals to you.

Honestly I still thought of *treasures* as a euphemism to help rationalize spending hard-earned money on something small and probably useless. I didn't really believe in treasure until the final hours of the Route 411 Sale. By the time we reached mid-Tennessee I was feeling yard sale fatigue. I couldn't look at one more picture frame or made-in-China toy that some kid had straddled and probably peed on. With two hours until my flight back to New York, something, some voice in my head, told me to pull off at one last nondescript sale in Englewood, Tennessee. At first it looked like so many of the others. There were Alan Jackson posters and Crystal Gayle eight-track tapes. But off in the distance a bit back from the other mounds of stuff, I saw a small setup that had just a few items on it. It called to me. As I walked over I saw the ninetheenth-century opera glasses first. They were in perfect condition and came with a slightly distressed kid leather case. Also on the table was a carved white mother-of-pearl hairbrush and a matching hand mirror. They were so delicate and lovely.

What happened next seemed like Jungian synchronicity at work. I spied a pamphlet made of parchment paper. It was aged but in good condition. It was a bound copy of a lecture given at Brown University on November 21, 1920, titled "The Arrival of the Pilgrims" by John Franklin Jameson, PhD. My jaw dropped. I went to Brown University and would be there the following week. Could this be real? Was this a true incidence of meaningful coincidence? I needed to know why on a rural road in Englewood, Tennessee, I was able to put my hands on an antique lecture from the college I attended which was located 939 miles away in Providence, Rhode Island. When I politely asked the owner about the origin of these items, Phyllis said she had decided it was time to do a little clean out and had found some things that belonged to a deceased family member. She told a bit of a jumbled story about a glamorous aunt in the family named Fanny McGregor. The family wasn't originally from Tennessee and she struggled with the name of the town in Massachusetts where they once lived.

"It starts with a *T* . . . Towtown?"

"Taunton?" I nearly shouted.

"Yes, Taunton. Cora wrote all this down. It is in her Bible, which I think is in a museum somewhere in New York." Who was Cora and why would her Bible be in a museum? A few more minutes of small talk and some quick note taking led to a long session down the Google rabbit hole when I returned home. Cora's Bible is not in a museum in New York but is now a part of the Old Colony Historical Society in Taunton, Massachusetts, one of New England's oldest historical societies. A few phone calls and a couple of newspaper searches revealed a story that goes something like this.

Phyllis's aunt by marriage was named Cora Gushee. She lived to be 103 years old. She and her husband had settled in upstate New York. She had been the historian of Youngstown, New York, and in fact there is a room named after her at the local civic center. "She was a great lady," according to the volunteer at the Youngstown historical society who was happy to send me some information on Cora. She was a church elder. She was a charter member of the Town of Porter

Historical Society. Early in her life she had been a farmer's wife, and she continued to ride her tractor in her eighties. She did not have any children of her own but raised her twin nephews when her sister died. And she was the keeper of the family history.

Cora's husband, Gordon Clark Gushee, was the son of Louisa Clark, a descendent of one of the oldest families in the United States. The Clarks, then the Clarkes, arrived in 1637. According to family notes, the Clarks had Mayflower cards. Louisa Clark married a bright young reverend named Wallace W. Gushee. He graduated from Brown University in 1891 and remained active with the university. So that solved the mystery of the lecture. When his fiftieth college reunion rolled around he wrote in the alumni journal, "If alive, I expect to attend Ninety-one's Golden!" He made it. Wallace's older sister, Fanny Gushee, was born in 1863. Fanny married Archibald McGregor. Fanny McGregor was the bon vivant in the family and spent time in Europe enjoying the finer things in life. Some of the items for sale were hers.

So how did these items wind up at a yard sale in Englewood, Tennessee?

Cora worked in New York until she was one hundred years old, and then retired. She moved to Tennessee to be near her family. You see, Phyllis from the yard sale is married to one of the twins Cora helped raise since they were little boys.

Eight years had passed since Cora was laid to rest in Tennessee, and Phyllis felt it was time to move on a bit. These were some of the things someone else might enjoy owning. Someone like me, who could not believe a nearly one-hundred-year-old lecture from my alma mater was sitting on a card table on a roadside in Tennessee. I was frightened to ask her how much she wanted for the lecture booklet. It looked so perfect and old. I braced for the price. "That's two dollars." Her trash was my treasure.

A week later I was at Brown attending a dinner where the chancellor of the university was celebrating his sixtieth birthday. He is totally devoted to the school and donates millions, sometimes anonymously.

He is a man who rereads the school's charter just for pleasure. His family is listed by *Forbes* as the forty-fourth richest clan in the United States. They are worth billions. I decided to give him the lecture as a gift. He lit up at the sight of it and kissed me twice as a thank you. He'd never seen anything like it. To Phyllis in Tennessee it was nothing much, just something taking up space. It had no value to her; it was worthless. It was junk. Yet to a billionaire from New York City, it was priceless.

2

PACK RATS
(HUMAN AND OTHERWISE)

"PLEASE DON'T LUMP us collectors in with *those* people." The plea was from a sixty-something former schoolteacher who heard about my research and approached me at a library. It was clear that she did not want to be associated with a group of people who were doing something in her mind that was, well, unpleasant.

She was not wrong to call for the delineation. Professionals working in the fields of psychology, life coaching, and organizing make a distinction between collectors and clutterers. Collectors "buy and sell according to a mission" and make "rational choices" when they buy.[1] There is a certain level of connoisseurship associated with collecting. Collectors keep their possessions in a controlled environment and display them appropriately. A study of 192 collectors from around the world noted that "items are treated with extreme care and are often employed ritually or on special ceremonial occasions."[2] One in three people collect something: coins for numismatists, stamps by philatelists, and shells by conchologists.

Formal collections date back to the Babylonians (2000 BC). In Europe the accumulation and display of collections for personal expression became popularized around the Renaissance.³ Collections were kept in a room called a *wunderkammern*, which translated into "cabinet of curiosities." A wunderkammern could be filled with bones, insects, art, or a mix of items—just about anything the collector deemed exciting. This kind of hobby-based collecting became wildly fashionable a century later in the Victorian age, especially among the British upper classes. The problem with some of the British collectors is they gathered things that belonged to other people. To this day (as of late 2015) Greece is still fighting for the return of a "collection" of figures called the Elgin Marbles. Lord Elgin, the British ambassador to Constantinople, "discovered" some statues at the Parthenon in Athens and decided to take them home for his own "collection" in the UK. Or, as the BBC put it, "He removed whole boatloads of ancient sculpture."⁴ Elgin sold the works to the British government in 1816, and the stone artifacts are still in the British Museum. Greece would really like them back. And by the way, in Greece they are known as the Parthenon Marbles, thank you very much.

Famous collectors include Sigmund Freud, who owned twenty-three hundred ancient Roman, Greek, and Egyptian artifacts.⁵ David Geffen, the cofounder of DreamWorks Animation, owns the world's most valuable private art collection, valued at $1.1 billion, which is approximately 20 percent of his financial worth.⁶ I know a television personality who has a million-dollar baseball card, just one of his large portfolio. Collecting is a mash up of conscious consumerism and passion. While psychologists note that collecting is an "unrelenting need, a hunger for acquisition,"⁷ at its most benign it is a hobby, and at its most extreme it can be an obsession. It is not a disorder, like hoarding.

Hoarding is its own distinct condition and is recognized as such by mental health professionals. Originally lumped in with obsessive compulsive disorder, hoarding was recently given its own classification in the *Diagnostic and Statistical Manual of Mental Disorders*

(*DSM-5*) published in 2013, thanks to investment in research and more awareness about its destructive nature. The *DSM* is the official guide for evaluating and coding mental health issues. It now describes hoarding this way:

> Hoarding disorder is characterized by the persistent difficulty discarding or parting with possessions, regardless of the value others may attribute to these possessions. The behavior usually has harmful effects—emotional, physical, social, financial, and even legal—for the person suffering from the disorder and family members. For individuals who hoard, the quantity of their collected items sets them apart from people with normal collecting behaviors. They accumulate a large number of possessions that often fill up or clutter active living areas of the home or workplace to the extent that their intended use is no longer possible.

Hoarding affects an estimated 2 to 4 percent of the population. It is an extreme condition. But as with most extremes, there are many people whose lives aren't endangered by milder similar actions. But while those lesser actions may not be destructive, they can be problematic in everyday life. When it comes to the accumulation issues, the Institute for Challenging Disorganization seeks to help them.

The Institute for Challenging Disorganization (ICD) began as the National Study Group for Chronic Disorganization in the early 1990s. ICD has a mission to educate, research, explore, and develop strategies to help train professionals who work with civilians who are overwhelmed by their possessions. These pros are on the frontlines researching and trying to understand why some people are more susceptible to clutter issues. The group researches the intertwining of identity and objects, especially possessions. It considers situational factors and brain-based conditions.

So what does it mean to be chronically disorganized? According to ICD, it is usually someone who accumulates "large quantities of objects, documents, papers, or possessions beyond apparent necessity or pleasure." Someone who is challenged by disorganization has probably tried, unsuccessfully, to change his or her ways. Factors associated with chronic disorganization can be as simple as environmental challenges like inadequate storage. Attitudes and beliefs including perfectionism often lead to things remaining undone or unused until the action can be accomplished "correctly." According to ICD, overscheduling, compulsive acquisition, information processing deficits, and disruptive life transitions can all lead to severe disorganization.

Linda Samuels, the 2014–2016 president of ICD, isn't antipossession at all. "I don't think it is so odd that we define ourselves by certain objects. If you think about your space, you have things around, colors you like. What you see is the variation in the volume. And whether the stuff is enhancing your daily experience or it is causing stress. That's the dividing line. The fact that we are attached to our things I don't find odd at all. Is it preventing you from living the life you want, doing what you want, causing problems with family? That's the slippery slope."

It is also a matter of perception, as she found out in her early days as a professional organizer. She had a client call her in a panic. The person was distraught about a desk. When Samuels arrived to evaluate the scene, her client had a few stray pieces of paper. That was the emergency. The story points to the role individuality plays into all of this. "It has nothing to do with what I see—it has to do with how they feel about it and how they perceive it. Whether it is a few pieces of paper or whether it is truly a room you can't walk in . . . that's where I am starting."

Samuels is a tiny woman with ringlets of black curls and an enormous smile. When we meet she has a bright folder with my name on it containing our correspondence and some information she thought I might like. Organized. She's bright eyed, energetic, empathetic, and sincere in a way that would flummox the truly cynical. Barely able to see over the podium, she is warmly greeted as she presides over the ICD annual conference in Nashville, Tennessee. The conference is a two-pronged event. There are professional organizers, social workers, and educators who are there to take exams to earn a certification from the group. Then there are hours-long lectures that will present new ideas and perspectives on what insiders call CD for short.

Dr. Russell Barkley spent four hours exploring the connection between attention deficit issues and chronic disorganization. Dr. Barkley is a clinical psychologist with a long pedigree. He was professor of psychiatry and neurology at the University of Massachusetts Medical School and is currently a professor at the Medical University of South Carolina. This was one of his last small, private conference lectures and it was titled "ADHD, Self Regulation & Executive Functioning." He wanted the group to consider that ADHD could easily be present in some of their clients. He discussed some of the behaviors associated with ADD and ADHD, such as poor persistence toward goals and being easily distractible, and how those behaviors might be a factor in their clients' concerns. He also made the case that ADHD can disrupt the executive functioning of the brain, and in turn executive functioning can disrupt the ability to control one's environment and "goal-directed problem solving," like cleaning out an overflowing closet. He supported the idea that you have to consider this kind of difficulty as "chronic" and said taking that perspective is most useful when trying to help someone with clutter issues.

Executive function is a term you hear a lot at these conferences and in education circles as well. It refers to the battery of skills that are directed from the frontal lobe of the brain. These skills fall into two main groups: the ability to organize and the ability to regulate your behavior, emotions, visual imagery, and self-guidance.

Barkley's thesis is backed up by practitioners in the field. Dr. Ari Tuckman is a psychologist and author whose focus is patients with ADD and ADHD. He sees a definite overlap with chronic disorganization and his area of expertise. "What I find with a lot of folks with ADHD [is] what I call pseudo hoarding, which is when . . . they wind up keeping too much. Not because they really want all that stuff, but more because there's a fear of getting rid of things—[a fear of] if I get rid of it, what if I need it? Which, you know, for a lot of folks with ADHD, has a little bit extra basis in reality." For his patients, the fear that they waited too long to return something or forgot to send back an item can lead them to keep things around. He also says the process of going through extra stuff is really onerous and overwhelming for someone with ADD or ADHD. "For a lot of folks with ADHD, if the elves came in the middle of the night and cleaned everything up for them, they would be thrilled, whereas the folks who are more on the OCD/hoarding end of things, they would be mortified that: Oh, my God—all those precious gems were taken away from me."

Dr. Barbara Jo Dennison, PhD in psychology, pointed to post-traumatic stress disorder, PTSD, as a contributing factor to chronic disorganization. PTSD happens when a person is exposed to a traumatic event, experienced, witnessed, or learned that the event resulted in the death/serious injury to self, family, or friend and had repeated extreme exposure to the details of the traumatic event.

She looked at what happens to the brain after a traumatic event and the problems that result—serious deficits in memory, focus, sorting, and decision-making. Everyone in the field, from junk removal guys to closet organizers, will tell you anecdotally that a traumatic event—a death, end of a marriage, loss of a job—can trigger problems with discarding things.

Two of the leading experts in the long-term scientific study of hoarding are Dr. Randy Frost and Dr. Gail Steketee. They cowrote the book that nearly every other book and reference paper about over-accumulation repeatedly refers to: *STUFF: Compulsive Hoarding and the Meaning of Things.* It should be noted that in their book they write of professional organizers that "their services are often helpful to people who hoard but insufficient for those with serious problems" and that chronic disorganization is "a euphemism for hoarding."

From a purely scientific point of view this may be accurate, but it is reminiscent of certain scientific benchmarks that don't always apply to real-life scenarios. Strictly speaking, people over a certain body mass index are considered obese. *Men's Health* magazine crunched the numbers and discovered that technically Dwayne "the Rock" Johnson, the former professional wrestler and action movie hero who is a sex symbol and a giant wall of muscle, is technically obese if you go strictly by BMI.[8] A candidate to join the New York Fire Department passed all the strength and agility tests, completing an obstacle course in seven minutes and thirty seconds when the required time to pass is ten minutes and twenty seconds. He was told his BMI was too high join and he had to lose weight. So is he really too fat to be a fireman? Is someone who is chronically disorganized always considered a hoarder?

Take for example Adam Brown.*

Wearing a lovely sage green button-down shirt, pressed trousers, and round glasses, Adam Brown greets me at the door of his apartment with a big smile and a small bag of trash. "I didn't clean up for you, but I just was headed to the garbage chute." I thought it was a good sign that he was taking out the rubbish; that meant the place might be cluttered but clean. He hurries down the hall and upon his return immediately invites me into his apartment. I wasn't really sure what I was walking into at 7:30 AM on a Friday the thirteenth.

The hallway is dark and it is hard to see at first. I could make out on the horizon stacks and stacks of books on the floor, creating a kind of biblio-fence down the right side of the long hallway. The book barrier takes up about a third of the width of the hall but it is clearly passable. "Here's the bedroom, and there's the TV, which is almost always on." This morning it's MSNBC's *Morning Joe*. The TV is directly across from his bed that on one side is covered with all kinds of papers, documents, bills, flyers. I'd heard about this from our mutual friend's six-year-old daughter Olivia. I thought maybe she was exaggerating when she told me Adam had a "desk bed" and that he only sleeps on one small side. Well Olivia's report was accurate. While it is a full-sized bed for two, only one person could ever put his head down and maybe squeeze his body onto the non-littered side. Two pillows are stacked at the head. The comforter is hidden somewhere so Adam uses a vintage sleeping bag that is a patchwork pattern of apples and lumberjack-plaid squares. "A dear, dear friend of mine—a well-known screenwriter, you'd know her—told me, made me get the URL . . . or what ever you call it of 'deskbed.com' or 'my desk bed' because, you know . . . ." I learn that *you know* comes to mean that someday he could start a website about his deskbed. Or maybe patent it. Or maybe it would be a name of a book. It could be one of the many projects Adam might take on one day. He points to boxes that have papers he needs to go through. His floor fan doubles as a hamper with a few shirts tossed on it, yet hung on the door are freshly pressed clothes. On his bookshelf are piles of nicely folded shirts along with three lovely leather belts sitting in tissue paper. He picks up some shirt boxes off the deskbed. They are from a high-end fashion house, and he confesses, "I mean, I have boxes of these. I don't even know how to say the name and they are covered in dust. I guess I was going to return them and ran out time." They are from Façonnable, where shirts can go for a couple hundred dollars. Adam works long days and has been in his new job at an investment house for a bit over a year. "I'm aware that my outside appearance, the Zegna suits and all, doesn't match what's going on in here."

Adam is charming. Interesting. Interested. He is a fifty-something Ivy League graduate who has worked at major financial institutions. He cares deeply about his family and his friends and their families. All around the apartment, tucked in nooks and crannies, are photos of his people. He is not married, but came close about a decade ago. He said he tried keeping the apartment clean during the courtship. After they broke up, the clutter reappeared. The next life-changing event was the death of his brother eight years ago. Adam still chokes up when he talks about him. He made one more attempt to clean the place almost exactly a year after his brother's death, when it is Jewish tradition to unveil a headstone. He wanted his family to be able to come into his place. That was the last time he made a real effort, and since then the papers, books, and odd items have dominated his space. As he walks me through the 750-square-foot, one-bedroom apartment he speaks at a rat-a-tat pace and is full of wit and funny asides. Adam alternates between being embarrassed about his apartment and accepting.

He points to the stacks and stacks of books he owns. The piles are organized by single subject. He has a shelf full of books about the Iraq war and another full of some of the best narrative nonfiction works that have become movies—*A Civil Action, A Beautiful Mind, Black Hawk Down*. He wants to write a book about presidential politics in the 1960s. His home is in one way very hopeful because it is an apartment full of possibility. But for now he lives in the land of the unfinished projects. And *everything* is a project for him. He points to a heap of Christmas cards and explains they are unopened—now months past the holidays—because he needs to consider what each one means. To his mind a card might lead to a dinner invite, a job opportunity, a new friendship. He has to consider very carefully how to respond to each one and until he has time to do this, they sit there unopened. "This may sound weird but I am a perfectionist. And if I can't get it done perfectly then I won't do it or I'll wait until I learn how to or figure out how to do it." This would explain the sixty-five books about screenwriting. He wants to write a screenplay, but he needs to know how to do it properly.

In the living room there isn't any place to sit that doesn't have something on it. He points to an older piece of furniture. It is an old fashioned desk that used to be his mother's. The drawers are full of family photos and tchotchkes. "Different things that have meant things to me. A lot of it is worthless, meaningless." He pulls out a plastic robin's egg blue toothbrush holder. "My mom wrote my name on it." He shrugs his shoulders and put his hands palms up by his shoulder, making the universal gesture for "WTF?"

Adam refers to himself as a hoarder and calls his apartment "terrible" and a "swamp." "I have one friend who won't stay here or come over. She always stays in a hotel." He actually tries not to spend time in his apartment. He loves to go out, see friends, tag along on family trips. His dance card is rarely empty. That said, he knows there's a moment every day when he realizes he has to figure out what to do after work, where he spends a considerable amount of time. "I am not a planner and not a decision maker. . . . Am I going to go home to this horrible apartment? I will find something to do. And something I want to do that might motivate me to clean up the desk. Maybe try to write something." He sighs as he points at the computer. It is on a desk that you can't really see under all the paper. "The computer is an amazing thing for a hoarder. I have folders and folders of articles that I've saved. I don't know that it is any better. They are somewhat organized. There are folders by topic . . . even to the point of a hierarchy of folders of structure and incredibly organized by topic. Writing research project. Actual projects. Subject topics. Then I have one hundred places that are marked, 'Go through this folder!'"

During the course of our conversation, without any prompting, Adam ticked off one chronic disorganization threshold after the other: perfectionism, traumatic events, attempts to remedy the situation, difficulty in decision making, negative impact on social life, shame. He also knows it is getting worse. He recognizes the domino effect. For example, in the middle of the night a few months back he noticed a leak in his kitchen ceiling from some pipe. It was 3:00 AM and he knew the super wouldn't come, so he just closed the door. Now that the pipe has been fixed the ceiling needs painting, but he knows he can't get someone in there to do it until he cleans the kitchen.

There's also the issue that he thinks this just may be who he is, and that if he cleaned up he would no longer be Adam, That Guy with the Apartment, as people know him and introduce him. That's how I met him, through a friend who said, "You have to see my friend Adam's apartment!"

"I have to say, I dine out on it a bit," he admits puckishly. He does perk up at the idea of working with a professional organizer, but wonders if this behavior is in his DNA. "I can remember unwrapping gifts . . . and my mom saying, 'Don't rip the paper . . . we can use it again.' My parents' garage down in Florida, there are jam jars filled with nails. . . . What I've learned is, I believe, my parents are hoarders, or what I believe are hoarders, whether they are technically or not."

His suggestion that his elderly parents have a problem is in line with the research around aging and holding on to items. Of the 13 percent of people over sixty-five who develop dementia, one in five exhibits some sort of hoarding.[9] The physical limitations and cognitive impairments that occur as we age can contribute to the accumulation of things and the inability to get rid of them.

There are also distinct attitudes about objects based on generational cohorts. Valentina Sgro has written and lectured on the subject extensively. She describes the current elderly generation born between 1922 and 1946 as the Veteran Generation. They grew up in the decades after World War I, during the Great Depression, and during/after World War II. At some point during their lives was a period of great rationing. Holding on to things, saving things, was what they were taught to do, and it was considered a virtue. Throwing out a perfectly good item was and still is blasphemy to anyone who grew up experiencing drastic measures like the Emergency Price Control Act of 1942, which set rations for food during the war so that Americans were unable to buy sugar, coffee, or meat without government coupons. The *New York Times* ran a fantastic series on Depression era survivors in their own words. Gladys from Florida wrote this:

My mother never threw anything away. If a sheet got worn, she would cut it up and put it together with another sheet. She mended towels, and when they frayed around the edges, she cut them up to make washcloths. The sheet got old and were worn out in the middle, they cut strips from the sides, narrow strips, and tied the ends together and put it on the loom and wove blankets. If they wanted color, they added narrow strips of fabric from old dresses.[10]

It is a common refrain that organizers hear. Lynn from Florida told me clients say to her, *Someone will use it someday* or *It belonged to my mom, my grandmother, my grandpa.* It is easy to understand the mentality. That is why there are garages with jam jars full of nails, like Adam's parents, or fill in the blank for the member of the Veteran Generation in your life. What was a behavior for survival during lean times can translate to troublesome habits given the available abundance of the last half of the twentieth century. Imagine what a Costco looks like to someone who had to stand in line for food?

Sgro's other presentation point about generational collecting habits is that the Veteran Generation takes its role as historians very seriously. "They view themselves as repositories of lore and wisdom." She found these folks are often obsessed with the past, and some of them see it as their duty to save everything for future generations. Another issue for members of this greatest generation is that they were very accustomed to order and rules. When those rules disappear after retirement, it can be unsettling. She said one way to help an elder with junk issues is to remember that they respond to structure, systems, and authoritative sources of information.

Parts of the population are cognitively vulnerable when it comes to the accumulation of stuff. The love of junk is the perfect mashup of the neurological and the behavioral. According to Dan Ariely, who is a professor of psychology and behavioral economics at Duke University, humans aren't wired to assess value. "We don't have an internal value meter that tells us how much things are worth. Rather, we focus on the relative advantage of one thing over another and estimate value accordingly."[11] Humans take from external clues (a Kelly Blue Book assessment of your old car), but sometimes internal processing (I love that car!) layered over reality leads to an off-base valuation.

Through his research, economist Richard Thaler introduced the endowment effect. His work revealed that people will consistently value or overvalue an item just because they own it. The aversion to losing the item pumps up the items perceived worth for the owner. I'd like to suggest this could also be called the garage sale effect. How many times have you seen a used item with a sky-high price tag and thought, *Really? You believe your old beach towels from Epcot Center are worth five dollars apiece?* The answer is yes, because the idea of losing the object gives it more worth in the eyes of the owner.

A recent neuroscience study backs up the idea of aversion to loss, even if the items are useless. Yale University researchers discovered that two areas of the brain that register anxiety and even pain were stimulated in certain people, mostly hoarders, when they were asked to discard a personal item. The areas of the brain, the anterior cingulate cortex and the insula, registered activity when "actual real time and binding decisions had to be made about whether to keep or discard possessions."[12] The possessions in this experiment were not family mementos or photos. The possessions were junk mail and newspapers.

It would be hard to discard something if you believe on some level it has feelings and emotions. It is what scientists describe as the human ability to decide that a thing is "worthy of moral care and consideration."[13] This anthropomorphizing of possessions led researchers at the University of Miami to find that "anthropomorphic tendencies were significantly associated with greater saving behaviors and the acquisition of free things."[14] It could be hard to give away that poor chair because it will be lonely without you.

Then there are people who retain things out of a sense of honor. Researchers at Texas A&M who studied what's known as product retention tendency describe a behavior which is "more closely associated with the waste avoidance tendencies of frugality, creative reuse, and environmental concern, whereas compulsive hoarding is more closely associated with the emotionally-charged product attachment tendencies of possession attachment and materialism."[15]

There's one contributor to junk-a-holism that is prevalent and hard to avoid: touch leading to ownership. The science supports what retailers have known for years. We've all had a sales person encourage us to feel a soft, fuzzy sweater or run our hands across the grain of a leather couch that's on sale. A purchase is more likely to be made if one holds the item, because certain brains are wired to take ownership upon touch and to feel connected to a thing just because of the contact with it. The writers of a piece titled "Please Touch the Merchandise" in the *Harvard Business Review* advised firms to read up on the latest science around touch and to consider how "physical warmth, weight, and hardness can influence consumer decisions. Arming managers with knowledge regarding the precise effect of specific touch sensations can further improve retail strategy."[16] Two researchers, one a professor at the University of Wisconsin–Madison School of Business and the other at UCLA Anderson School of Management, noticed that the attorney general of Illinois warned shoppers about haptic manipulation and being pressured to handle merchandise during the holiday season. They sought to investigate the premise. Subjects, 231 in all, were presented with a Slinky and a mug on a table about two feet away. Some were asked to touch the items, play with them, and handle them. The other group was told hands off. At the end of the session when asked if they felt any ownership of this mug or could own this mug, those who touched the items had indeed grown attached to them. The non-touchers were indifferent or not committed at all.

The length of time you hold something can also affect how you feel about it. A project called "The Power of Touch" revealed that participants who held mugs longer were willing to pay over 60 percent more for the mugs than participants who held the mugs for shorter periods.[17]

The ICD has its own name for this behavior and Samuels has seen it in her work with clients. "There is something called kinesthetic sympathy. I notice that when someone who does tend to get emotionally attached to their things, if they touch it, they become even more attached." She has developed a workaround. "So if I am working with someone new and we are deciding what's going to stay [and] what might be a candidate for going, I'll ask permission to touch something. If everything they are touching stays then I say, 'Is it OK if I hold it while you decide? Let's see what happens.' And very often that makes the difference."

One astute organizer from Calgary boiled it down to one sentence about why her clients keep unnecessary items close by. Deidre said, "To them, it's not a thing. It's a memory."

"I am careful about the words I choose," Linda Samuels says slowly. And she is being careful in sharing this with me because she knows the name of this book. She does not use the word *junk* about her clients' things. "I don't even say 'throw out' or 'trash.' I will tend to say things [like] 'edit your possessions' or 'let go' or 'release.' I'm trying to honor even the things they decide [to throw out]. I don't make those judgments. Let's just say we are talking about clutter; what is clutter to one person is an end goal to another." She feels it is important to be clear about this particular issue. "For me as an organizer, I have to be really careful with my words because *junk*, when you are working with CD clients, it is an insult."

Pack Rats

You really shouldn't be too insulted if someone calls you a pack rat. It's not just an inventive name for a person who likes to store randomly acquired items. Common white-throated wood rats, scientific name *Neotoma albigula*, are 1) incredibly cute, and 2) serve a bigger purpose. In leaving behind their jam-packed homes, pack rats have helped archaeologists look back thousands of years via the fossilized matter those rodents tucked away. So you can drop that information next time someone looks around your garage and tries to use pack rat as a pejorative.

Pack rats are small, furry, and cartoonishly adorable creatures. They look like the successful result of a scientific experiment to genetically engineer a rodent to resemble a kid's stuffy toy. Weighing in at just under a pound, they have round, chubby little bodies, brownish fur, black button eyes, and circular ears that stand out like hand fans. Pack rats have fuzzy tails, unlike their much less appealing city cousins, Norway rats, whose hairless, whip-like rudders are creepy. Pack rats are passive loners. They just want and need to collect things to bring back to their nests.

Tom Van Devender was the senior research scientist at the Arizona–Sonora Desert Museum in Tucson, Arizona, for twenty-six years and he knows pack rats. "I think they're very opportunistic. Most of them are real generalists. They'll go out and they'll try something. They'll try anything that's there. So, they may decide, 'Well, I don't like this' and drop it." The southwest is the home turf for *Neotoma albigula* and Van

Devender has conducted numerous field studies of their habitat. Even though he is a scientist he doesn't use the Latin name for the species or call them wood rats, as other scientists do. He prefers to call the animals pack rats, a nickname they have been called for a century, although one scientific journal wouldn't publish his work if he did.

What does he make of their collecting tendencies? "I think it's innate." Van Devender recalled an experiment with a baby pack rat who was separated from its parents. The rat, raised without the nurturing of mom and dad rat, was put in an aquarium alone. It immediately went to work building a house with what was made available to it. Van Devender calls them natural snoops. "They'll see shiny things and bring them back. One time I was doing a little studying about strips of shiny things. I realized that if they got really interested they'd just keep going further and further. I think that's curiosity."

Although the pack rat is the most well known of the collectors in the animal kingdom, other species do it as well. Legend has it that intelligent crows called magpies also like shiny things, though recent science has questioned that claim.[18] The reputation is so enduring that an opera by Gioachino Rossini called *La Gazza Ladra*, which translates as *The Thieving Magpie*, uses the bird's kleptomania as a plot point to create drama. There is one real-life documented case of a magpie making off with the goods. Imagine how devastated Julia Boaler of Sheffield, England, was when she realized she couldn't locate her large pear-shaped diamond engagement ring. She and her fiancé looked in sink drains, pulled up the carpets, and turned their car inside and out. Years later during a spring clean up of their yard, they found the sparkler in an old magpie nest.[19]

There's no debate that some animals collect things to propagate their species. The male satin bowerbird builds a tunnellike nest out of plain old sticks but then decorates his bachelor pad with found items that are mostly blue because female bowerbirds really have a thing for blue. The males will bring back blue pens, bottle caps, and key rings to tuck into their nests, setting the stage for what they hope comes next. The goal is to attract a ladybird to make baby birds.

For protection, the decorator crab, a variety of spider crab, will grab pieces of shell, sponge, and seaweed and fasten the items to their backs for camouflage. Survival drives these creatures.

"Wiffle balls. They really like wiffle balls," says Kris Brown, who is also known around Tucson as Mr. Pack Rat. A forty-year veteran of the pest control business, his job is to get rid of pack rats who have decided to make their homes in and around human houses in the southwest.

As someone who is called in to dismantle pack rat dens, Kris has pulled all kinds of things out of the nests.[20] He keeps the winners in a display box at his home office. "The best nest as far as interesting stuff is always where there's little kids [in the homes] because [the rats] take the kids' toys." His treasure box is full of, among other things, a rubber duck, a Barbie with the hair chewed off, a phone handset, a political rally button for Fife Symington (the former governor of Arizona who was indicted for fraud), car keys, half a Ken doll, a Double Bubble wrapper, the motor from a Swedish erotica vibrator, lots of balls of all sizes, a piece of a beer can, a baby shoe, and a mousetrap, suggesting that at least one pack rat understands irony.

Pack rats originally lived in the arid desert mountains in the south and mountain west. They created dens in rock crevices and boulder piles as protection from their natural predators. As humans moved into the desert, pack rats saw even more opportunity for protection and hydration in the lovely gardens planted by landscapers. Pack rats really don't want to set up shop in a human home like other rodents. Kris says if a pack rat gets stuck in a house it will destroy the home trying to claw its way out. They care more about their own dens than yours. They prefer your lawn. Humans have made it so darn inviting with all that cacti and those sprinkler systems making water so easily available. Kris explains, "Pack rats are limited by their habitat. There's only so much habitat. When you build a house and put in roads and streets, you suddenly create a lot more habitat. The runoff from the streets, the irrigation, you get a lot better environment."

"The spawn of Satan" is how one homeowner described them. Another found it amusing when he stumbled on a pack rat and tried to shoo it away with a shiny wrench, only to have the little critter play tug-of-war and try to take it.

So every day Kris Brown and his team get in their white trucks, some with big trailers full of gardening equipment attached to the back, and head out to some tony neighborhoods that have unwanted guests. The suburban sprawl has altered the natural food chain in the desert. He points to all the lawns as we drive to a job. "People get rid of the rattlesnakes. People use poison. The owls die and go away. There's not as many owls. So, the pack rat population can kind of get out of control. And so you kind of reach a critical mass where someone has to do something. They're damaging everything. They're everywhere. And a lot of times, that's when people call us. They've just reached their critical mass. We'll go to a job here where there's thirty-four nests to an acre. That's not natural."

There were actually thirty-five traps at that job. It was a beautiful house, situated in the foothills. When you looked up it was all blue sky and red rocks. When you looked down it was all pack rat nests and cactus. The nests look almost like beaver dams of sticks, plant debris, and cactus. Kris's son and his helper have already sweated through their shirts after a morning of using pole saws to whack through prickly pears in order to excavate the homes nestled underneath the cacti. It was 103 degrees by noon.

The reason the nests have to be destroyed is because trapping the animal alone does little good. If a pack rat is merely evicted, another will readily move right in, start decorating, and continue building. Kris has even seen live animals living with pack rat skeletons in some of the really big dens. Pack rat homes usually have little nests with chambers: one for food, and one for sleeping where you might find cushion stuffing taken from some unsuspecting patio furniture. Kris has pictures of one site where a pack rat took an entire mop to make a nice bed for itself.

As promised, the nests reveal all kind of weird treasures. In one morning we found an Oreo cookie wrapper, a packet of Sour Patch candy, a piece of Styrofoam coffee cup, and a small white ball, possibly from a pool filter. Sometimes a client asks Kris and his crew to keep an eye out for some specific thing that has gone missing, maybe car keys or dog tags. "I made a hundred dollars once!" Matt remembers. He was offered the reward to find an arrowhead that had gone missing from the man's patio. His father had given it to him as a boy so it had great sentimental value. Matt went to work. Sure enough, there was a pack rat nest fifteen feet away. Matt removed the nest, carefully sifted through all the debris, found the arrowhead, and collected the C-note.

Kris goes from cage to cage looking for critters. Sometimes there are two little eyes looking up at him. Sometimes there are four feet in the air because the pack rat has died from the heat—but never from poison. Kris does not use poison because it will further corrupt the natural food chain. A rat dead from poison means an owl will soon be dead. The other reason is because pack rats often don't even like to eat the colorful poison—believe or not, they just collect it, like anything else. Kris has found nests full of the stuff. So the rats are either really stupid or really smart. The big problem is if the pack rat takes the poison but he doesn't make it to the nest with his noxious booty, which happens a lot. "A client called us because her dog ate some of the poison. Big vet bill. The neighbor was using the poison. And the rat would go over and poison his food and collect all this. And sometimes he'd get distracted and drop a piece, which then the dog found."

Kris uses a simple mixture of oatmeal and peanut butter to lure the pack rats into the cages. The little guys who are caught will be euthanatized and then frozen. Kris donates the rodents to a local avian shelter for wounded owls that are unable to hunt. While at first it seems kind of cruel that these furry folks meet their maker in a toolbox fashioned into a homemade gas chamber, it could be seen as a course correction. Humans have gotten in the way of the natural cycle of prey and predator, so Mr. Pack Rat helps put it back on track.

Prevention is key to keeping pack rats from invading your space. You can't repel them. They aren't afraid of much. The best way to not get pack rats is not to be a pack rat. Kris chuckles at the thought. "Just the irony of people that collect junk get animals that collect junk because they create an environment." That's right—a patio with stuff on it, an old grill, a shed with stuff in it all look like big FOR RENT signs to these little hoarders. Kris shows me photos of a home where he did an extraction. "This is a person that is creating a problem. They put a sofa on the back porch. And, well . . ." The next photo shows a pack rat nest underneath the couch, cushion material pulled out with a stash of orange rinds and tin foil. In another case, someone who left an unattended BBQ grill slightly open returned to find it overflowing with mesquite beans, hundreds of crescent-shaped pods. The pack rat had turned it into its own bulk supply store.

Pack rats aren't dangerous themselves. They can attract some unwanted guests, though. The kissing bug is a common parasite that enjoys a pack rat, and the bug's bite is very dangerous for 2 to 4 percent of the population. Also, rattlesnakes are attracted by pack rats. But mostly they just annoy people.

So Mr. Pack Rat's calendar is full. He is always busy, because at this point the rats aren't going anywhere and people aren't going anywhere. "Pack rats are native American rats. And they're wild animals. They are not commensal rodents. But they'll take advantage of anything we give them. But they don't need us to survive. They survive just fine on their own. But we've moved into their territory, and what pack rats need more than anything, because everything in the world wants to eat them, is shelter and protection. So, they build these sometimes elaborate nests. . . . And part of their survival is they reuse those same nest sites generation after generation."[21] The fact that *Neotoma albigula* have been around for tens of thousands of years has helped members of the scientific community in an unusual way.

Kate Rylander is a biological technician and paleobotanist with the US Geological Survey, the USGS, in Tucson, Arizona. "I'm working on Nine Mile Canyon, which is a project up in Utah, where we're trying to figure out the last fifty thousand years of vegetation change." She is a bubbly blonde with a soft, high voice who gets very excited about a hardened piece of a pack rat nest, part of what's called a midden. Midden means, quite literally, garbage pile, and it is the term used to describe the pack rat dens lodged in crevices and all the matter around it. As she shows me around her lab, there's a lot to be found in a nondescript beige trailer.

"It doesn't take much to do science. All that you really need is a microscope and a question." And the questions for Kate and her peers are *What is in the nest?* and *When was it put there?* What looks like a bunch of sticks or a piece of hardened mud to a civilian eye is a trove of information for scientists like Kate who spend hours examining the material through a space-age microscope. She rolls her desk stool from station to station to stare at slides with tiny portions of what some pack rat packed away thousands of years ago. "I start identifying it. You're learning what kind of botanical material is collected. It also has pieces of bones, perhaps from the rat itself, families that have lived before. Sometimes, it even contains archaeological material. It contains insect material from anything that flew in and got stuck in the midden while it was being made. And then we do all the analysis and we come up with an idea of what this particular sample looked like. We take the material out, and we date it for radiocarbon dating." Because pack rats don't venture farther than three hundred feet from their homes, the matter inside is from the immediate area. That is how the middens give scientists a proxy record of the time about specific material found at a specific site.

Kate loves to teach schoolchildren about it. One part of her lesson about how middens survive for thousands of years almost always results in a room full of gigglers because it involves a certain bodily function. "What happened is, the rat went into the cave, collected lots of food for itself, nesting materials. It climbed up into a crevice, made that area really nice, and then started peeing on it, as animals would. Because the pee is of a quality that allows it to preserve the botanical materials, he pees on it over time and eventually leaves. It takes on a very hard and rocklike appearance, but it's preserved like that in caves and crevices all throughout the southwest, South America, and so on, for thousands and thousands of years."

I am like one of her students, minus the giggles, and my interview with her has turned into a field trip to her lab. Kate has a microscope, a petri dish, and some tweezers all set up for me. She urges me to look through the instrument even though I'm not sure what I'm looking at or looking for on the slide. She wants me to see what she sees and why it gets her so excited. "So, what you're looking at is about three thousand yeas old." That is pretty cool. Still, the sample looks like tiny twigs and leaves floating on the bright white backdrop. Each one is a little bit different from the next. The pieces of debris are small even with the powerful microscope. "I've done it, like, seven-x power, but it goes all the way up to seventy-five power—seventy-five times the image that you're seeing. I've got everything from *Juniperus osteosperma*, which is a particular kind of juniper tree, to the *Pinus edulis* or the pinyon, to saltbush, which is *Atriplex*. Also, it's a cactus. Now, that's a pinyon needle." Once she shows me what each individual piece is she hands me a small, pointed wooden stick and tells me to start sorting. It is wild to pick and choose pieces of ancient plant life from thousands of years ago. While it is a forensic mission for scientists, to me it isn't that far off from rummaging through that three-hundred-mile-long yard sale looking for a great discovery.

For scientists the purpose of sorting any one of the thousands of samples in Kate's lab is to be a detective. Many times they are trying to find out why a certain species disappeared over time. Kate gave me this sample for a reason. "We have this particular kind of juniper, but I also have three other kinds of juniper. But today, in the area, there's only one kind. Why did the other three disappear? So, you'll want to know, OK, so where did *Juniperus scopulorum* go, say, in a particular midden series? It likes usually a little bit cooler, moister area. So, it's not there today. What could that mean?"

Kate and like-minded scientists from both private industry and from funded labs believe these middens can help provide some clarity about shifts in climate.[22] One of the scientists in this camp, ecologist Dr. Kenneth Cole, suggests that "plants responded rapidly to climate change if they were able to move uphill, but plants migrating northward took up to ten thousand years to adapt," and "the rate of warming now is very similar to what it was then. What we see happening in the middens is happening to the world."[23]

At this remote and quiet USGS facility Kate takes me to a temperature-controlled room where there are industrial shelves full of plastic bins that in turn are full of plastic-bagged samples from middens all over the country. There are samples from Sheep Creek Canyon in Wyoming, Cottonwood Canyon in Utah, and Rhodes Canyon in New Mexico. Many samples were collected by Julio Betancourt, a leading expert in the field, and his colleague Tom Van Devender, who also collected samples housed at this lab. And collected means these researchers climbed up onto the rock faces to find and remove these middens. Now experts, like Kate, painstakingly work through the samples, cataloging, comparing, and analyzing the data.

"You'll be able to take the materials that you see in these middens and do the analysis, find out what's in these middens, and perhaps say something about the future based on what you saw in the past."

The more you learn about pack rats, the easier it becomes to draw parallels between their actions and those of humans who also like to bring home shiny things. While there is limited funding for work like Kate's, it is probably impossible to earn a grant to study the relationship between Neotoma species and the Homo sapiens species—though it could be worthwhile. Rats are consistently used in scientific experiments related to human beings because they are biologically and behaviorally similar. As one scientist from the National Institute for Health said, "Rats and mice are mammals that share many processes with humans and are appropriate for use to answer many research questions."[24] Is it fair to compare a person with a clutter problem to a rodent? It is tempting: A pack rat picks up random things it likes, stores them for no other reason, builds a bigger home over time for its things, and will continue to do this in its home or anyplace it calls its home. How different is that from someone with a storage unit full of Beanie Babies? Are we like pack rats, adapting to our new environment that allows us to buy more and store more? Is someone who buys a case of pasta from a big box store all that different from the pack rat that crams mesquite beans into an open car trunk? Is there a similarity between a pack rat bringing dangerous poison into its nest and the hoarder who continues to fill an already dangerously packed house?

I asked three different experts if "pack rat" is an apt description of someone who holds on to a lot of stuff. They all said yes. "Sure," said Kris Brown, Mr. Pack Rat. "They're hoarders. And just like people, some rats are lazier than other rats, so they may not care."

3

JUNK AS ART
Q&A WITH VINCE HANNEMANN,
CREATOR OF THE CATHEDRAL OF JUNK

"An ongoing (and climbable!) backyard sculpture
that turns one man's trash into everyone's treasure."

—*LONELY PLANET*, ON THE CATHEDRAL OF JUNK IN AUSTIN, TEXAS

AT NEARLY THREE STORIES high and an estimated sixty tons, the Cathedral of Junk is a creative, chaotic colossus. Every inch of it is made from interconnected pieces of junk. It's a three-dimensional collage of found objects. If I listed each item it would fill an entire book. It has the appearance of a funky fort. You can walk in it, wander through it, and climb on it and never have the same experience twice. The cathedral is visual pandemonium, yet it inspires a surprisingly serene scene. While visitors try to take it all in, they tend to speak in whispers if they speak at all. There is an undercurrent of worship going on at this shrine of stuff. Most people just look—up, down, and all around.

The Cathedral of Junk lives in Vince Hannemann's backyard. He is its creator and keeper. Tall and thin, he wears thick, square black glasses and has brown wavy hair. The rangy, loose-limbed artist has distinct knuckle tattoos reading J-U-N-K on one hand and K-I-N-G on the other. When he holds his fists together and outward, he silently announces who he is.

Hannemann started building the cathedral in 1989 when he was in his mid-twenties. Initially he used objects he found on his own. As the story spread about the guy building a temple of scraps and castoffs, people began to bring material to him. He has told reporters that he once received a chainsaw in the mail and someone even donated a prosthetic leg.

The Cathedral of Junk has become an attraction for the imaginative traveler who wants to experience more in Austin than the Sixth Street music scene or the LBJ Presidential Library. The online reviews from Yelp and Google are revealing.

Amanda, TX
Oh what a magical wonderland that inspires child-like awe & gives a new perspective on our throw away society.

Deb, UT
Who it is "cool" for? Visual Artists. This is ART. Not just a junk heap in a yard. There is a method to the madness, a color theme, vignettes of items that belong together and a juxtaposition of a few that don't.

John, CT
One of my favorite finds were a giant batch of old action figures from the 90s, which included WWF wrestlers, the original Ninja Turtles, and Trolls. There was also a large shrine dedicated to cats. Also found a couple cool old motorcycles and kept finding old surfboards everywhere. On our way out, we talked to the "Junk King," who was a relaxed, really cool guy.

Jane, CA
This is a joke. The owner is an asshole and definitely not worth the ten dollar "donation." So unimpressed with him and his yard full of junk.

Russ, CO
I was so impressed by the Cathedral of Junk that I wandered in a stupor-wonder the whole time I was there. It is impressive. It is arty. It is inspirational. It is unique.

Karina, Washington DC
This place is a palace of old crap you'd find at the city dump—and that's not a [totally] bad thing! It's amazing how

everything is held together—concrete, wire, duct tape, who
knows what.

David, CA
A placid refuge in a residential neighborhood where the
residue of technology and commercial culture is carefully piled
into a tranquil and provocative shrine. Once you get by the
curmudgeonly owner/artist, breath deep, relax and take it all in.

Paul, TX
This is a neighborhood of single-family homes with
children and dogs and we would love it if you would go to
Disneyland instead of coming to our neighborhood.

Hannemann claims that at one point he had over 10,000 visitors
a year from all over the world, which works out to about 30 visitors
a day. If he is even close in that estimation, the narrow residential
street where he lives has seen a lot of activity. The cathedral has
become in demand as a venue for plays, photo shoots, and even a
Bank of America commercial.

When Hannemann started the project, his backyard abutted a
field. Now there are houses all around. Some of the residents in the
south Austin neighborhood felt overwhelmed by the crowds, and in
March 2010 someone filed an official complaint with the city. For
seven months it seemed the cathedral might be closed down. An
inspector was dispatched to the property to take a look at the tower.
The city decided Hannemann needed a building permit, a certificate
of occupancy, compliance with setbacks, and to follow standard public assembly code enforcement.

At one point Hannemann became so disgusted with the bureaucracy
that he told reporters he was going to just dismantle his work because
the rules were changing what the cathedral was. His position raised an
interesting question: what *is* the project? Is it a piece of art? Is it a sculpture? Is it a building? Is it an external expression of one man's mind?

Local supporters committed themselves to saving it, whatever it was and is. Fund-raisers were held to help cover legal bills. Some rolled up their sleeves and pitched in to help make some of the changes the city required. Parts of the structure were dismantled and tons of debris were removed. The national media reported the story with an odd observer's curiosity, while the local media framed it as old-school cool Austin versus new money Austin. The city and Hannemann reached a deal and the cathedral remained with a few changes.

You have to make an appointment to visit the cathedral today. I called seven times to schedule one. I left messages six times explaining why I wanted to visit and that I wished to interview Hanneman for my book. No messages were returned. On lucky call number seven, Hanneman picked up the phone. He told me I could come by the next morning. I asked him if I could interview him and he said yes.

Pulling up to this quiet street I thought maybe I had the wrong address. But then I saw a few other folks looking around curiously. One group was European and the others were hipsters from California. We all converged upon the driveway of a small, unassuming, single-level home. Hannemann asked for a ten-dollar donation. We each paid and he told us to just go in and how to climb up the back of the structure. Hannemann was wearing black pants and a black-and-white striped referee top.

The cathedral is really incredible, as in it is barely believable. It is a testament to Hannemann's vision and skill that he could take all this junk, and it really is just junk, and marry it together in a way that makes so much sense but no sense at all. As you walk through a passageway and under a pergola of used bike spokes, hubcabs, bed springs, and crutches, you feel like you could be walking from one dimension into another. There's deliberate staging of some items. There are silos of old CDs that are glittering vertical rainbow prisms. There are rake tines lashed onto car fenders with maybe a half-naked doll positioned in between. Certain sections seem to have a story to tell. A toilet bowl full of battered rubber ducks is both amusing and eerie.

I spent about an hour exploring the structure before I introduced myself. The interview was short and sweet and sour. His story was interesting but his mood shifted several times during our conversation. He shut me down after about ten minutes. Hannemann says he is often misquoted by the press, so here is the full Q&A of the interview, unedited, including my sometimes bumbling questions. It is short, but somehow it made me understand the Cathedral of Junk and its creator's motivations a lot better.

Q: Your mom coined it the Cathedral of Junk?
Vince Hannemann: Mm-hmm.
Q: What did you call it before that?
Hannemann: Yard Space 11.

Q: And what's your mom's name?

Hannemann: Linda.

Q: Linda. Linda called it that. Do you have a personal definition of the word junk? When I say junk, what does it mean?

Hannemann: Well, junk is not trash, you know? Junk is something that could be reused, you know? Some—junk is something that's broken, but it does not—it's not valueless. So, you know, junk, you keep around. Trash, you get rid of.

Q: When you originally started—did you go out and claim stuff for Yard Space 11? Or was it stuff that was already around and you looked at it and thought, I can do something . . .

Hannemann: No, there wasn't anything here. I started by collecting. But after a little while, people started donating stuff.

Q: And do—is there one material you like to work with, where you find really it sort of speaks to you, versus another kind of material?

Hannemann: Old stuff.

Q: Yeah. I like the glass. I think the way the glass catches the light . . .

Hannemann: Sure, if it's shiny, I like it. It's not much more complicated than that. Everybody likes shiny stuff, right? Well, maybe not. I don't know. I won't speak for everybody. I said everybody liked money the other day and somebody wanted to argue with me. It was like, well, whatever.

Q: Well, it'll never be unpopular, let's put it that way.

Hannemann: Whatever. That's not true. There's always haters. Doesn't matter what.

Q: This is true. You had a couple of music videos that were shot in here. Do you remember what bands?

Hannemann: Oh, God, no. I don't care.

Q: When someone approaches you about shooting in here, do you have any sort of rules?

Hannemann: Previously, I've been yes, yes, yes, yes, yes about everything. And now, I'm no, no, no, no, no.

Q: It just has changed? What's changed?

Hannemann: None of your business.

Q: OK, that's a fair answer. What kind of tools do you need? And what kind of tools do you use?

[*Hannemann holds up his hands*]

Q: Just your hands?

Hannemann: Just hands. And—yep. . . . So, let me ask you, what are you doing?

Q: What I am doing is, I'm writing a book about junk, because I'm really interested in America's relationship with it right now. There are people like you who gave a beautiful definition. And there are people who just want it out. They want a completely clean home. There are people who can't part with it, who have an emotional attachment to it.

Hannemann: I know. I watch that show, the *Hoarders*? I just got the frickin' cable TV, and it's like, disgusting. It's like, it's worse than a drug. It's horrible. But yeah, like, *Hoarders, Buried Alive*, and shit? I watch that stuff and I'm like, Wow, what is it about those people and me that are just like, the same thing? And you know what it is? It's that emotional attachment to that shit.

But I'm not a hoarder.

Q: No, you're not.

Hannemann: But I still have an emotional attachment to this shit.

Q: But you've expressed it in a sort of a . . .

Hannemann: Ah, whatever.

Q: An interesting way.

Hannemann: So, what? That doesn't matter.

Q: And I think it's sort of interesting that there's a business— there's a whole business of this, to come out of junk—of junk removal, of junk . . .

Hannemann: Well, yeah, because America's—like, even with economic crisis and all this crap, whatever, you know, like, storage containers are—that's like, a growth industry. Like, people are— they're going to like, their house is going to be foreclosed on, right? Whatever. And they're not going to realize that they've been like too huge of a fucking lifestyle and everything's cost too much, so they're just going to try to hold onto that crap and put it in a goddamn storage container. You know?

And somehow, they're going to be able to go back to this unrealistic, bullshit lifestyle and spend like, I don't know how much money just to—yeah, $3,000 to save $200 worth of crap.

Q: **And also, then, there's the stores that just make stuff to keep your stuff in. It's the great George Carlin routine about your house is the place to put your stuff, and like, make . . .**

Hannemann: Right. Well, America's got the great—best stuff in the world. And now, here we are being lied to. Here's the deal. They're like, "Oh, my god, this is the seventh billion person born on the planet. The planet can't handle it. It's China's fault. Oh, my god, those overpopulating people." All this crap. There's not enough to go around. How's the planet going to handle seven billion people? And yet, we're using ten times as much crap as seven billion people need and throwing it away.

So, you're telling me there's not enough shit to go around for everybody? Bullshit. That's bullshit.

Q: **How did word spread about . . .**

Hannemann: I don't know. Word of mouth. How does that work?

Q: **Yeah? Did you just—the—were—you're building it and people stopped by to check it out? Who were the first people to sort of realize what was going on? Friends?**

Hannemann: Oh, man, it just—yeah. You know, word of mouth. I don't know how to—you know, one person talks to another. Then, of course, I started this before the age of the Internet. But once the Internet hit, it's all over. You know, I don't have a website. Right? I don't know how you heard about me. It wasn't from me.

Q: **Nope.**

Hannemann: It was from somebody else.

Q: **Yep.**

Hannemann: And now, this is the kind of shit that I have to do all day. I don't like it.

Q: **Oh. OK, well, I appreciate you taking . . .**

Hannemann: Well, as a matter of fact, I'm going to swear it off. I'm just about done doing this kind of stuff. I really, really hate it.

Q: I appreciate it. Oh, something that I read that was interesting
that I hope it's true. You mentioned, people have some type
of emotional reactions.

Hannemann: Oh, yeah. Man, you know, they won't believe me
about this, but it's true.

Q: Oh, I would.

Hannemann: I had this lady come over the other day, and she sees
a red cardinal out here. "Oh, my god," she's like, "Oh!" Bird
signs, you know? "Oh, it's a red cardinal, and ohh!" All this
crap. She starts crying and I was like, OK, it's OK, it's OK. It's
just a red cardinal. Blah, blah, blah. And she—and we start
talking about numbers, and this, that, and the other thing.
And I'm—I kind of like whatever. You know, a lot of people
do. I point to that, that the numbers on the house were 4422.
Ahh! Ahh! Oh, my god. Big hugs, slobbery kisses and shit. It's
like, Oh, my god.

Q: Wow.

Hannemann: Oh, let me tell you one other freaky thing. It's 4422,
but the—all the different lots have different numbers, whatever,
you know, lot 1, 2, 3, 4, whatever? This is lot number 13. Ahh!
Unlucky number. Ahh! Red cardinal!

I'm sorry. I hate to make fun—

Q: Oh, no. It's just sort of—it's sort of interesting. It's sort of
interesting. What I—my impression of it is, it's a sort of—
it's a—it speaks to possibility. What you can do, it's possible.
Look at this. Somebody else thinks it's junk or crap. You've
made it into something new. It's possible to be something
else. It can be turned into something else. I find it very hopeful. I think it's cool.

Hannemann: I'm glad you think that.

Q: I really do. I'm not just giving you bullshit. I really—I didn't
know what to expect.

Hannemann: Oh, no. I've heard that. It's nice. It's a nice thing to
hear.

Q: Can I ask, are there certain—I see, you know, like, everybody's
going to see what they want to see. I see moments of humor

in there. You know, like, dedicated by the women the irons on top of it, like, the irony. Like . . .

Hannemann: Well, as long as that's what you see, but that's not where it comes from. [*His voice had a distinct edge to it.*]

Q: OK. I didn't realize. I looked at that and there was something else I saw, and I thought—Oh, and the throne, how there's a phone next to it, like the Batphone. There's an old, beat-up phone. And that made me laugh. I don't know if that was intentional or not.

Hannemann: I know. I know. What you see is like, you know, peacefulness and humor and whatever and all that shit, it comes—it all comes from exactly the opposite.

Q: Oh, you'll have to explain that to me. I don't understand that.

Hannemann: It comes from a deep well of dissatisfaction, long-ing . . . you know, all negative emotions. It all comes from negative crap.

Q: Internal . . .

Hannemann: Internally, right. So—and that's a—it's a way of work-ing out negative crap, OK? [*His voice is raised. He is clearly agitated.*]

Q: Yeah.

Hannemann: So, you know, like, Adolf Hitler wanted to be a painter, right? And he was trying to work out that negative crap. Maybe he might have been able to work it out if somebody was like, "Gee, I really like your pictures." And maybe World War II could have been prevented if somebody just said, "Dude, you need to be an artist."

Q: So, after you work on the cathedral . . .

Hannemann: So, I think what happened is that somebody told him, "Dude, you suck as an artist. You need to find another way to make a living. You are pathetic." And he was like, "Fuck you all! I'm going to kill every last one of you fucking Jew bastard art motherfuckers. Do you hear the deep well of hate and dis-satisfaction that's inside of me?"

Q: Uh-huh.

Hannemann: That's where that comes from. So, if you want to think it's funny or this, that, and the other thing, go ahead. It's peaceful and crap? Go ahead. And that's what you get from it? Go ahead. But I'm telling you, that's not where it comes from.

Q: Do you feel better . . .

Hannemann: No! That's it. Over.

Q: OK. Thank you.

End of recording.

II

WHO HAS IT?
AND WHY?

4

FROM AUSTIN TO AKRON
JUNK BUSTERS USA AND TRASH DADDY

Junk Busters USA: Austin, Texas

Agnes. Irene. Bertha. These three ladies are large, in good shape, and looking for some action. Agnes is the youngest and a fine choice to be a guide for a day of junk removal, Austin style. She's revved up and ready to roll by 7:00 AM with two handsome young men, Scott and James, along for the ride.

Agnes is a cab-over style truck that can hold eighteen cubic yards of whatever can fit in her. "This is the least stinky cab," according to nineteen-year-old Scott, who will be managing the schedule. Agnes is part of the Junk Busters USA fleet. The name of the company is an homage to the classic 1984 movie *Ghostbusters*. While the Junk Busters can't get rid of poltergeists, they will take just about anything else. The trucks are painted the same acid green as the pesky apparition Slimer, who was a breakout star in the film. The company logo features the word JUNK smack in the middle of a red circle with a backslash, much like *Ghostbusters* movie poster, and "Who ya gonna call?" is written on the side of each truck, a reference to the film's theme song. One very happy and creative Junk Busters customer took to Yelp to review the company by writing new lyrics:

> When it's time to give
> Your couch the heave-ho,
> Who ya gonna call?
> Junk Busters!
>
> When it's time for your
> Old loveseat to go,
> Who ya gonna call?
> Junk Busters!
>
> Don't wanna hoard my junk
> Don't wanna hoard my junk
> JUNK BUSTERS!

The Junk Busters team has a very clear system. They work in pairs; one guy drives the truck and the other navigates, checks the schedule, and makes contact with the client. The goal is supreme customer service while maximizing time. James, a student at Austin Community College, puts the up in upbeat. He calls each client, happily confirms the job, and lets the customer know the out time is about thirty minutes.

Scott and James are all business as they go through their checklist of things they will need for the day: a dolly, tool kit, clipboard, buckets, and Super Big Gulps containing forty-four ounces of caffeinated, sugary fizzy water. They won't really stop until the end of the day. The only breaks they take are to fill up for gas, hit the bathroom, or pick up lunch from a truck stop. My stomach learned the hard way not to trust a nineteen-year-old dude who tells you that a particular gas station has the "best taquitos." The stops are brief. It takes them about fifteen minutes to refill their sodas, grab a smoke or a vape, and stick something fried in their mouths. These guys never stop moving.

"Maybe we will get some good donate-ables today." James is optimistic about the first job of the day. They are headed to a repeat customer. Junk Busters has been to this particular house five times already, helping a young family clean out before a move. "We had a whole truck of donate-ables time. Her husband just told us to get rid of it." Donating is not as easy as it sounds. Junk removal folks repeatedly lament about how picky some of the name brand donation centers have become. The Junk Busters will often go to churches and other smaller entities first because they are more willing to accept certain items. James keeps a list on his clipboard.

In professional junk removal there are a few different categories: recyclables, things to donate, scrap metal, and the truly worthless dreck that can't be used anymore. That stuff usually goes to the landfill. It is what James calls "actual junk." No one likes to take stuff to the landfill, especially in eco-aware towns like Austin. It is the least desirable option, both environmentally and economically. The more a removal company can offload via recycling or donation, the lighter the truck will be when it gets to the landfill, where trucks are charged by the weight of the load. The lighter the load, the more profit for the company.

The reason this particular multi-visit job has been a bonanza for donations is because the home is located in the second-wealthiest zip code in the Austin area, just west of downtown. It is a five-bedroom, six-bath, new construction with a pool and a 912-square-foot garage. The family who lives there is moving to a slightly larger house in the same picture-perfect neighborhood. The pretty young mom is using the move as a chance to rid herself of things she says her not-so-small-anymore children have acquired. At this point she greets the Junk Busters like old friends. They already know the layout of the now-almost-empty house. She points and they pick up a pile. Point and pick up. Point and pick up. Bags of clothes. Legos. Many Legos. Many, many Legos.

As the guys remove the boxes and bags from the home, a pile is growing on the lawn. When the igloo-shaped doghouse is placed on the mound, James starts to look worried. The original quote was for about a quarter of a truck and this pile was moving well past that point. The pricing strategy is almost the same for all companies. The client pays by how much of the truck is filled: a quarter of a truck costs X, a half a truck costs Y, and a full truck costs Z.

The refrain of "Oh, and one more" is heard again and again as this woman keeps finding things she doesn't want to schlep into the new home. It is a common occurrence. Most people underestimate their loads. She keeps bringing out items. Hangers. Cushions. A microwave. And then there's the upright piano; it isn't a piece of junk by anyone's standards, yet it will not be making the trip to the new house.

This is clearly going to be a bigger haul than originally quoted. He hasn't put anything in the truck yet because he has to plan it out. "It is a lot like Tetris." Tetris is a puzzle-like video game developed in the Soviet Union in the 1980s. The player has to carefully maneuver brightly colored blocks into interlocking patterns by manipulating the pieces. James played a lot of Tetris when he was a kid. "I destroy at Tetris. You really gotta know Tetris to pack a truck. You got to break down the boxes, not letting any air in there. Really filling it and packing it." He stands back and tilts his head one way and then the next. He looks back and forth at the pile. He starts to make decisions about what needs to be nestled in, strapped in, wrapped up, or lashed down. "It is more art than science. I see it in my head." I didn't have one handy to test this out, but I am fairly certain James could do a Rubik's Cube in less than two minutes.

All the guys who work on the Junk Busters trucks have a special skill. There's Frank, who is the brainy former mover. He was hired for his chill temperament and superhero spatial relations. He seems to have a secret power to shape-shift furniture through the doorways of some of Austin's smaller arts-and-craft-style homes. Scott is a country boy, and when it comes time to take down a barn, he is the man. "I'm in charge of demolition," he says proudly. "It is really important to control the fall." Finally there's Chase. He is quiet and thin. His complexion suggests that he is both young and into fast food. Chase likes to drink French Vanilla International Delight coffee creamers for a treat. He grabs them at fueling stops. He peels back the foil from the little blue cups and just pops them in his mouth. The kind with no refrigeration needed. Shake Well. UHT processed.

Steve Welhausen, the founder and owner of Junk Busters USA, saw something in Chase. It was the same thing he looks for in everyone he hires. Chase is a good kid. "So we start with the character, 'Are they good people?' I want good people. Personally, I don't care if they can bench press four hundred pounds. If they're not good people, people I can put in someone's parents' homes unsupervised and still sleep at night. That's kind of the defining factor that we start with, and sometimes they're younger than they are older. They have no bad habits. But unfortunately, a lot of times, they have no habits, good or bad. But one of the gentlemen, Chase, that you met, to put it in context, as far as common sense, street smarts, we were getting gas one day. And he had just started with us. And I said, 'I'll swipe it, and you fill it up.' 'Uh, how do you operate it?' He had never put gas in a car. And then he finishes pumping it, and he's, like, 'Now what do I do?' It's, like, 'OK, we're going to teach you this. This is where it goes.'" Now just past fifty, with smiling eyes behind his glasses, Steve is a soft-spoken, straight-talking teddy bear of a Texan. He has a sharp mind and strong convictions.

He wanted to give the young man a chance and some guidance. Steve taught him to shake the customer's hand and to make eye contact. He reminded him that you don't spew your dipping tobacco into an empty soda bottle in front of a customer. This is the kind of mentoring that Steve believes is important. He seems to enjoy the opportunity to help a young person who hasn't had certain advantages. He always knew that when he had his own business, he would run it the way he always dreamed a company could be run.

"After corporate America for twenty-five years, I always made little notations of how things were done right, and how things were wrong, more wrong than right. And I put them in the back of my head, that if I ever did start my own company, I'd call on all that experience and bring it to bear, so to speak."

In 2004 Steve's wife, Betsy, saw an opportunity. When they needed to get some stuff out of their house, a job that was a little bit bigger than the two of them could handle or had time to handle, the Welhausens looked for help. As they remember it, they could only find what they describe as "two creepy dudes and an old, beat-up truck. The kind of guys that know the Texas Department of Correction's school song forward and backward." Betsy wondered if the time was right and if by using Steve's skills they could do better. She remembers, "He was in high-tech at the time. And I don't know, he was kind of burned out, I think. And he has always put such a professional spin on just whatever he's done. He's just a good people person. And he, you know, takes good care of people, business relationships, and personal, and everything else. I saw an article on 1-800-GOT JUNK. And kind of brought it to his attention, too. And I think just the combination of those two, we were kind of like, 'You know what? He could do that.'"

Steve went into research mode. He would get up at three in the morning and scour the web and business books to figure out how to do this. The main thing he learned was that the field was wide open. "It is rare. If you think of any other industry, they've been around fifty years. There's four hundred competitors—carpet cleaning, AC repair, pest control. And when I did the national search, it came up blank, except for that one company." Rather than be intimidated, Steve saw a potential flaw in their franchise model. "GOT JUNK? still, to this day, has a very FedEx, big corporate America feel to them. You cannot, in my humble opinion, get a warm fuzzy, or it's challenging to. At least not in my area; it might be different, depending on the franchise owner, somewhere else in the US. So we want it to be like Southwest compared to GOT JUNK? being American Airlines. A different feel—and not take ourselves too seriously, and I think that's reflected in not only the website, but how we do business." Their marketing results in what might be called the double-take-then-smile method.

Junk Busters' motto is "Satisfaction or twice your junk back." Steve's official title is CJO—Chief Junk Officer. For him it is ultimately about the customer's experience. "I train the employees on, 'Let's have coffee with them.' Let's have that tone in our conversations with them, like you're talking to your neighbor, or having a cup of coffee with a good friend. And that's kind of how we built the company up. But better value, more personable, more than anything else."

One thing Steve realized that the big guys perfected was the junk removal vehicle. The trucks were awesome and he wanted one. When it comes to business, Steve follows Picasso's belief that good artists copy, great artists steal. "I actually tracked down who made the GOT JUNK? trucks out of Alberta, Canada. And I called up there, and got the owner of the company on the phone. And they were processing, like, five a week to GOT JUNK? and I said, 'Well, I'm starting a recycle company down here in Austin, I was curious if you'd build us a truck.' And he's like, 'Recycle? Do you want to put bins on the side?' And I was, like, 'Uh, no, we would like them in the back.' And it was so funny. And he drew it for, like, twenty minutes, and he goes, 'Do you just want me to build you a truck like the other guys?' And I said yeah. He said, 'I'll make a couple of changes to it, and we'll ship it to you.'" From the first moment he considered the idea to when the business opened was four months. Irene was his in the summer of 2004 for $45,000. Bertha joined in 2005 and Agnes came along in 2007.

By the time they are ready to move the piano, Irene arrives with Frank and Chase. Steve pulls up in his car behind them. He wants to make sure the piano gets out in good condition and that this very good customer is happy. The plan is to give the instrument to a member of his church. The family has a talented son but they can't afford a piano like this one. The client said yes to the unorthodox donation chain.

James pulls Steve aside and explains that the job has grown and how it will certainly exceed the estimate. Steve nods patiently and just tells him to go with the original price. It is one of those moments that someone who spent his life in corporate American loves. He is the boss. On the spot he can make the decision to cut a repeat customer a deal. James shrugs. He later tells me, "He truly believes in customer service. Even if it cuts into his own money." While a young go-getter guy like James seems a little confused by the choice, Steve Welhausen knows what he is doing.

And James knows that Steve knows what he is doing. That's why he has been in business for about a decade. Steve is a pioneer in junk removal in the Texas Hill Country. Each and every one of the guys who work for Junk Busters has great admiration for their boss. Scott, who has worked fifteen or sixteen jobs, says Steve is the best boss he's ever had. "Steve is the reason I am here," Frank says. Steve credits his wife, Betsy, as the reason that he can be the boss he wants to be. "We never would have made it without her support, marketing, and ideas, and thoughts, and no way we would have made it past the first year without her."

Rolling down the highway, the guys tell stories like old war vets. They remember their first hoarder house. For years the owner had engaged in a practice known as the "shop and drop." The person would buy something, then just bring it home and never even open the bag—just drop it on the floor and never touch it again. They found loads of purchased items that had not been used with tags still on, in bags so old they were disintegrating. At another job they found a huge dog statue that they put in the front passenger seat as a gag. It turned out to be worth $500. Then there was the divorcée who was the executor of her late ex-husband's estate. She wanted to clean out a storage unit that she never knew her husband had rented. "We show up. They open it up and it is full of porn! *Playboy. Hustler.* Videos!" James can't stop laughing as he tells the story. Apparently the gentleman had this unit for about fifteen years. He spent closet to $20,000 to keep his stash hidden. James remembers the woman being furious and just wanting it all gone, but her son was a bit wiser. He spied a first edition of *Playboy* from December 1953 with Marilyn Monroe on the cover. Copies of that edition have sold for as low as $7,040 dollars and as high as $39,000.[1]

Irene and Agnes pull up to a cul-de-sac to unload the piano. When they are parked in a normal middle-class neighborhood with normal driveways rather than in front of a McMansion, you can see how huge the trucks really are. Carefully, the four Junk Busters get the piano off of Irene.

The family is clearly moved by the donation. With a little bit of encouragement from the guys, Scott jumps on the stool and opens the top of the instrument and gives an impromptu concert. He begins to play and sing the John Legend smooth jam, "All of Me." He has a warm, husky voice that fills up the room. The piano sounds great, and so does Scott. And because we are in Austin, live music capital of the world, of course the junk removal guy plays the piano and can sing! "You're gonna hear about me one day," he says with a big smile when we get back in the truck. He was in a band, but the two other guys got a great offer to tour, so they left. "I don't blame them."

Scott couldn't go because he has a lot of responsibilities. At nineteen he is helping to raise a niece, and his fiancée has a rare neurovascular disorder. He is working to put her through school to become a sonogram tech. "We gotta do for ourselves. We didn't have anyone to pay for college or buy us a car when we were sixteen. We have to take care of ourselves. So I may have to put my dream on hold." The plan is that once she is established and can be the breadwinner for a while, he can pursue his music. He still has an occasional gig and is excited because he was just booked for a wedding.

Everything about that one morning of junk removal, from the minimansion to the piano-playing worker with a tough life story, sums up the town of Austin, Texas, these days. Tech industry boom. College kids. Musicians with day jobs. Other Junk Busters calls on the docket for the week reveal the rest of the story: an office clean out, a barn clean out, a quote for a hot tub removal, and a college grad who needs his couch gone because he is upgrading. If you look at a town's junk, it can tell you a lot about what's going on locally. In 2013 Austin was one of the fastest-growing major cities in the United States. Metro Austin saw its population jump by nearly half a million people in the first decade of the twenty-first century.[2] One demographer published an astounding finding in 2014: 110 people move to Austin every day.[3]

The growth has created some problems. Traffic is insane. Traffic is the enemy to professional junk removal because time on the road is time away from a job. Steve decided the workday would start at 7:00 AM and end by 3:00 PM in an effort to avoid having trucks trapped in a bumper-to-bumper jam, not making money. And there's an ongoing fight for the soul of the city. The "Keep Austin Weird" campaign, created by folks who helped foster the creative, fun vibe of the place, is fighting to keep the city from becoming too sanitized and generic. City originals are also fighting to keep the area from being carved up and sold to the highest bidder. At a local bar, I overheard an older Texan who had clearly never been acquainted with sunscreen tell the bartender, "Some realtor told me I lived in Travis

Heights? What the hell is Travis Heights?" According to a real estate blog, Travis Heights is an "eclectic historic neighborhood."

All the development is good for a junk removal company. However, one particular challenge is that Steve has done such a good job with marketing, logos, and his website that some people think Junk Busters USA is national chain—and that's not necessarily a good thing in Austin. People like to spend money locally. Steve explains that he had to tack USA on the name because of other businesses with the same name. He then concedes that maybe his site looks a little too slick. He has recently amped up the locally owned angle, but he does not begrudge the city's growth. It has saved the company. He jokingly says he thought he was a genius from 2004 to 2008. Things were going great. He added trucks, had an office, and even tried to expand into San Antonio.

"We had a fourth truck on order. We had more employees than where I needed to put them. We had a nice big office. We had people answering the phone. Yeah, times were good. Yeah, we were knocking down some pretty good numbers every day, running two trucks solid, three trucks, possibly, yeah, three trucks. And it was like somebody threw a switch." The financial collapse in 2008 almost killed Junk Busters. The jobs just dried up. Steve had to downsize, fast. The office went. The San Antonio branch was closed. Some people who needed to be laid off were. They stayed open, but things changed. Now Steve works from home and has created a virtual office. And not all days go well.

The day after the feel-good piano donation, they stumbled on an office clean out from hell. After a Texas drought, it rained. Biblical rain. Eanes Creek flowed over Bee Cave Road, so it was closed during morning rush hour. This made the second truck forty minutes late.

Dollies were needed to haul big, industrial-sized trash cans full of old office supplies, memos, papers, and boxes. "Where did you put the pliers, bro?" Scott shouts, realizing the dolly has blown a tire and they still have many file cabinets to remove. The tire needs replacing.

There was a fair amount of grunting even from big Frank. Then James sliced his hand pretty good on some metal. This was all before noon.

They work out a system where one of the guys loads stuff into a thirty-two-gallon can, two other relay it up to the truck, and then James figures out how to load it. This office clean out requires them to walk down a muddy embankment and through the basement. They were suspiciously eyeing the ground for poison ivy.

The recession may not have closed down Junk Busters, but poison ivy once did. Steve shakes his head as he retells the story. "We get a call from a guy who says he tore down this barn. Can you come haul it away? And we were out there for, like, three days hauling just lumber and all sorts of stuff. Never saw a poison ivy bush. And a couple of days later, somebody broke out. The next day, another one of the boys broke out, the next day the other boy broke out. And I am horribly allergic to poison ivy. I can go in our backyard and there can be one plant in the back end of the property, and I will come down with it. We shut the whole company down for, like, four days because we were down with it. We're like, 'We're going to take Benadryl, we're going to turn the lights down, we're going to lay in bed and moan for days,' because we couldn't get ahead of it."

No poison ivy here, just mud and heavy files. "I can tell what kind of day it is going to be by looking at my shirt." James's shirt was filthy. He had to change by noon.

But most days are not that dramatic. They are small jobs that make people's lives a little bit easier. "I just want it gone, gone, gone," is what the woman said as she waved her hand at the old red barn behind her. The house had a FOR SALE sign. "I just got to the point where I was tired and I couldn't find a habitat for it." "It" being all the stuff in the barn. They tell her, *No problem*, quote the price, and let her know to wait in the house. They will come get her when they are done. Sometimes it is easier when the client doesn't watch. James likes the look on their faces when they come back and whatever space that had been jammed with stuff is empty and broom clean. It took about twenty minutes to get a barn full of plywood and old tools in that condition. He and James look back at their work.

"When it is all gone. That's the magic."

It is a different kind of magic and junk, city to city.

Trash Daddy Junk Removal: Akron, Ohio

Brian Kaiser is on a reconnaissance mission for an upcoming eviction "set-out." Driving a big, shiny, black 2006 Dodge Ram 3500 truck with dark-tinted windows and no company logo, Brian sets off to a part of Akron that has seen better days. Brian's business, Trash Daddy Junk Removal, is often hired by real estate agents or rental agencies to remove the belongings of someone who will be getting the boot for not paying rent.

"When you [the property owner] evict somebody, the bailiff sets an appointment." Brian knows the ins and outs of the law better than some agencies. "We have to be there during the appointment. If the people are there, he [the bailiff] kicks them out. And then we set all their stuff on the curb or the front yard or driveway. And we have to make sure that we bag it, what can be bagged. If it's a couch, a fridge, we can't, obviously. But things, we have to take respect with their stuff and put it out there respectfully. And then we have to wait twenty-four hours from the scheduled time of the eviction set-out. A lot of Realtors don't understand that. They think we can pull up, load all of these people's stuff in our truck. Well, we're liable to be sued at that point. So, those are some issues that we run into." Another issue is that the deadbeat tenant might not be too happy he or she is being asked to leave. This is why Brian or one of his lieutenants does an initial drive-by of the property in an unmarked vehicle, to see if the house is still inhabited or if there are any dogs or signs of illegal activity. "We've had them to where we've actually had the sheriff out before."

Trash Daddy doesn't shy away from the rougher side of junk removal. It can't, given the economic conditions in the Akron/Canton, Ohio, area. While Austin's junk reflected its go-go economy, Akron's reflects an economy gone-gone. In the 1920s Akron was like Austin, a thriving metro center that was called the Rubber Capital of the World. Jobs were plentiful and the paychecks were healthy because Akron was the base for five of the six biggest rubber and tire producers, including B. F. Goodrich Company, Goodyear, and Firestone. In the 1970s and '80s it suffered financially as many rust belt cities did. In 2010 the unemployment rates in Akron and Canton were among the highest in Ohio. Recently there has been increased energy around civic revitalization. When a burst of fracking doubled natural gas production in Ohio, the area felt a bit of an economic boost. According to the census, by the end of 2014, the Canton/Akron unemployment rates were in line with the state and national averages.

As a result there are a lot of different kinds of folks living in a small area. There's a series of satirical maps on the web of US cities called "Judgmental Maps" because the maps describe a city's neighborhoods with brutal insider-y honesty. The Akron map includes neighborhoods like "Ruined by the Freeway," "White Upper Middle Class Heaven," "Deer," "Mostly Dorms," "Avoid After Dark," and "People Who Are Born and Die in the Same House."

Brian confirms he has an eclectic client roster. For example, the day after one of these set-out drive-by investigations, Brian's team helped out a well-coiffed suburbanite in a stunning 1920s three-bedroom home who repeatedly offered the team lemon ricotta cheesecake and tea. She was beginning a second career as a romance novelist. "One day I'm in a million-dollar home, and one day we're in a very, very bad area. So, with the way the economy has changed, we get a lot of eviction clean outs because people aren't paying their rent."

The evictions are not pretty. His guys have encountered threatening situations with irate evictees. Some of his guys carry Tasers on these jobs.

It can also be tough emotionally when there are children involved. Brian has two adorable kids of his own, so his heart hurts when a child is part of an evicted family. He reminds himself that whoever owns the property or works for the company that is renting the property has to make a living and has his or her own family to feed. "A lot of times, I've been able to develop the ability to diffuse the situation and help them know that I understand what they're going through and I feel bad that we have to do what we have to do. So, we try to maybe take them away from the situation, pull them out of it, talk with them. We'll laugh and joke around and try to get their mind off of it. But those can be scary sometimes."

On this particular drive-by, every third or fourth house on the street looks abandoned or seriously dilapidated. He finds the address and slows down a bit and peers out the window. He takes note of certain things. No car. No animals. "The blinds are drawn, nothing out of the ordinary." Or so he thought. A few days later Trash Daddy shows up for the removal. As Brian waits for the bailiff to arrive, a guy he recognizes who owns a small asphalt company in the area approaches him. He's the renter and the evictee. Brian has to set out the stuff of someone he knows. The man told Brian he'd been in jail for pistol-whipping his ex-girlfriend's new boyfriend, who's an alleged sex offender and was spending time around his child. Afterward Brian sums it up: "This is a crazy business."

Thirty-eight-year-old Brian Kaiser is a P90X-loving conservative Christian family man who founded Trash Daddy after putting a $75 advertisement in the local paper offering "All kinds of hauling." He had a commercial driver's license, a 2000 Dodge pickup truck, and a little flatbed trailer he used for his stump grinding business. Brian's wife, a nurse who is smart, sensible, and smokin' hot, thought he was nuts. That was in 2006. Now he has three trucks, nine trailers, and has expanded into Columbus, Ohio, as well. He also has a name that's hard to forget and far more innocent than it sounds. In Brian's case, it is just about being someone's dad. Brian had been in the business for a few years under the name All Hauling. One day in 2010 his son wanted him to stay home and play. Brian told the then two-year-old, "Sorry, Bud, I have to clean up some trash for someone." His son looked up at him, smiled, and said, "You're the Trash Daddy." He liked the name, designed a logo, and put it on his trailers, T-shirts, and website.

Someone else liked it, too. One day Brian did an online search for his company and discovered his entire website had been stolen by a guy in Abilene, Texas. It was a bold case of web plagiarism. They guy copied and pasted every part of the site, except for the part about his son naming the company, and then slapped his own phone number on it. Brian had made a rookie mistake and forgotten to trademark Trash Daddy.

Brian admits that in the early days he was learning as he was going. He had to quickly figure out the EPA guidelines and the health department rules. He didn't realize he couldn't just scrap a refrigerator, due to the Freon. He also had to get used to all the different ways people treat their stuff that might not be in line with his personal value system.

"The newer generation is so wasteful. We've gone into places and the people just say, 'Yeah, all that stuff in that room goes.' And it's literally six months old or whatever, toys that we just watched our kids say, 'We want that!' And they're already throwing it away! Then we've seen the green people. People call them the tree huggers, those people who are interested in saving the environment. They're very concerned, 'Where are you taking that?' I mean, they almost grill us like we're on trial. And they want to know. So, you have all these different facets of people. And sometimes the wealthy are very green. And then sometimes maybe the poor are the wasteful. But to watch their nature and their thought process is really, it's sad in a way, so to see that their life revolves around those material items, even though they're junk or nasty stuff."

While he has made a career for himself digging through debris of an urban landscape, Brian considers himself a farm boy at heart. "Growing up we milked fifty-five cows twice a day. We weren't the big fancy computerized milking parlor. We still actually walked up beside the cow, got kicked by them, and then once they were done kicking us, then we put the milkers on and let them milk."

Brian Kaiser and hard work have been acquainted for a long time. Growing up the youngest of three in Lewisville, Ohio (last census population count 176 people), he didn't go to college, but the life lessons he took from his truck-driver dad and stay-at-home mom have been as vital to him as an entrepreneur as any economics course. "The farm aspect really played into affecting all this because I learned the work ethic of getting up at four in the morning, doing milk, and then after you're done milking, you go work all day or you go to school. And you hurry up and get home and eat at four because you've got to milk by 5:00 PM. And then, you want to go out and have fun if you can stay awake. Plus, you've got to be back at 4:00 AM. Cows don't care about Christmas. I missed part of my own graduation party because I had to go milk. And that's played into a huge effect in this business because at nine, ten at night I've been outside in the [barn] spotlight storing a trailer to get ready for tomorrow morning because you just do it. And I've seen some of the guys that have worked with us like, *You guys are nuts. What are you doing?* And the mentality, I guess, was a little different."

As the Trash Daddy website explains it, "We can help with Clutter, Downsizing, Evictions, Divorce, Foreclosure, Hoarding, Remodeling, and more." What the heck could *more* be? Could anything be worse than any of the other situations? I learned the answer was yes when Brian's right-hand man, Casey, and I went on a call for an estimate.

It was a pretty nice neighborhood and not too far from NBA star LeBron James's house. We were a little early, so to kill some time we did a drive-by of the palace where the Cleveland Cavaliers superstar lives. Casey once did a job for his next-door neighbor. Brush with fame.

We arrive before the client, having easily found the compact two-story home up on a hill. We turn into the long driveway. Everything looks OK from the front. But once we pull around the back, we drive right into what looks like a small municipal dump. A burned and now soggy brown fake suede couch is leaning against the side of the house. There are random bedsprings strewn about and dirty, broken children's toys in a heap. A car approaches and out emerges a very forlorn and stressed middle-aged woman with ash-blonde hair and an ashen complexion. She is the definition of unhappy. She unlocks the door and leads us inside the house.

There are three old beds and a couple dressers that need to go. Going from room to room you can't help but notice that the previous occupants let kids write on the walls with black marker. The place could have been a set for a horror movie. I half expect some maniacal-looking toddler with a knife to pop out of a closet and threaten me with some menacing catch phrase like, "Guess who's getting a time-out now!"

Cat feces are here and there. "I think the cat is still in here," the owner says as she peeks into some closets. I hope not. Before we can ask what the hell happened here, she offers the sad tale. She was a novice landlord. It was the first time she had ever rented her house. She'd moved into her late mom's home and wanted to wait a bit to sell this place, hoping the economy would improve. The renters had been there about a year and a half. They stopped paying two months ago. "A neighbor called me and said there's a moving truck in the driveway." She contacted the renter who told her, yes, they were leaving but she'd get a Dumpster to clean out the stuff. By the time the owner got there the renters were gone.

It looks like a classic abandonment job until Casey opens the one-car garage. Inside is a mountain of full garbage bags. The stench is overwhelming. Casey looks long enough to get the dimensions and quickly count how many bags from the floor to the celling and how many across. "OK . . . you can close it," he says as politely as possible. The renters not only didn't pay their rent, they also didn't pay for garbage collection. About twenty yards away was a circle of gray cinderblocks. It's a makeshift fire pit full of half-burned trash. Perhaps the renters had planned to incinerate all the stuff that was in the garage but, as Casey pointed out, they clearly were not Mensa members.

"Guess nobody told them you can't burn beer cans."

The woman sat down at the picnic table and said to no one in particular, "I can't believe people would do this."

It takes Casey a few minutes to calculate how much time, how many men, and the approximate volume of the job. When he gives the woman a card with the price there's a bit of sticker shock. The estimate to get the house, the garage, the fire pit, and the yard completely clean would be $1,300 dollars.

"I didn't know it would be that much," she says softly.

Casey gently explains it would probably take five guys about five hours to clean this up right. "The garbage pit is a real menace. We don't know how deep it is."

She says she has to think about it. Casey doesn't push it but explains that she should just give a call when she's ready and they will make this all go away. He wanted to close the deal, but the woman just wasn't ready. It's no problem. Trash Daddy has a lot of work right now. Once we got back in the truck the phone didn't stop ringing.

10:31 AM
Trash Daddy: Hello, Trash Daddy. Casey speaking.
Q: What's the price on your Dumpsters?
TD: For fifteen feet, about $275 [for] seven days.

Q: How big is it?

TD: About four feet tall, fifteen and a half feet long, and seven feet wide.

Q: How long do I need to let you know in advance?

TD: As soon as possible. All my Dumpsters are out now, but I should have some back by mid next week.

Q: OK, thank you.

10:38 AM

TD: Hello, this is Trash Daddy, Casey speaking.

Q: Hi. I have the remains of a yard sale to get rid of. . . . How do you do what you do?

TD: Well, it is an $85 minimum to pick up something. And then we measure by cubic yard.

Q: What do you do with it?

TD: We donate it.

Q: OK. I'll get back with you.

By 10:50 AM he has taken five calls but hasn't booked a job yet. "Everybody is price shopping today."

10:51 AM

TD: Hello, this is Trash Daddy, Casey speaking.

Q: Do you recycle old TVs?

TD: Yes.

Q: Do you pay for them?

TD: No, we charge to get rid of it. It costs us money to dispose of old TVs.

[Silence. Line drops]

The abrupt end to the conversation leads to a little bit of sarcasm from a normally good-natured guy. "Yeah, that's right. I make a living hauling things for free."

There are many people who still don't really understand what professional junk removal is and why they would pay to have someone take the stuff away. Even the big franchises aren't heavily represented in the

mountain west because people have space to keep their old things or they haul it themselves. And then there's just general suspicion. "Some people assume you are going to sell their stuff," Casey explains. He remembers that one of their competitors tried the resale idea as a business model. "For a little while we were being underbid by a guy who came in at about half of our quotes. He was selling the stuff. It must have burned him out. Housing it. Moving it. He went away after a few months."

Brian is very aware of skeptics of this business. There are a lot of sketchy people hauling junk. He is a walking billboard for his company. Brian himself is immaculately dressed, pretty buff, with a shaved head, soft voice, and a steady, strong gaze. He has rules about how his team behaves and how they appear. No smoking or cursing or spitting on the job. He wants a client to feel safe enough to leave him with a key code to their garage or home, and some do. In fact, we went to lunch one day after leaving the site of a job only to find the owners sitting behind us and his team back at the house hauling away. Many of his guys are related to one another or are friends of friends, and he has high expectations of them. He runs his family-friendly business like a tight ship.

"First how we stay competitive is we try to make sure everybody is uniformed. To look more professional, I think. People feel security when we show up versus if we're . . . like, we have a guy that we see at the dump all the time, and he has [what] we call the Craigslist Special truck. He bought it for a thousand bucks. He put some unpainted plywood on the sides. And he's out there hauling against us. And he hauls for half of what we haul. And he shows up in usually sweatpants, flip-flops, and old tank top. And I mean, I'm very scared about who comes to my house. I'm very paranoid because I know I've heard stories. I know what happens with people. They get their house cased. They walk through. They see how a place is set up. They see [if you] don't or do have security, do or don't have a dog. So I think the uniforms have kept us more professional, which brings us above people. Our trucks, we have customized our trucks. They're a little different looking. Everything's a little lifted and tinted windows and just a custom look."

He is hoping his clean cut/dirty jobs model could lead to a Trash Daddy franchise. To buy a franchise from one of the big national junk removal chains you need around $100,000 to qualify, while another requires $50,000 in liquid assets but a net worth of $200,000. "A hundred thousand liquid capital! How many people do you know who have that—especially in these times?" was Brian's reaction when he started researching the idea. He wants to disturb the franchise model by offering a low financial barrier to entry. He dreams of offering a franchise financing option with the hope of encouraging the guy who doesn't have an MBA, or even a BA, to get into business for himself. He has one hardworking fellow named Mike working a few jobs in Columbus to see if there's a market there. He's expanding his reach into Cleveland and Youngstown. "I think I have an opportunity to offer to all these—you know, some dad that's working for $25,000 a year and he's got that just, I'm-going-to-tear-it-apart mentality, but he never gets that opportunity. So that's why I think leaving our prices lower as far as to buy in, to never get as high as the other guys—not to take them from them, but to give them an opportunity. To say this is what you need, start bare bones. And I don't expect you to make X amount of dollars. You don't have to send me so much per month. Some of these franchises, it doesn't matter if you make anything. You're sending them a $5,000 check every month. I think that the American dream of owning your own business is still there. We can do it. I did it and didn't go to college, didn't have any business training. I just did it. And just through a ton of hard work it's been working. I think that aiming toward that and the family values, kind of the Chick-fil-A type of a mentality, you know." He refers to the company several times during our interview. Brian admires Chick-fil-A's longstanding infusion of faith into its business plan.

Brian strives to live and to work with his values intact. When he finds himself face-to-face with people in their darkest hours, some of whom made their own misery, he tries to bring his Christian principles to bear. Respect. Honesty. Generosity. After a brief discussion of Chick-fil-A, an opponent of gay marriage, Brian quietly shares that he has done jobs for gay couples even though some friends have asked him why. He notes that "they have needs too, . . . they are good tippers," and in his mind it is the Christian thing to work with people with whom you don't necessarily equate yourself.

As a competitive, modern entrepreneur who would love to see his franchise dreams "blow up," he struggles with his ambition and his morals. "I've heard the term used before that if your competitor is drowning, you don't reach for them. You stick a funnel in their throat and pour a five-gallon bucket of water down. And so, that's hard for me to—we have to look at the faith end of—I look at this as a bigger picture. So, people are looking at me, *OK, he's a businessman or whatever. But what's his integrity?* And that's bigger for me. I would rather, if I have to lose this business, be known as a person who has integrity versus if I had to cheat and do anything like that because it's not worth it. And I'm not going to lose that, not so much reputation and impressing men, but to know my beliefs and my faith. I answer to a higher power. I answer to God, so I've got to do what's right."

5

DEFINING YOUR TERMS

T HE WRITER-PHILOSOPHER-HISTORIAN VOLTAIRE wrote, "If you wish to converse with me, define your terms." It is a good rule but not an easy one to follow if the term is *junk*. Peter Sokolowski, editor-at-large for Merriam-Webster dictionary, observes that the word junk is a bit unusual. "Junk is one of those words in English that's just an English word." Junk doesn't have some strange history like the word "tragedy," whose origins have something to do with goats, or "muscle," which comes from the Latin *musculus* which means "little mouse" because biceps were thought to resemble squirming mice under the skin. Sokolowski says about junk, "There's no convoluted history."

Junk was the original name for reused rope or cable on sailing ships. The *Oxford English Dictionary* puts this first application around the fifteenth century, and this definition remained intact for centuries.[1] "You may make your ship fast with any old junk" was the advice given to eighteenth-century seamen according to the *OED*. In a nineteenth-century guide for naval cadets a nuance appears. A differentiation is made between good junk and bad junk. The good stuff was from old cables and the bad came from cord that was no longer up to the task of binding or holding anything together. In the guide a note was made that sailors should look carefully because twice-laid rope made from hand yarns could be useable, but to beware because they could also be "made up from junk, or condemned rigging and worthless."[2]

It was around this time that junk went from referring to spent bits of rope to a noun that could apply to anything value-free. The word *junk* experienced "meaning migration" according to English professor emeritus from the University of Maryland Jeanne Fahnestock. That's when a word's original meaning organically evolves. Fahnestock says, "Users extended the term to non objects, so now that even ideas, comments, proposals, and just about anything can be labeled junk in informal contexts." She goes on to add it has even changed forms. "By conversion, the term was also pressed into service as a verb, 'to junk.'"[3] Over time, as wordsmiths played with sentence structure, in addition to something being classified as junk, junkiness could also be an object's identifying characteristic or become a compound noun, as in the case of junk mail, junk science, junk bonds, and junk food.

Junk Food

Labeling snacks, drinks, and even meals as *junk food* has been attributed to Dr. Michael Jacobson, PhD, of the Center for Science in the Public Interest (CSPI). One source says the term was casually used in the 1960s, but Dr. Jacobson is the man who popularized and legitimized it. The way he remembers it, "I suspect that the truth of the matter is that people had been using the term junk food in ordinary conversation, but I apparently was the first one to put it in print around 1972," shortly after he cofounded CSPI. Jacobson's focus was educating the public about nutrition and food safety. He began to publicly call out certain eats as junk food, specifically fare with no or low nutritional value and, in his words, "Products like diet soda that are not high in calories but are concoctions of a raft of worthless chemicals."

Junk Bonds

After the fall of financier Michael Milken in the 1980s, *junk bond* was a common term. Milken and his firm, Drexel Burnham Lambert Inc., discovered there was money to be made on newly issued bonds with dodgy credit that offered high yields. Investments that once had stellar credit but had lost their luster had been around for years and were known by a much lovelier name, "fallen angels."

These new investments had iffy reserves from the get-go. The actual connection of "junk" to "bond" was used by the *Wall Street Journal* on March 27, 1975, in an article titled "One Man's Junk Is Another Man's Bonanza." The writer describes the investment folks involved in this racket as "junk traders and dealers," but it isn't until the fifth paragraph that the words *junk* and *bond* find one another. For years, junk bond would appear in print as "junk" bond or "junk bond," but by the mid 1990s all need to qualify the term was gone.

Junk Science

Calling a finding *junk science* is a way to describe data or evidence that was not developed using solid scientific methodology, unsupported by peer group analysis, or science that has been misused or become outdated. The term has become a political football and a legal sand trap. Sometimes opposing sides manipulate and cherry-pick science to support a certain view. The book *Galileo's Revenge: Junk Science in the Courtroom* brought the term junk science into the nomenclature in the early 1990s. The book's title refers to astronomer and physicist Galileo, who was put on trial in 1633 and convicted of heresy for daring to suggest the Earth revolved around the sun.

The possibility of junk science going unquestioned led to a recent dramatic change in Texas law. Texas is the only state in the country with what is often referred to as "junk science legislation" on the books. The statute, SB344, went into effect in 2013 and allows people who have been convicted to have another day in court if there is evidence that questionable science was used to convict them, if an advancement in science disproves some evidence which led directly to their conviction, or if there is proof that questionable expert testimony based on now-bad science lead to a conclusion of guilt. At least four people have been released from prison since the law went into effect.

Harvard scholar, scientist, and journalist John Bohannon recently exposed the amount of junk science and unchecked science being touted as the real thing. In 2013, over a period of ten months, he submitted an incredibly flawed article about a cancer wonder-drug to a host of open-source online journals. When I asked him how warped the paper was, he let out a rueful chuckle. "The paper was *so* bad. You want to talk about junk science. The paper was absolutely trash." He used a fake name and passed himself off as a scientist named Ocorrafoo Cobange from the Wassee Institute of Medicine in Asmara. A twenty-second web search reveals that Asmara exists—it is the capital of Eritrea—but the Wassee Institute does not. Of the 304 open-source journals that received the paper, 157—roughly 50 percent—published it. It blew Bohannon's mind. "I made sure there is enough bad science, I don't care how lazy you are, if you are a real scientist and you read this paper you would never accept it for publication. The data did not support the conclusion and I didn't use the right controls at all. It shouldn't take more than five minutes to know this is a bad paper."

After the initial shock of it all he became deeply disturbed by the brazenness of these journals that ask scientists to pay to be published and whose editors clearly do not care about the quality of the content. "It's really depressing." His tone was noticeably grim. "What we all want is to trust science, because science itself is based on trust. That's how this whole thing works: we trust each other! If I do a particular experiment, you shouldn't have to wonder if I did the experiment if my analysis and data holds up." He went on to add, "The problem with junk science and junk journals that publish it is it is polluting the pool of knowledge. The longer this goes on the more everything is getting degraded. We are losing trust in what scientists are saying."

Junk Mail

"Junk Mail Stirs the Ire of Congress" was an article in the December 26, 1954, edition of the *New York Times.* Now a lot was going on in this country in 1954: School desegregation. McCarthyism. The first US nuclear sub was commissioned. Yet junk mail had the country and Congress in fits. What started as a fifteen-month trial to fill the post office coffers wound up as a mid-century smack down that gave birth to the term "junk mail."

Certain businesses always had what were called sucker lists. Dating back decades, an entrepreneur or company could purchase a list of people to whom they could send enticements. It was early direct marketing. The catch was that all of this type of mail—these "circulars, catalogs, printed matter, and merchandise supplies"—was sent out at a different postal rate than letters or newspapers.[4] It was called third-class bulk mail and it needed to have an actual address on it, which is why you needed the sucker's name and information.

In an effort to reduce a deficit, on August 21, 1953, the postmaster general allowed an extension of a practice that already took place in rural communities where there wasn't door-to-door delivery. The 1953 plan allowed a business to send to the post office as many circulars or flyers as were on a given route. The mail didn't have to be specifically addressed. It could say Occupant, Patron, Household, or Addressee. The mail carrier would just leave it with the rest of the person's mail. Less time sorting and increased use could lead to some much-needed cash for the postal service, which dubbed it "patron mail."

Politicians called it "a countrywide headache."[5] At the time post office policy was dictated by Congress, and it listened to its constituents. People threatened boycotts. Unions got involved. A letter to the editor of a local paper questioned the practice: "Has anything been made public about the analysis of the New York Post Master concerning late delivery of mail and whether or not this is being made worse by 'junk mail'—3rd class bulk mailings without addresses?" It was signed Cranston Williams, Newspaper Publishers Association, and dated December 7, 1954. You'll notice Mr. Williams's job title. The newspaper lobby hated patron mail. It believed patron mail was robbing papers of advertising dollars, essentially bypassing the middleman, the print advertising section. The lobby was behind much of the bad press about the ruling and it started to refer to the mailings as junk mail.[6]

From coast to coast, local municipalities big and small are still trying to fight junk mail. In the fall of 2014, New York City rolled out a Stop Junk Mail campaign in conjunction with Green NYC. The city's sanitation commissioner told a crowd at Union Square Park, "We have two billion pieces of junk mail delivered to New Yorkers every year, and a huge amount of that still does end up in landfills."[7] An environmental advocacy group called 41 Pounds (www.41pounds.org), after the amount of junk mail it claims one person receives each year, will contact direct marketers on your behalf to have you removed from lists—for a price. It hopes eliminating junk mail will reduce the number of trees and the amount water used to make paper that winds up being tossed out. There are other websites that will provide a similar service for free. Even two of the US government's own agencies, the EPA and the FTC, have webpages dedicated to rolling back the tide of junk mail. Meanwhile, their half-sibling agency, the independently financed US Post Office, recently launched "a new integrated marketing campaign to promote easy-to-use and affordable direct mail and shipping services to America's small business." So while the government gives and takes away physical junk mail, we as individuals are left to deal with perhaps the most invasive and unregulated type of junk mail of all.

Spam

If you look right now at the junk or spam folder of your e-mail account, it is likely full of offers from online retailers you've frequented. Or you will see outrageous subject lines like: G-U_C..C..I -..W-A-T_C_H_E S--_A..T-_ C..H_E A-P-_..P_R I_C E. This unsolicited junk e-mail is called spam after a Monty Python skit set in a small restaurant. The waitress, a hearty fellow in drag using a falsetto, repeatedly announces what's on the menu. Almost everything has spam in it. Everything. The waitress starts reading off the list. "Well, there's eggs and bacon. Eggs, sausage, and bacon. We have eggs and spam. Eggs, bacon, and spam. Eggs, bacon, sausage, and spam. Spam, bacon, sausage, and spam. Spam, eggs, spam, spam, bacon, and spam. Spam, spam, eggs, and spam, spam, spam, spam. Spam, spam, spam, spam, spam, spam, baked beans, spam, spam, spam, and spam . . ." Some Vikings who also happen to be eating at the diner (because it is Monty Python after all) seem delighted by the menu and start chanting a song about spam, "Spam, spam, spam, spam . . ." for a good two minutes. At one point an old lady shrieks, "I don't like spam!" yet everyone keeps saying it. It pretty much defines how people feel about unsolicited incoming e-mail.

The use of the word spam to describe a repeated, unwanted message was popularized in 1993 when a user accidently generated around two hundred messages on a user board. One of the peeved receivers was a witty writer and software trainer, Joel Furr, who called the influx Spam, and the name stuck. But the first actual unsolicited e-mail coming directly into someone's inbox dated back fifteen years earlier. Who would think of such a bizarre scheme?

Gary Thuerk would. He made history on May 3, 1978, when he sent out an unsolicited mass e-mail that has now earned him a place in the *Guinness Book of World Records* as the person who sent the first junk e-mail. Years later Thuerk recalls he was having an ordinary day at work until he noticed a young man looking at him quizzically as he read a magazine article about the ARPANET, the precursor to the Internet. Thuerk remembers the conversation vividly: "He says, 'Oh, well, this says you sent the first e-mail spam back in such-and-such.' I went, 'Let me see that.' That was *PC World*. So that was their twentieth anniversary issue. And that was like 2003 or 2004, something like that. And that was when I got exposed and all of this came up. So, I had told some of these young whippersnappers, I said, 'Hey, you'd better be nice to me. I was one of the original spammers.' And they look at me like, 'What are you talking about?' Then all of a sudden like, 'Oh, it's the father, the padre, the grandfather of it.'"

Thuerk, who is funny, energetic, intelligent, nerdy, clear-eyed, and now in his golden years, must have been a dynamo four-plus decades ago when he was working as a marketing manager for Digital Equipment Corporation (DEC). He had a strong grasp of the technology and its possibilities. The 1970s were an exciting time in the history of computer science and the Internet. Apple Computers had just been founded. These new networks connecting universities and research sites were creating all kinds of new needs. Thuerk was helping develop and market commercial-grade support products for the evolving field of e-communication.

"I wanted to tell people about a wonderful new product that I thought up. The product was coming and we had a plan to get the word out. This was in the day when a long-distance phone call was a big deal. At the time there were only about twenty-six hundred people on the ARPANET." He laughs at how small and antiquated it seems.

Thuerk describes almost every detail of that time over coffee in the clubhouse lounge of his retirement community in the Southwest. He recounts the days leading up to his creating something that is now so ubiquitous it is responsible for 70 percent of e-mail traffic: "So, I got out the ARPANET directory, or like you'd call a phone book, and a yellow marker." He found the names of four hundred people he thought might be interested in his new product. "My product manager, he got to type in all the addresses while I wrote the invitation." It took as long to type in all the names as it did for him to create the invite. Thuerk opted for all caps. He wanted it to feel like an invitation to a wedding reception, familiar with a hint of expectation.

> Mail-from: DEC-MARLBORO rcvd at 3-May-78 0955-PDT
> DIGITAL WILL BE GIVING A PRODUCT
> PRESENTATION OF THE NEWEST MEMBERS OF
> THE DECSYSTEM-20 FAMILY; THE DECSYSTEM-2020,
> 2020T, 2060, AND 2060T. THE DECSYSTEM-20 FAMILY
> OF COMPUTERS HAS EVOLVED FROM THE TENEX
> OPERATING SYSTEM AND THE DECSYSTEM-10
> <PDP-10> COMPUTER ARCHITECTURE. BOTH THE
> DECSYSTEM-2060T AND 2020T OFFER FULL ARPANET
> SUPPORT UNDER THE TOPS-20 OPERATING SYSTEM.
> THE DECSYSTEM-2060 IS AN UPWARD EXTENSION OF
> THE CURRENT DECSYSTEM 2040
> AND 2050 FAMILY. THE DECSYSTEM-2020 IS A NEW
> LOW END MEMBER OF THE
> DECSYSTEM-20 FAMILY AND FULLY SOFTWARE
> COMPATIBLE WITH ALL OF THE OTHER
> DECSYSTEM-20 MODELS.
> WE INVITE YOU TO COME SEE THE 2020 AND HEAR
> ABOUT THE DECSYSTEM-20 FAMILY AT THE TWO
> PRODUCT PRESENTATIONS WE WILL BE GIVING
> IN CALIFORNIA THIS MONTH. THE LOCATIONS
> WILL BE:
> TUESDAY, MAY 9, 1978 – 2 PM
> HYATT HOUSE (NEAR THE L.A. AIRPORT)
> LOS ANGELES, CA
> THURSDAY, MAY 11, 1978 – 2 PM
> DUNFEY'S ROYAL COACH
> SAN MATEO, CA
> (4 MILES SOUTH OF S.F. AIRPORT AT BAYSHORE, RT
> 101 AND RT 92)
> A 2020 WILL BE THERE FOR YOU TO VIEW. ALSO
> TERMINALS ON-LINE TO OTHER

DECSYSTEM-20 SYSTEMS THROUGH THE ARPANET. IF
YOU ARE UNABLE TO ATTEND,
PLEASE FEEL FREE TO CONTACT THE NEAREST DEC
OFFICE
FOR MORE INFORMATION ABOUT THE EXCITING
DECSYSTEM-20 FAMILY.

At that time the ARPANET was not supposed to be for commercial purposes. It was funded by a branch of the military and national Department of Defense to improve communication and research. When the DoD got wind of this rogue missive a high-ranking official called and chewed out Thuerk's boss—who wasn't angry, by the way. Not everybody complained. One engineer told him, "He said, I'd rather get this than the junk e-mails we get coming around telling me about somebody's party." The engineers at one university were not happy at all to find that the e-mail had clogged the server and the administrators had to delete the unsolicited e-mails one at a time.

Thuerk says that now spam and unsolicited mass commercial e-mail are the same thing and can take different forms. "It can be messaging, but e-mail, so short messages are also the same effect, texting. . . . All direct marketing e-mail is spam."

During his successful career he has had moments when he realizes what he unleashed. He really felt the pang when he found out about the infamous "Green Card e-mail" of 1994. "The second famous e-mail, spam, the second famous spam. Sixteen or seventeen years after mine, so we've moved to the nineties, here in Phoenix we had a guy who got together with the local UUNET, Usenet, UUNET, if you remember those. They weren't really the Internet. They were local networks. Same concept, but they really hadn't hooked in yet. And, he [the lawyer] got together with one of the administrators or the system guy, and said, *Listen, I want to send this e-mail to everybody you have.* They wrote it and they sent it out and it went to all the people in Phoenix that were using the system. And . . . it was real spam, and it was an announcement that, *Hey, listen, I am an immigration lawyer. We offer these services. Here's our name and number. Come see us. We can help you."*

The service was some very expensive help filling out a very simple postcard to enter in a lottery to obtain a green card. According to the cofounder of the Coalition Against Unsolicited Email, the lawyers were "a husband-and-wife law firm [who] decided to join the lottery frenzy by pitching their own overpriced services to immigrant communities. But these two were not your run-of-the-mill hucksters. They were innovators with a penchant for technology."[8] They were a bit infamous within legal circles and eventually lost their licenses to practice law. "I knew from that point on that the lawyers were involved and everything was going downhill." At this point Thuerk makes it clear that unsolicited e-mail is not homogenous. "So this shows you the difference between good marketing and bad marketing, OK?" His explanation sounds quite a bit like the nautical advice given about the good and bad rope given centuries ago. He believes his e-mail was the good kind of spam. "OK, mine, I found the target. I selected something. I went hunting with a scope and a deer rifle. This guy, he went up to the top of the tallest building in the world. He had these flyers printed out. I'm right at my target, designed, just know what I've got to do. Get that message sharp, to the point, do it. Versus just throw it out there and maybe someone will respond."

Thuerk does believe that ordinary folks have to take some responsibility for the spamming they receive and that they are not just on the passive receiving end. He says it isn't an invasion of privacy because we invite unwanted e-mail. "A lot of people get spam because of what they do on the Internet. They just do the things. They don't think about the things they should be doing. I've been telling these people that back in the nineties—don't give out your personal information. I don't do my banking online. I don't know anybody in the banking industry, I mean executives, that do banking online. Everything you're doing. And the people, they just don't think about it. They don't understand. I try to tell people about that kind of stuff. Your privacy is, when you go in your house you want to just take off your shoes and put on bunny slippers and that. And the world has no reason to know that. You like to have a chocolate thingy, whatever, just before you go to bed at night. That's a privacy thing, OK, getting into the bedrooms and that." His point is your privacy ends when you start researching chocolates to eat and then order the chocolates online at night, giving out your shipping information, credit card, and e-mail address. At that point you have ventured out of the privacy zone. A funny example is when I Googled the definition of spam, I got spammed with a pop-up advertisement on how to get rid of spam.

Thuerk has a sense of humor about his place in history. He does sign his e-mail FoS, as in "Father of Spam," but he is serious about his security. During an interview it is customary to ask someone his or her full name and birth date or age. He wouldn't comply. He said he never gives anyone his birthday or age. Yet he was willing to talk a bit about his life as a semi-retiree. He consults with companies about Internet security. His wife is doing good in the world helping teach at-risk children. But even the man who unleashed digital clutter into the world confesses to having a common terrestrial problem. He told me, "We had to get rid of a lot of that stuff when we moved. Actually, we gave away most of the stuff in our house. . . . We're downsizing, but we still have too much stuff."

Too much stuff? The man partially responsible for filling up your inbox has too much junk in his real life.

Other Junk

Finally, it should be mentioned that the modern uses of *junk*, all by its lonesome, stray far from its origins or original definition. The slang forms range from grimy to uncouth.

If someone is looking to score some junk it means they want to partake in the euphoria-inducing and life-destroying drug heroin. In *Trainspotting*, the Academy Award–nominated film about heroin users, main character Mark "Rent Boy" Renton laments, "The down-side of coming off junk was I knew I would need to mix with my friends again in a state of full consciousness. It was awful." The origin of this use of the term is that addicts would search for scrap metal to sell to junkyards to get enough money to buy heroin. Those metal-grubbing addicts became known as junkies and the drug as junk.[9]

In the last two decades of the twentieth century, junk took on two sexually related meanings, one for women and one for men, providing some sort of bizarre gender equality.

"Junk in the trunk" became a way, generally considered positive, to describe a woman with a voluptuous derriere. The saying can be attributed to a little-known rap duo called Duice. The group hit the Billboard chart once, and only once, reaching number 12 and selling two million copies of a song called "Dazzey Duks" in 1993. The lyrics extol the virtues of women who manage to fill out or fill up very, very short shorts—those cutoff jean shorts named after Daisy Duke, who just-barely wore them on *The Dukes Of Hazzard*.

> What started the trend of them Dazzey Duks
> Ever since the summer of the '90s
> Girls had a deal with the future behind.
>
> See many terms they use to express
> We're talking about the butt cheeks not the breasts.
> Baby got back, *the junk in the trunk*
> She got a six pack or a hell of a rump.
>
> Yo, need some fries with that shake
> See many terms they use to relate.

Yes. So many.

The use of *junk* associated with the male anatomy was the subject of an entire article in the venerable Gray Lady, the *New York Times*.

Yale-educated linguist Ben Zimmer traced the euphemism back to a writer named Ethan Mordden, who he reported used it in a magazine piece called "The Hustler" in the 1980s.[10]

When I found Mordden, he explained he had been writing about gay life for a magazine called *Christopher Street* and he had used the term in a bunch of stories. Like all good writers he took information and observations from his real life and weaved them into his work. "I had a friend who was very colorful and made up language. His name was Rip and he was the kind of character you didn't want to waste." Mordden knew immediately what Rip meant the first time he used junk to describe a man's genitals and that the euphemism had to be in one of his pieces. "There was logic to the sound and context and what he meant. It was like in the fifties, when hip, cool jazz guys spoke their own lingo. This was a playfully, sneaky way of expanding the language. You could tell what Rip was saying if you were a good listener."

Often employed by radio shock jocks to avoid FCC issues, junk was mainstreamed in 2010 when a man at a TSA checkpoint recorded his opposition to a newly instituted and somewhat invasive pat down procedure. Eleven months earlier, an aspirational lone-wolf terrorist smuggled explosives in his underwear onto a flight from Amsterdam to Detroit. As a result, in the name of improved security, TSA agents began to engage in extensive searches using the backs of their hands to pretty much pat down the part of a person that underwear traditionally covers. When a TSA agent told a young man at the San Diego International Airport that he had to submit to one of these searches, the man turned on his phone's video function and recorded the episode. It went like this.

> TSA: Do you have anything in your pockets?
> MAN: I don't think so; they had me take it all out.
> TSA: No belt? No nothing?
> MAN: Nope. No belt. No nothing.

TSA: Do you have any external or internal implants that I
need to be aware of?
MAN: No.
TSA: OK, I am going to be doing a standard pat down on
you today. Using my hands going like this on your body.
Also, we are going to be doing a groin check. That means
I'm going to place my hand on your hip, the other hand on
your inner thigh, slowly go up and down . . .
MAN: OK.
TSA: We're going to do that two times in the front and two
times in the back. And if you'd like a private screening we
can make that available for you also.
MAN: We can do it out here, but if you **touch my junk**, I am
going to have you arrested.

Considering this video went viral and the story, including the junk
reference, was covered by nearly every major news outlet, maybe we
need a new compound noun for the twenty-first century: junk news
including squirrels on water skis, the wardrobes of celebrity children,
and Twitter fights between reality stars.

6

SPACE JUNK
Q&A WITH DONALD KESSLER,
FORMER NASA SCIENTIST

———————

IN 2013 THE BEAUTIFULLY terrifying film *Gravity* received myriad accolades, including seven Academy Awards. Its star, Sandra Bullock, was named best actress by multiple film critics' associations for her role as Dr. Ryan Stone, a medical engineer stranded in space when her spacecraft is badly damaged by orbital debris, commonly referred to as space junk. She spends the short, tense film trying to get back to Earth and away from the large fragments hurtling through space.

The only truly harsh critics of the film were some very precise members of the scientific community who poked at the film's astro-accuracy. Are the International Space Station and the Hubble Telescope positioned so that someone could travel between them, as Dr. Stone did in the film? No. In space would her tears float away dramatically as they did on screen? Never. But the action that propels the movie is based on a troubling truth. There is enough orbital debris and space junk whizzing around at incredible speeds to cause serious problems and potentially disable satellites that are integral to the way we live.

NASA describes space junk as "all man-made objects in orbit about the Earth, which no longer serve a useful purpose."[1] There have been approximately forty-five hundred launches since the beginning of space exploration. According to NASA, as of mid 2015 there are roughly twenty-three thousand pieces of debris at least 10 cm (3.9 inches) in size zooming around the lowest Earth orbit at speeds close to 17,500 miles an hour. If you recently downloaded a song or movie, it is likely a satellite somewhere in this orbit was involved. It's the same neighborhood as about twelve hundred working satellites that control things like GPS and weather monitoring systems that predict hurricanes. It is also where all the manned space flights have ventured and any future space exploration or commercialization would likely take place. That is, unless it becomes too unsafe because of space junk, and some scientists believe we are at that point right now.

The big junk is tracked by government agencies and the US Air Force, but the small stuff is rogue, often undetectable, and dangerous due to high speeds. A marble-sized piece of junk in low Earth orbit travels at such a high velocity that, were it to make contact with another object, would have the same effect as a grenade.[2] If you include all the upper orbits, there are about half a million pieces of debris out there. Simply put, humans are sending too much junk into space and just leaving it there, making it more dangerous for humans and making a potentially rich resource unavailable.

The biggest offenders are the United States, Russia, and China. There have been a series of incidents in the past few years and these are just the ones we, civilians, know about. In January 2007 China successfully tested an antisatellite missile by sending it to destroy one of their weather satellites. The result was an enormous amount of debris blasted out into orbit, around three thousand traceable pieces. Two years later, there was an accidental collision between a piece of space junk—an old, nonfunctioning Russian satellite—and an active

US commercial communications satellite. Experts say those two collisions alone are believed to have wiped out years worth of work that had been done to address the problem. This proves the point that it doesn't take a lot of space junk to make a lot of trouble. That Russian collision caused problems for years. A couple of whoppers could set back the efforts to clean up space and make it safe.

In March 2012, a significant amount of debris was headed toward the International Space Station (ISS), and it was detected too late for the station to maneuver out of the way. The threat was real enough for the astronauts to be deployed to the Soyuz space capsules in case they had to escape from the base. The $150 billion investment has had to engage in debris avoidance maneuvers (DAM) four times between April 2011 and April 2012. The astronauts have had to "man the lifeboats" a least three times in the past nine years,[3] including as recently as July 2015.

The international community is taking this issue seriously. The United States has its own national space policy that in part addresses space junk by calling for "strengthening measures to mitigate orbital debris." The European Space Agency (ESA) has begun implementing a plan called e.Deorbit, which will send a "space janitor" to retrieve what it calls derelict satellites. However, there is no official governing body that is the space cop. Various recommendations have been made through the United Nations and through individual agencies about how to build spacecraft and satellites that 1) can be built with shields to absorb the impact of incoming debris, 2) not leave anything behind, or 3) find a way to do something with the debris that is there.

Japanese, Swiss, and American companies are developing all kinds of far-out solutions for the latter. The theories include building nets to catch it, lasers to shoot it, robots to sweep it up and capture it, and parachutes to drag it back to Earth. At the heart of most solutions is to use space's self-cleaning powers and pull the junk into the lowest orbit, where it will one day burn up upon reentry—though some larger pieces won't fully disintegrate and will fall to Earth. The chance of someone being hit by space junk is infinitesimal. Most of it falls into the ocean, though a few large pieces have made it to land. However, their real danger is out there, not down here.

In 2011 the National Research Council, part of the National Academies of Sciences, reported that we were at the space junk tipping point.[4] How did it get so out of control? Wasn't there someone who could have predicted the danger of too much junk in space?

Well, there were a few, and the best known is Donald Kessler. In 1978, while working at NASA, Kessler published a paper predicting the exponential growth of the debris as the result of collisions. The media dubbed his hypothesis the Kessler Syndrome, although he never called it that or promoted its use. But he does understand that a catchy name draws attention to the problem and that's his main goal. He prefers to talk about the actual facts and consequences of space junk, why we can't afford to let out of sight be out of mind, and why the space program needs to be financially supported.

In his slow, southern drawl, Kessler can make this complex, scientific problem understandable: "It was sort of like you were living in a neighborhood and you didn't have a dump, and every time you got a new car you just stuck the old one in your backyard. Got a new refrigerator, you put the old one in your backyard. That's essentially what is happening in space."[5] His work was taken quite seriously, so much so that NASA established an Orbital Debris Program that still exists today, and the design process of spacecraft changed to reflect the threat.

Now retired, Kessler works with several independent research groups to keep the focus on the problem and to help find solutions. He does this and still gives interviews because he feels it is his responsibility. He has contributed to several films, like the Imax documentary *Space Junk* and *Collision Point: The Race to Clean Up Space*, and yes, he has seen *Gravity*.

Q: What was it about space that attracted you?
Don Kessler: Well, to me it's the secret of the universe. It's where we all came from. It's our origins. I was mainly interested in

the planets because that was a possibility where there was other life, and it—it just grew from that. When I went to NASA, they gave me several choices. They said, "Well, we got this meteorite group, we got this lunar sciences group," and I just said, "Well, meteorite sounds interesting," and that just turned out to be the key to understanding the debris environment.

Q: In your opinion, what qualifies as orbital debris, space junk?

Kessler: Well, anything that's not serving a useful function.

Q: So, it's like regular junk.

Kessler: Yeah. But, legally, there is no legal definition of it. Consequently, that's probably a failing of the international law. At the time, they just didn't envision space junk when those rules were written.

Q: Why wasn't space junk considered an issue early on?

Kessler: Well, there were these concepts, and to me it was we were misled by our understanding of the solar system. And, you know, "space is endless," and that was the general impression. Nobody had really begun to realize that we were concentrating so much material in low Earth orbit where there wasn't much room, and they weren't paying attention to not only how they were doing it, but what was going on after they left the things in orbit, and the fact that they weren't adhering to the laws of the universe, essentially.

Q: So, it was just this misguided notion that there's a ton of space in space?

Kessler: Yes. And, you know, that's sort of the nature of all environmental issues. You start off thinking you got plenty of room, you don't need to worry because the oceans are endless, the air is endless, it couldn't possibly end. It just—and after a while, you run out of space.

Q: When you sat down to write your paper—which I attempted to read, I understood parts of it—what was your initial goal?

Kessler: It was to draw attention to the fact that if we didn't do something different, we would create an environment that was self-perpetuating and that we needed to change the way that we operated in space.

Q: And the way you described it was you wanted people to understand the possible consequences of "continued unrestrained launch activities." What did you mean? Just that we just keep going as we're going, and we don't do anything preventative?

Kessler: Right, exactly. And, of course, when they did the *Space Junk* movie, I remember the narrator was surprised to learn they just turn things off, leave them in space. And, of course, the only thing that will bring an object down is in the lowest parts of low Earth orbit. Below about five hundred kilometers, you'll reenter within twenty-five years. But if you're above that, say, between five hundred and one thousand kilometers, it can be centuries before things reenter. And if you're above one thousand kilometers, it can be billions of years before things come down because there's no—there's insufficient atmosphere at those altitudes. So, it would continue to accumulate. There's no question about that.

But it gets to the point in low Earth orbit—where most of the material is—it's a question of how fast this debris is being generated verses how quickly it's being emptied by the natural atmosphere. There's a term I started using, the *critical density*, at what point do you reach that where you're going over this critical density so that things, even if you don't put anything else up there, the collisional process will generate debris faster than it can be removed? And my calculations and most of the calculations from the rest of the world, except for France, have come to the conclusion that we've already exceeded that critical density in low Earth orbit. And the only way you can bring it back to an equilibrium is to remove some objects. The number that NASA has come up with is that you need to remove five objects per year for the next one hundred years, or a total of five hundred objects. . . . Now, whatever you put in space, you have twenty-five years after you're finished using it to get it out of space. And the way that's usually done is in low Earth orbit, if you're above five hundred kilometers, you just use the last bit of fuel to drop it down to below five hundred kilometers, and it will reenter naturally within that twenty-five years, so . . .

Q: Are those rules part of the UN rules on orbital debris?

Kessler: They are—yes, they are. They've accepted now all the way through. We formed an organization called the Inter-Agency Space Debris Coordination Committee, IADC for short, that has fourteen member nations all over the world. One of the things I'm doing now is I'm representing NASA on that group. And through the IADC, we—everyone has agreed that, yes, we—the whole world should conform to these rules. And they have recommended them to the United Nations, and the United Nations has accepted them in principle, but they haven't added any numbers to that. They say, you should get out of orbit as soon as you can, something of that nature, rather than saying the twenty-five years. But the rest of the world pretty [much] uses that number of twenty-five years.

Q: What is it about the twenty-five years?

Kessler: Well, it was kind of an arbitrary decision. When you run the models, whether it's twenty-five years or immediately, there's very little difference. And when we came up with the rule, part of what we were looking at is we had to do something that was inexpensive. I had people in the military approach me afterwards who said, "Gee, if I had known you were going to give us twenty-five years, we wouldn't have been against the program so much." It's a cheaper way of doing things. You keep the expenses down. And that's what we were mainly concerned about early in the program. Because if we started telling people that we were going to raise their cost significantly, we wouldn't have gotten anywhere. And, so, it was a compromise. And we're still feeling that the twenty-five years is sufficient, but the problem really is, well, there's no agency or anybody to enforce that rule. We even referred to them as guidelines, but within the United States, NASA, for example, is bound by them; ESA is, as I said, they're bound by them. But they can still go to the secretary of state and ask for a waiver. And they have been doing that a lot in the past, but there are now people within the military, within NASA saying, no more waivers. We're getting serious.

Q: What was the first piece of orbital debris, space junk. Was it the first Russian launch?

Kessler: Yeah, Sputnik.

Q: Sputnik, is that true?

Kessler: Yep. Some of those very early launches are still in orbit. I think Sputnik was launched at a pretty low altitude and reentered fairly quickly, but there was an elliptical orbit I know is still up there. But, gosh, nobody . . . I mean, some of my colleagues, they were convinced that there just wasn't an issue with satellites colliding with one another.

And that was true very early in the program, but what they didn't do is look, well, how is this going to progress? Because what happens is that when you're looking at collision frequency generating debris, it goes at the square of the number of objects that you have in orbit. You double the number, you quadruple the collision rate. And when I wrote that it was at one collision every seventy-six years, and there were roughly less than five thousand objects in Earth orbit. Today there are three times that many. Three times squared is nearly ten—factor of ten—squared, and three squared, and you end up with ten times collision frequency, which is once every 7.6 years, which is pretty close to what everyone's predicting today. That's what you would expect with catalogued objects. So, it will continue to increase that way—it will increase as the square—you can get there fairly quickly because of that.

Q: I'm not sure what the right language to this question is, but are there certain launches or missions that create more debris than others, more junk?

Kessler: Well, there have been. For example, there for a long time, nobody really worried about the shroud put over a space craft. They just dump it overboard. They had explosives and cables that would come off. And now most of those things are tethered to make sure that they don't do that.

Q: Does space junk ever decay in any way once it's up there?

Kessler: There are some forms of decay; for example, you put up a plastic, there's enough atomic oxygen in the upper atmosphere that it will slowly oxidize. And you'll see these satellites that look like they're gold. They're actually covered with Mylar, which is a plastic surface, and the atomic oxygen will eventually—and they're very thin—over periods of years, that will eventually eat away and you'll see pieces of the Mylar come off. Same thing happens with paint. Paint flakes end up coming off. But other than that, the only other mechanism for eroding the surfaces is actually either meteorites or debris hitting those surfaces and taking hunks out of it all. And, of course, in the long term, that's exactly what everything will end up doing.

Q: An average collision, what would be the result?

Kessler: Well, an average collision really could be catastrophic because the smallest of the trackable objects are really not massive enough to catastrophically break up another satellite, but it would generate a lot of debris. And the only hint that you would have that that was going on is you may see a few pieces come off of a satellite. . . . And these are pieces that [are] ten centimeters, or roughly a softball size and larger, but not as massive as a softball. But—we see that happening quite frequently—there are satellites, for some reason, that are generating fragments.

Q: So a small collision could be more problematic than the occasional catastrophic one.

Kessler: That's right. We're just not seeing them because we don't have the sensors to be able to determine what's going on. But the catastrophic ones do get people's attention because the whole satellite breaks up. It's, like, you might as well have put a hundred pounds of TNT in it and blown it up. So the numbers that I use now, you end up with about a hundred fragments that are large enough to go on and cascade and cause another catastrophic collision, plus hundreds of thousands of centimeter-size objects that are capable of stopping just about any satellite from functioning, and then plus millions of millimeter-size particles that are capable of causing a satellite to stop functioning depending on where it hits, and it has [happened]—depending on whether or not it has shielding on it. For example, on the International Space Station, partially, when that was being planned, the debris issue was developing to the point that we could supply them with enough data that they planned to put shields on their spacecraft that would protect the habitation areas against roughly one-centimeter debris and smaller. And they, of course, they do collision avoidance against debris that's ten centimeters and larger, but in between one centimeter and ten centimeters, there's—they have no protection.

Q: In your opinion, what's been the collision of space junk or the incident that's been the most troubling to you?

Kessler: Well, what we don't know is most troubling. Since the end of the shuttle program, the shuttle has always been looked at as a reusable vehicle, so it has to be inspected after every flight, and one of the things that you discover when you inspect it is it's got craters on it. Some of those craters require some repair. And we started very early in the program analyzing the source of those craters and using that as data for our models as to what the real environment is. We'd rather have raw data to define the environment like we did during the meteorite days where we flew satellites and actually measured the meteorites penetrating surfaces. We've never purposely done that with debris yet—and I think that's a big failing of the space program, not having done that.

Q: So the shuttle was an unexpected sort of space spy in a way. Because it came back with all this information that you didn't necessarily—it wasn't sent up to get this information, but it came back with it about orbital debris?

Kessler: We also repaired the Hubble Telescope and we brought some pieces back, and that has provided data. But by far, the best has been the shuttle. And within the last couple of years, they finished the analysis of the shuttle data. And one of the things that it's showing is a large number of millimeter-sized particles, larger than we expected, that are stainless steel in origin, and they're—we don't know where they're coming from. And there could be something going on; for example, the collisional cascading phenomena that I have come up with is the big stuff, and it gradually grinds it up into the little stuff.

This—there could be a phenomena going on where the little stuff is eroding the surfaces of spacecrafts so much now that it's creating an increase in debris from the smaller end. So, you got both ends started clawing away at each other. That's pure theory. But these stainless steel particles could be a symptom of that, and that's one of the things that we're trying to—that NASA right now is trying to get a grasp on.

Q: One of the things that I found so interesting was the idea that it's hard to come to a solution about what to do because of international issues.

Kessler: Yes.

Q: Because space doesn't belong to one country. Do they really know whose debris it is?

Kessler: That's one of the jobs of the space command, to identify the country of origin of everything they catalogue. In fact, their ground rules are it cannot become part of the catalogue until you know what country it came from. And so, consequently, there's an awful lot of stuff waiting to be catalogued because they're not sure where to assign it. But if you go to the US Space Command Catalogue, you will find literally a couple of thousand objects associated—several thousand—with the Iridium Cosmos collision that says this came from that collision.

So, they do work toward doing that, but the problem is that the way international law is set up, it's different than the law of the sea. The law of the sea says if there's an abandoned ship and you get a hold of it, it's yours. But the law in space is that you're always responsible for it; even if it's abandoned, no one else can go up and touch it or you're breaking the law.

And in severe cases, a nation might even consider it an act of war because by getting even a dead satellite, you're trying to learn how they're made or, you know, learn some secrets.

Q: So, if the US figured a solution for space junk it can't go get a Russian piece of debris and apply the solution.

Kessler: That's right, [not] without the cooperation and the blessing of the Russians. And, of course, there are ways around that. Russia is a member of the IADC. And, so, consequently, they could work together. In fact, they could easily, whatever nation develops the technique to do it could say, OK, here it is. Here's the technique to do it, you use it, you go—you take care of it. And because it represents a danger to everyone, I really don't see the downside of any nations saying, OK, yeah, I'll remove my own debris, especially if somebody else pays— helps pay for it.

Q: What's the possibility of a piece of space junk falling and landing on the Earth somewhere?

Kessler: Oh, it does it all the time.

Q: Oh, we just don't know about it?

Kessler: We just—right. The small stuff mostly burns up, but there are—there is a material in there like titanium and some other metals that have a high melting temperature, and they consequently don't burn up, and they do represent a hazard on the ground. But you're more likely to get hit by a natural body reentering or an airplane falling on you than you are by space junk.

Q: The danger, in your opinion, is the collisions that happen in space. It's not what happens on the ground here.

Kessler: Yes. The astronauts would much rather . . . if they had a choice, just surely, purely from a hazard standpoint, they'd be a lot safer on the ground than in space. In fact, right now EVAs [Extravehicular activity, a space walk] are [meticulously] planned. They don't want to spend a lot of time in EVA because [a] millimeter-size particle could penetrate the space suit.

Q: So, why do we have to clean it up?

Kessler: Well, it depends on our infrastructure; what it really boils down to, it's going to get more and more expensive to put things in space. Because you can get around all of this simply by adding shielding to the spacecraft. And that's what the space station did. And one of the satellites that we looked at that's being planned to be launched, they didn't plan to add shielding, and we evaluated it and said, *You need shielding*, and they said, *Oh, OK*. But they didn't like to do it. One of the requirements that we have on them now is that you've got to be able to do this maneuver—after you finished using the satellite, you have to be able to drop it down to less than twenty—so that it reenters within twenty-five [years], if it's not functioning, you can't do that. So, you have to assure everybody that it's going to be functioning—that least only one chance in one hundred that it won't be—and consequently, they end up having to add shielding just to be sure that you're able to reenter it within the twenty-five years.

Q: So, the preventative measures cost money.

Kessler: That's right.

Q: And avoiding space junk is costing money at this point.

Kessler: That's right. And with time, that amount of money will continue to increase because you need to add more and more shielding. And it doesn't pay off in the long term because the more mass, the fundamental problem is you got so much mass in Earth orbit all going in different directions, and the more mass you add, it's like adding fuel to a fire. It's going to want to grind up sooner or later. And, so, consequently, it's not a long-term solution. The long-term solution, if you're planning to use space in the future, is you've got to have a different way of managing space. And one of the first things you have to do is ensure that whatever space you're operating [in], that it represents a stable environment—a sustainable environment. And right now, we don't have that.

Q: Recently we both have seen all these solutions popping up. Let me run a couple of them by you. You tell me why they would work or why they wouldn't work. The vacuum idea?

Kessler: Vacuum?

Q: . . . of vacuuming it up?

Kessler: *(laughter)*

Q: That makes you laugh.

Kessler: Well, when they use the term vacuum cleaner, for a long time I laughed at that, too, because you, you know, you can't— a vacuum just doesn't work in a vacuum. You're not going to suck anything up.

Q: How about the idea of lasers; the idea of zapping the junk with lasers?

Kessler: The problem is you got to get rid of the big stuff, and most of the people that are proposing lasers are only going after small stuff. And that's just temporary. I mean, for example, this laser cannon that they want to put on the space station, it will have a range of one hundred kilometers. So, you're not doing very much. What some people will [use] the lasers [for is moving] the big stuff, and the way they do that is they shoot a beam at it and vaporize part of the surface, and that vapor . . . then acts as a jet that that then propels it hopefully in the right direction, which is to make it drop down to a lower orbit and eventually reenter.

Q: The solar sail, the idea that it would drag it down into the orbit?

Kessler: The only way that you could cost effectively do that is put the solar sail on it before you launch it because you don't want to go up there and attach it. You could do that. But, yes. In fact, there's one company called Tethers Incorporated that actually is building an attachment you can put on any space craft, and it drops a tether down, and that acts like a silver sail in the sense that this tether then can use the Earth's magnetic field to generate electricity, and that electricity—the process of generating that electricity—takes energy out of the orbit and actually causes it to reenter more quickly. So, it acts in principle, like a solar sail. [With] a solar sail you're using the sun to slow it down, and in this case, they're using the Earth's magnetic field to slow it down.

Q: Of all the solutions that you've heard, which seems the most plausible and the most practical?

Kessler: Well, the most plausible is to just use the old-fashioned technique of going up and grabbing it and bringing it back—using something like the shuttle to go get it. And, you know, that is the most expensive. Even if you had one lodge—bring one object back—and you're only doing five a year, we're launching things into space seventy-five launches per year.

Q: You just have to budget in cleanup? If you're going to be doing this, it's going to be the cost of business; you have to budget in cleanup if you're going to be involved in space exploration.

Kessler: Exactly. Yep. And once you have that capability, then even satellites that say, well, I don't want to follow the twenty-five-year rule. OK. Well, you're penalized, you know, 10 percent of your budget you're penalized, and we'll pick it up for you. It's part of our satellite servicing capability. And you can minimize that cost, too, by planning where you put them.

Q: Of all the things that you predicted in '78, what's come true?

Kessler: Just about everything. When I go back and look at that paper, I surprise myself of how accurate it was.

III

WHEN DID IT BECOME BIG BUSINESS?

7

JUNK VETS
CHICAGO, ILLINOIS

"If you want somebody who's going to get the job done,
hire a veteran."

—PRESIDENT BARACK OBAMA,
STATE OF THE UNION ADDRESS, JANUARY 20, 2015

"I just knew that when I was getting into something
I was going to go full force in it, and I did. And I'm doing it.
It's just neat. By far, other than being in the Marines,
this is the best job."

—HECTOR CABALLERO JR.

I N THE SPLIT second when an Internet search serves up a list of junk removal companies, the potential customer has to decide whether or not to click on a link. As one business writer characterized it, to immediately connect with the consumer online a vendor "must reach inside their brain and pull a lever."[1] So what association could sway the average person to trust your company right away? What image could quickly telegraph to a client "Hey, we can come into your home and you'll feel safe and respected"?

Military branding is a perfect match for selling junk removal because of the attributes often assigned to veterans: loyalty, honor, hard work. The shorthand of the military affiliation is universally understood. After all, junk removal is a business model that requires an almost unreasonable comfort level—you have to allow complete strangers into your personal space and let them touch your things.

The founder of JDog Junk Removal of Pennsylvania says the appeal is knowing that a veteran-owned business will understand ethics, punctuality, and respect.[2] Businessman Jerry Flanagan, whose nickname was J Dog when he was in the army, wanted to help other service people start their own enterprises. He came up with the idea of offering junk removal franchises to active duty, reservists, and families of service members. For these folks he offers a full package with a designated territory, web support, and marketing plans. The latter includes the look and image of the company. Workers suit up in uniforms that resemble fatigues and the trucks are painted camouflage. The JDog logo is a gruff-looking bulldog wearing a captain's hat and, of course, dog tags. The bulldog has been an unofficial symbol of the marines since Brigadier General Smedley Darlington Butler, a double Medal of Honor recipient who introduced the English Bulldog as a mascot after World War I. His name was Private Jiggs.[3]

In Vermont you can call Grunts Move Junk. The CEO of the company served in the army and the COO was in the air force. For those in the know, a grunt is an infantryman, what the US Army refers to as "the backbone of the army." It is also, of course, an onomatopoeic word applied to work that is tedious, requires more brawn than brains, and hard enough to make even a strong person groan. Grunts Move Junk fully embraces its military theme. The tri-level pricing structure is as follows: "The Private," a small haul; "The Sergeant," medium-sized removal; and for a big load, "The Captain." The haulers wear army-green shirts with an "I [Heart] Veterans" logo on the back. They drive military-jeep-style trucks sporting a US Army star with a big gold G in the center. On its website the workers are rated on charm, height, and dance skills.

Fire Dawgs is owned and operated by veterans *and* firefighters in Indiana. It opted to play up the first responder aspect of the company with bright red trucks and uniforms and cute Dalmatians on the logo. However, the superhero military man branding isn't a sure path to success. The Junk Fighters of Kansas City, Missouri, another responder-based company, went out of business in 2013.

You wouldn't immediately peg Hector Caballero Jr. as someone who served unless he happened to be wearing short sleeves. On his right arm is a simple tattoo, two words written in script, Semper Fi, and on his left forearm, Semper Fidelis. It is Latin for "always faithful" and has been the marine's motto since 1883.

Hector met a recruiter when he was nineteen. "They had these flashcards. There were like twenty of them. He said, 'Pick out seven things that are important to you.' And there were things like leadership, integrity, honor. You know, I'm not trying to be all cheesy, but I was picking them out and he [the recruiter] was like, 'You could be a marine. Think about it.'" Not even of the legal drinking age, Hector made a decision that changed his life. "I was moved by it. And I joined." A young, big, tree-trunk of a guy, a Mexican American with closely cropped dark hair and a killer smile, Hector was ready to go.

He served for four years as military police and garrison. He was stationed in Okinawa for a year. He broke up fights on bases and responded to plane crashes. At one point he trained and became part of the Special Reaction Team (SRT), which is like the SWAT team of the marines. A career highlight for him was providing support and security in the Philippines for the fifty-year commemoration of the Leyte Gulf landing, the largest naval maneuver of World War II.

Once he was honorably discharged, Hector had a few different jobs and even owned a bar for a while. One day he thought he'd hit on the path to small business ownership that didn't involve booze and fried food. "I remember coming home from the bar one night, and I was thinking, I'm driving home, and I had a couple other rental properties at the time, and I wanted to continue renting properties. And I saw the port-o-johns and it clicked in my head. I'm like, real estate is all over the place! You don't have to pay taxes, you just collect rent on it. I was really fascinated by it. I went so deep into it that I had port-o-john magazines coming to the house. I mean, I had so much literature. I had a list of eleven portable toilet companies. I went down a list. I found one that wanted to hire. Got hired. They hired me on. They relied on me for everything because I was the most reliable guy. I wanted to learn everything." But what Hector learned was you couldn't trust the real estate market. Construction dwindled when the economy collapsed in 2008 and his idea went down the toilet. (I couldn't resist, and if you knew Hector, you'd know he'd think that was pretty funny.)

"I remember I just quit because I'm like, 'I'm not even going to think about it.' And then I was watching CNBC. My wife was making dinner. I'm like, 'Oh my God. I got it. This is it. I'm going to do *that*.'"

That was junk removal.

"You know, I did everything in a week. I called the lawyer and said, 'Hey Tony. I want to get incorporated.' 'OK. I'm on it. What's the name?' I said, 'Junk Vets.' And then called the insurance company and said, 'I need insurance.' Got it. This is it basically. Got my vanity phone number, 855-JUNKVET, and then—my brother, a steel worker, I asked him, 'Can I use one of your trucks?' He was like, 'Yeah.' So, he leased it to me for a while. . . . I took it in, got it painted, got my website, and I was in business."

Hector's can-do attitude is what military recruiters cite as a natural resource. Experts say that veterans are good for business because, as one executive put it, "The military is perhaps the best institution in the nation for teaching highly sought qualities such as leadership, teamwork, mission orientation, and integrity."[4]

Hector agrees and believes his time in the marines plays a part in what he does every day on the job and how he runs his business. "One thing that is a big misconception about marines, a lot of movies portray them as like, you know, loud and fighting. We're tough. We're fighting, but you know, they don't portray the professional department. It's the biggest group of professionals no matter what trade you're in. Whether you're in infantry or you're a military policeman, they train you how to be professional. . . . Don't slip up and swear. Don't say anything out of line, and just be aware of what you're saying. I think about that. I don't want to slip up when I'm dealing with a customer. I don't."

Hector's boss is tough and business minded, but fair. He has to be; Junk Vets is a one-man band. When Hector has a big job he does his best to hire other veterans and service folks to help. "I was just like researching other companies and I'm like, 'What do I got that's unique?' You know what I mean? I just couldn't think of anything.

And then I just go and think in my head. I'm like, 'I'm a veteran. . . . Then I wanted to model it after a veteran-owned business, you know, hiring vets. That's what I'm looking to continue to do hopefully. But it's not possible to hire only vets, you know?"

He's had a few successes. But there was one failure to save a former brother in arms that haunts him. An old friend of his, we'll call him Ted, did not make the same kind of productive transition to civilian life that Hector did. It is hard for Hector to talk about it. "He was the Marine Corps. When you think of pitch-perfect marine professionalism, he was hard core. He was just a great dude. Everybody looked up to him. Everybody respected him." The two were in the same living quarters and they became very good friends. "We were like brothers. We became so tight. We did everything together. We worked together. We'd go out partying together. We'd wake up in the morning hung over and go get breakfast and then go to work. Then we'd go back to the barracks. We had that lifestyle. It was just work hard, and play hard. When we got out of the marines he never stopped. He just got really out of control. He called me crying, like, 'Dude, I don't know what to do. I'm going to die. I'm withering away.' I'm like, 'Dude, come here right now.' I wired him a bus ticket, and he was on a bus. He came to town and I said, 'Come over to my house. Spend the night at my house this weekend, and then we'll continue treatment.'" Hector had hoped he could help his friend get back to work and that he could get the guy on his feet. "I picked him up from the bus station, and I knew immediately we were going to the hospital. It was that bad." Ted lasted for about a month and then left.

Hector's drive for helping out others is a big part of what he does. His childhood friend helps run a halfway house for people who have worked their way through substance abuse rehab. It was started by a firefighter to help other service folks with addiction issues, and it has expanded to be a workable solution for all kinds of people trying to reclaim their lives. Hector often tries out guys that his buddy, also a recovering addict and an alum of the house, thinks would be good on the job. This buddy, Mike, worked with Hector on many jobs in Junk Vets' early days. He knows the healing power of helping others in need, especially those whose lives have been overtaken by their junk, in a way that sounds a bit like the people who have been overtaken by their addictions. "The people are overwhelmed. It is needed for people who are in trouble. People who just bury themselves. They are afraid to get rid of stuff. Objects [of] sentimental value. People are afraid of losing what they have, so they collect and accumulate."

Veteran or not, Hector was working on Memorial Day weekend. Junk Vets is a low-fi operation: he has a cell phone, a notebook, and his truck. He had a few jobs booked, and a third emergency one came in at the last minute. They all had one thing in common: all of the homes belonged to folks who were born when a man could be president for more than two terms.

A whippet-thin and lighting-quick lady in her seventies was waiting in her driveway as Hector pulled up the truck. It has a red cab, the hauling box painted blue with white lettering: JUNK VETS. The woman was neatly dressed in a white leisure suit and white running shoes. Her thinning but well-coiffed hair was dyed a fawn brown. She led Hector to an immaculate garage. She'd already organized what needed to go but was still a little embarrassed by the piles she wanted removed. "I had forty years of clutter!"

If she only knew what most garages look like. Her garage was a junk hauler's dream. No vermin. A swept floor. No sharp edges. She had completely staged what she wanted taken away. She ticked off her list of things to go: the gutters, an old table, some leftover decking. Pointing to the back wall, she apologizes for not making the objects more accessible. "There are these weights over there in the corner. I couldn't pull them out. What can I say, I'm a hundred-pound weakling!" She was maybe one hundred pounds with a brick in each pocket, but this lady had a strong spirit. She was a fast talker, zipping over to the right corner of the garage to show Hector the frames on the screen door and bopping over the left to point out a tire. "I always said, next year, next year . . ." She finally decided to get started with the garage but she had not tackled her attic yet. "It is a crawl space. It has all my kids' stuff. A baby mattress for a baby's crib. My baby is thirty years old." She laughs. When asked why not let Hector head up there and at least haul away the ancient baby crib mattress, she says quite seriously, "Well if she had a baby, we could use it."

It was an interesting comment. A woman who until that moment was making rational, clear decisions about life's leftovers expressed an unrealistic attachment to a mattress that most likely would not meet twenty-first-century safety standards. It was probably harboring mold, could sag in a way that increases the risk of SIDS, and was likely not fire retardant. Yet in her mind, an agile mind, that mattress was a connection to her "baby" and the promise of grandchildren to come.

The job was completed in about twenty minutes.

"I can't believe I got rid of all that stuff. Some of it after forty-five years!" Does she know any veterans? Yes, her husband had been in the air force. "You are a godsend!" she told Hector as she paid him. She was really happy. "I swear I didn't pay her!" Hector chimed in. He was clearly pleased that his customer was thrilled. He told me earnestly, "I promise, it wasn't an act!"

That nice lady was what we all hope for our parents, and even ourselves as time marches on. She was living in her own home. It was clean and fresh and so was she. It is a real blessing for those who get to live the last years of their lives as she is.

Others are not as fortunate, as was made clear by an emergency call that came in at 10:16 AM. The person on the other end was a little panicked and short on details. Hector tried to get the caller to tell him how much needed to be picked up so he could give him a quote. Hector asked nicely but repeatedly, "Well, what kind of stuff ya got?" From his face, it seemed Hector was not satisfied with the answers he was getting. He quoted a price based on the vague description. After he hung up, Hector had a feeling.

The location was an assisted living senior home. A harried-looking but exceedingly polite overweight black woman in her forties

met us at the loading dock. She'd discovered at the last minute that
her mother had to be out of her apartment by the end of the month,
which was in four days. She'd done all that she could in the space
but now she just needed the rest gone. She was clearly in distress.
As she leads us up to the apartment, a few heads popped out and
a man asked Hector, "Are you going to Mrs. Madsen's*?" Hector
stops to tell the elderly man, "I am not sure, sir. I am working for
her daughter today." Everyone in the facility seemed to know about
Mrs. Madsen.

Hector's fear turned out to be right. There was a *lot* more stuff
than the woman's husband had said on the phone. There were three
couches, two chairs, a mirror, mops, brooms, silk flowers, four bags
of clothes, and a fake fireplace. And when we got there, the daughter
mentioned the storage locker. Storage locker? Hector later told me
"Sometimes I feel stupid when I underbid. But she seems like a nice
lady. She has trouble." He ultimately didn't charge her extra. It really
should have been double the quote but she only had the cash that her
husband gave her based on his elusive phone conversation. Maybe
the husband played Hector, but she was close to tears. It was easy to
understand why. The state of the room told the story. It smelled of
urine and stale food. It was easy to imagine that it had been a nice
living space once, but that over time Mrs. Madsen, probably telling
her children she was fine, was too proud to admit or maybe too sick
to realize that she was living a life that was slowly degrading.

Hector and his team worked in silence. There wasn't much to
say. This was sad. He looked at the couches and whispered to me,
"Man, I hate old furniture. Old furniture is really heavy." In the
midst of all this trash was a beautiful art deco pearl pin on the floor
in the corner. Was it accidentally left behind? Was the initial clean
out so frenzied that many other beautiful pieces were now in a box
or Dumpster somewhere? Or was it just a sign sent to remind us that
someone who was loved lived here, someone who had a life where she
would wear a pin like this to church or out to lunch? "Thank you so
much," the woman says when I hand it to her. "It was my mother's."

One thing Hector always remembers is that the things he picks up belonged to people and the people have life stories worth remembering. He is a big fan of junk and the stories that come with it. He has been known to ask questions about things that catch his eye, and with the client's permission he will often keep stuff they want gone. On a quick trip back to his house to hug his baby boy and bring his pregnant wife lunch, he shows me some of the treasures he has pulled from the trash. In his living room are two sexy gray leather club chairs rescued from a removal job at the Austrian consulate general's office on tony Michigan Avenue. His kitchen island countertop is high-end black butterfly granite saved from a construction job clean out. We head down to his basement and he shows me hundreds of baseball cards he pulled from one job. He has a box of beautiful stopwatches. He loves the tales behind each item and its original owner. He has a whole bookshelf in the basement taken up by boxes of autographs. It is an eclectic mix including Mel Brooks, Bob Barker, Buddy Ebsen, Barbra Streisand, Red Buttons, Jim Carrey, Barry Williams, Kenneth Tobey, Tim Matheson, and MC Hammer. It all came from a garage clean out of an older couple. Hector was amazed at what the husband had amassed. "This took a lifetime, you know?" Hector never saw the man, only his wife and son. Apparently she was fed up with her husband's hobby and talked him into getting rid of it all. "He was fascinated about Hollywood. We found Hollywood contracts, canceled checks from producers. I told the son, I want to meet your father, but he said no. There was something weird about it. I got the sense there was some depression going on."

We head out to his garage, which Hector knows is in need of a junk intervention. The original plan was for his wife to sell some of the stuff online, but Hector III arrived, and now Jacob is on the way. So for now, there are stacks of items like a five-foot gumball machine. Hector relays the backstory on each piece he has saved. His garage is a bit of a junk museum, and he is the curator. "I'm gonna show you something really cool." He grabs a bag and pulls out some fantastically ornate sequined glitzy gowns. The story behind the frocks is a reminder why not all junk is created equal.

He got a call from a woman who was moving her elderly parents from Chicago to the East Coast. Their doctors suggested they would fare better close to family. It was a big job. "We cleared the house, like eight Dumpsters," he remembers. The final bill was $3,600. All through the work, Hector noticed the older couple were watching his team and not saying anything. "Here's this little old lady and old man sitting there and they're just quiet and minding their own business. I'm cleaning out the attic and I'm coming across all these costumes, stage costumes, pictures. I found this picture. It was the most beautiful lady. She was in her twenties. She was gorgeous. I brought this down. I told the guy, I'm like, 'Sir, you wife's pretty now but she was hot back then.' He was like, 'Oh, yeah. She was a looker. She was a good-looking girl.' And he's like, 'You know, she was a jazz singer.' And then we sat there and started talking. She was like, 'I'm going to be on channel eleven tonight.' And I'm like, 'Really?' And she goes, 'Yeah. They're going to interview me.'"

Because he stopped to talk and to listen to the quiet elderly couple, Hector discovered he was cleaning out the house of Chicago jazz legends Eddie and Geraldine de Haas. Geraldine was described by the *Chicago Tribune* as the "first lady of Chicago Jazz." Her husband was a bass player of great note who performed with Chet Baker, Roy Haynes, and Miles Davis. Geraldine Bey started her career as a smooth alto jazz singer with her siblings in a trio called Andy and the Bey Sisters. They toured all across Europe and released three albums. They had regular gigs at some of the legendary jazz clubs, including the Blue Note (where, Geraldine says, Marlon Brando hit on her). Her brother, Andy Bey, had a late-in-life second act as a solo artist while Geraldine settled in Chicago and made it her business to keep jazz coursing through the city. She established the South Shore Jazz Festival. She went on to save a local cultural center, and she created the Duke Ellington celebration in the heart of the city that went on to become the Chicago Jazz Festival. Before they left

Chicago they were honored with a big celebration by some of the city's most famous musicians. It was covered by the local news with great reverence.

By the time Hector got to the house the most precious items had already been donated to a jazz museum. "The daughter said, 'Hector. Take what you want, because if it's in there, don't even tell me. We've already given the jazz museum enough.' So, I got a chance to get out those costumes." So what is a five-foot, ten-inch former marine going to do with a petite jazz diva's stage gowns? He has no idea, but to him they seemed too special—Mrs. de Haas seemed too special—to throw them away. "I don't know what to do with them. I think someone would appreciate them, you know?" That's the tricky thing about junk and junk removal; it all meant something to someone at one time.

He recently found himself at a moral crossroads. Hector showed up for a job and realized he was removing the belongings of a very famous Chicago basketball player. The player had gone through a bitter divorce, had just remarried an actress, and now his ex-wife decided to just chuck all the belongings of the house she got in the settlement. Signed photographs with other superstar players. A college jersey. Thousands of dollars worth of sneakers. Hector tried to contact the player to see if he wanted it all back but was blown off by the handlers. He is struggling with the idea of selling it. "This is worth a lot of money, you know. It could mean something for my family." Last time I spoke to him he was still deciding what to do. He was particularly bothered by what to do with all the photos of the man's family because to Hector family is everything.

Hector's love of the past and love of country is fueled in part by his family's history. After a few long, dirty days, Hector takes me to the bar he used to own on the South Side. It is part of who he is and his family's story. There is one noticeable thing about this bar and its clientele. It is an accent that I'm sure only exists in the 234 square miles that comprise Chicago. When the older fellas at the bar talk, you hear the flat Chicago *A* and the stubby-sounding *D* for the *TH* diphthong, as in "da Bears." The voices are also laced with a Mexican accent and cadence. It's a mash up of two distinct sounds that support the other's quirkiness. It was strange to the point of distracting, but clearly everyone in the bar was used to it. Many of these guys had worked with Hector's father in the steel mills when they were pioneers.

His father, Hector Sr., was one of twelve children who worked on a farm in Texas. "That was back in the time when they were exploited. 'We'll pay you. Just pay you enough to eat.' That kept my aunts and uncles out of school. They don't know any better. My uncle Art came to Chicago and found work in the steel mills and called back. So, my grandpa just took a chance."

By the 1950s Chicago's West Side had become a beacon for Tejanos like the Caballero family.[5] Mexicans were successful in the steel mills and became an important part of the Steel Workers Union.[6] Hector's father, uncles, and the local fellows at the bar were among those men. "I am so proud of where my family came from. I go to Mexico a lot. It's part of my heritage or history, but one thing that my dad has taught us, not really in words, but in his actions. You've got to understand why our ancestors left [and] came to this great nation. The opportunities here are amazing. It's all what you make of it. It's not really opportunity. It's acknowledgment of opportunity."

Hector decided to seize the opportunity to start a business hauling junk. Junk has him living the dream. "It's an honest day's work for an honest day's pay and it's not bad money. Of course I want to get bigger, but I don't want to be huge. As you know, time is everything. I have time to wake up and have breakfast with my wife and then wake up my kid. Got to go, kick ass for a couple of hours, come home, and then I do a job the next day. It's just the coolest every day."

Well, not every day. One job in particular haunted him for a week. He filled two thirty-two-yard Dumpsters and three fifteen-yard trucks and let the scrappers have the rest. It started out with a phone call from a woman who said her mother owned an antique store and that Hector could keep any of the "antiques" he removed. It was the old bait and switch.

"All donateables first, household items . . . and then trash in the back," Hector tells the guys he's picked up for work today. They were all wearing the red, white, and blue Junk Vets shirts and so was I. One fellow was quiet but knowing, a slim, blond young man, Eric, who wants to chat about Monsanto and its genetically modified seeds. He listens to a lot of NPR and plans on attending a protest that his friend posted about on Facebook. He has a sort of lonely look, the kind that inspired our waitress at lunch one day to give him a free cookie—no one else, just him. The other fellow barely said a word. They were both in recovery and recommended by Hector's friend for this day of work where no one would be home. They could work at their own pace.

The woman opened the back door to let Hector into her mother's home. "My brother was going to help, but no . . ." She waves Hector toward the stairs to the basement as her voice trails off. Hanging on the heavily wallpapered stairwell were faded family photos from the early 1970s, judging by the width of the gentleman's lapels and the length of his sideburns. She won't go down there anymore. Really, she can't. There is a mountain of stuff at the landing. The basement was filled to the ceiling, which was a little over seven feet tall. The room was the length of the house, about fifty feet long and back about twenty feet deep. Hector had to climb over the top of the mound to see where the mass ended. He slipped and slid. It was a little bit like watching a kid climb up a snowy hill. He had to dodge chairs, wicker magazine holders, bags, and bins holding who knows what.

"This really shouldn't be legal," Eric said under his breath.

As for the antiques? Well, the woman owned more of a curiosity shop and the entire inventory was upstairs in the living room. Hector called for a Dumpster—a big one.

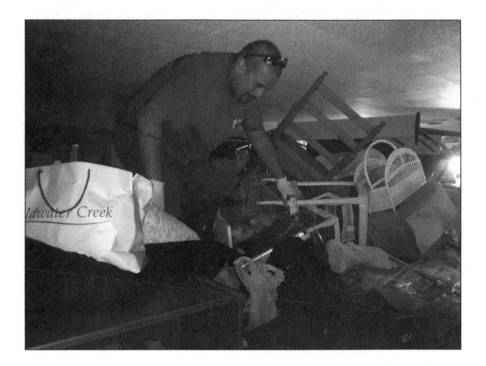

"It's all gotta go. I totally gotta disconnect. I just can't . . ." The woman's voice trailed off again as she wrung her hands. She seemed unable to complete a thought. She was becoming more and more emotional as she paced around near the door. Hector knew in his heart she didn't mean everything. After a quick conversation with her he told us to keep on the lookout for Bibles, wedding albums, and any important papers.

Hector explained why you have to have a little talk with clients before diving in: "You have to have communication skills with people because you're in their house and you're going through their life, you know? You can't just be some straight-faced, no-personality guy and go in there like, 'OK. I'll take . . . ' You've got to communicate with them and really connect with them and take their stuff out. A lot of people have lost their parents and you're watching them crying as you're taking their stuff out. We're the final guys in the final process of life. This is it."

Any thoughts about things being salvageable or donateable disappeared when it was clear that the bottom layer of the pile was soaked. There was water damage on almost everything. In some ways it made the job easier. This was a bag-and-toss job. Everyone gloved up and put on facemasks and started to fill heavy-duty contractor bags. We stuffed and stuffed and stuffed and started a conveyer line to get the loads out of the basement, up the stairs, to the yard, and into the Dumpster.

Going through the junk mountain was a bit of urban archaeology. The excavation revealed details of this family. As I placed items in the bags, I felt like I was watching someone's life in reverse. The outer layer consisted of the necessities of growing old, such as walkers, bedpans, and crutches. Next was a layer of toys of a variety and vintage suggesting they belonged to a grandchild, circa 1990s. A few more layers in revealed the good times when this family had money for family vacations to Jamaica and brought back straw purses and hats. Their luggage was cardinal red. There were citations for best employee. There was a big yard sale sign. Hector referred to this process as "peeling the onion." He meant that going through the many layers you find out about the people but initially I thought it was because this process could make you cry. Both are true. He said in most clean outs he can identify what life-changing event triggered the accumulation. The trigger is whatever item is found at the very end of the job. It could be an obituary announcement or a bassinet or a wedding invitation.

Looking around the house, it was a place that once held a lot of love and laughs. There were funny little signs here and there, the kind you would find at a church crafts fair. In the kitchen was a plaque that read "One nice person lives here. One old grouch." Close by was another sign that said, "Your warmth radiates onto all others around you." There were faded wallet-sized school pictures of little children on the refrigerator. On the wall right by the back door was a cutesy pink-and-white wall hanging, two rectangles held together by ribbon. The lettering was a swirly script and the sign said, "Eat

Like No One Is Watching. Shop Like the Bill Will Never Come." The sign helped make sense of what had been going on in that house. The over-collecting of calories and debt bares a striking resemble to the accumulation of stuff. A little is not so bad, but a lot can create distress. Seize the day can go wrong.

In the basement we did find a Bible and some wedding pictures, and we put them all aside. "Making progress," whispers Eric. "It is still nasty." Nasty was right. It was right around that point that I noticed the rat traps in the house and decided to do the rest of my reporting from outside. The Dumpster was nearly full. There was an enormous teddy bear near the top. You could see the furry feet sticking up over the edge. The neighbors watched through their windows and expressed concerned that leaving the Dumpster overnight would lead to some unsavory Dumpster diving.

By the end of the first day we could see the floor. The back wall was now visible. There was a full bar back there. Clearly this had been a boom-boom basement party room at one point. The very last things we found against the wall, the center or bulb of the onion, as Hector called it? Photos. Books and books of family baby pictures. Did starting a family set off the inclination to not let go?

At the end of the day everyone was tired and dirty and ready to be done with it. On the ride home Eric, the youngest of the crew, looked out the window and said, "Once you turn fifty you should just have to start giving things away."

8

BUSINESS AND SHOW BUSINESS

Business

Plastics!

Plastic bins changed the lives of two guys in Texas. They had decided to go after a dream of starting their own business. At the time they were coworkers in the paint section of a department store. The fellas first considered homemade furniture, but a research trip to a commercial trade show led to an idea that perfectly matched an emerging need: there they saw stackable Akro bins made of industrial grade polymer. The bins vary in size and are used mostly to store inventory. You've surely encountered them at a doctor's office holding things like syringes and the cups the nurse orders you to fill to the line.

Seeing the potential of introducing commercial-level organizing systems into civilian homes led Garrett Boone and Kip Tindell to open the Container Store in Dallas in 1978. A decade later there were seven Container Stores across Texas. In 2015 there were seventy Container Stores with an average size of twenty-five thousand square feet. By the time this book is published there should be seventy-nine stores in twenty-eight states and the District of Columbia. The stores are filled with things you didn't know you needed, such as a hair dryer holder, fasteners to keep rolls of wrapping paper in place, a clear plastic soda can holder for your refrigerator, and bed risers to boost your frame a few inches off the ground so you can then store the Container Store's specially made shallow underbed boxes you have filled. Full disclosure—a few years back when the Container Store signed a lease a few blocks from my home I was giddy with anticipation and walked by the location at least one a week until it opened, just to check in. For Valentine's Day my husband gave me flowers and a Container Store gift card.

The company's estimated take for 2014 was $800 million—and that was actually down considerably after a blockbuster IPO in 2013. The stores' workers are known for being highly compensated, twice the normal retail worker, and specifically trained. Where most retail sales folks ask, "May I help you?" and "Have you found what you are looking for?," Container Store workers are often encouraged to say, "What space are you trying to organize?"[1] For sixteen years the Container Store has been voted by *Fortune* magazine as one of the top one hundred companies to work for—and, yes, the stores carry Akro bins. Boone and Tindell were right.

The legend goes that early on someone walked into the original location and asked, "Are you the store that sells empty boxes?" On one level it is true: the Container Store simply sells receptacles. But it actually sells more than that. It sells potential and the promise of order and, in turn, serenity. It sells the possibility that your home can be free of confused masses and messes. It also means that your things might not be junk, if they are stored in a proper place or in an attractive vessel.

In the early days, one Texas journalist was fascinated by the store. Gaile Robinson from the *Forth Worth Star-Telegram* interviewed Mr. Boone in his home to see if he practiced what he advertised. Robinson walked away with this impression of the enterprise:

With every volley of the Container Store catalog, and each new store opening—20 to date—it becomes more and more apparent that there are scads
of organizational devices one "simply must have." Owning these things is
rationalized because they are obviously essential to life. Never mind that
being organized is a personality trait—buying the tools with which to be
organized is a shopping trait. Procuring Elfa shelves, the marvelous wire
shelving from Sweden, . . . does not necessarily mean that organization
will happen. All it means is Boone and Tindell get a little richer.[2]

I contacted Ms. Robinson in 2015 and asked what left her with
this impression.

"I wrote that? I'm often surprised when old stories come back to
haunt me," she said. "The first Container Store was in Dallas, just a
few miles from where I lived at the time. I thought it was the most
brilliant store I had ever come across and stimulated their cash flow
with my enthusiasm." As for her take on the company's success across
the United States all these years later? "I don't think Americans have
the need of additional storage as much as other parts of the world,
we just have too much stuff and we'd like to hide it, store it, or
disguise it in a decorative way. I'm an offender. I'd rather buy more
clear plastic shoe storage boxes and stack them to the ceiling of the
closet than truthfully address whether I really need two dozen pairs
of black shoes."

Three other storage solution retail stores started around the same
time, Hold Everything (1985–2006), Organized Living (1985–2005,
now a manufacturer), and Storables (1981). An entire retail genre
emerged because people needed a place to put all the stuff they accumulated and wanted to feel good about it, or at least like they were
being proactive about it. You see it at junk removal runs. Remember that job in Chicago that filled two thirty-cubic-yard Dumpsters?
There were sixty-two blue Rubbermaid storage tubs full of things
pulled out of that basement. At almost every house where a junk
removal company makes a call you will find plastic bins. Storage

supplies are to junk what Spanx are to middle-age spread. It is all still there, just squished in. In the wrong hands, containing culture just prolongs a problem, but in the right hands, in the hands of a professional, it can be a revelation.

"The Container Store supports a whole industry," one professional organizer told me. And vice versa. Professional organizers are like the Justice League of Clutter, swooping in and making things right and orderly once again. Or maybe for the first time. They create systems and teach their overwhelmed clients coping skills. They have different areas of expertise. Organizers can specialize in aging clients or small business organization.

What organizers really do was unclear to a writer named Alan Henry. He decided to crowdsource his research by posting a question to his Twitter followers on October 3, 2014.

> Alan Henry @halophoenix
> Has anyone actually had experience with a "professional organizer," or is that just BS on design/real estate shows?

Here are a few of the tweets back:

> Whitson Gordon @WhitsonGordon
> What the shit is this a real thing

> Jack @NinthBatter
> Well if we have food stylists does professional organizer really seem that strange?

> Jim Zakany @Jim_Zakany
> Yes. My wife is a borderline hoarder and they've really helped her.

> Alan Henry @halopheonix
> @Jim_Zakany Ah, good to hear it. Did they actually come and do work or make suggestions for you guys to do later?

Jim Zacany @Jim_Zakany
@halophoenix They work w/her, hands on. I stay out of it.
Both decultter & organize.

Alan Henry @halophoenix
@Jim_Zakany Interesting! Thanks—I may be flippant about
the idea, but I have an idea and they sound really helpful!

Jim Zakany @Jim_Zakany
@halophoenix I can't help her (she won't let me). She needs
a third party. Well worth it for some people.

Jeff Angcanan @Jeff_Angcanan
@halophoenix 3 boxes: Store, delegate, purge. There. You
owe me money.

Ultimately the author went on to write a thorough piece about
professional organizing for the website Lifehacker. It included a very
nice rebuttal to the naysayers from an organizer named Julie Bestry.
Her retort was, "Some people might think what we do is helping
people who are too 'lazy' to do things for themselves. I'm sure such
people cut their own hair, make their own clothes, and tutor their
own children in calculus without any difficulty. But I'm afraid the
rest of the world is a little more interdependent."

Bestry is one of the four thousand members of the National Association of Professional Organizers, known by the acronym NAPO.
It began with a small group of organizers who occasionally met in a
California living room to share stories and strategies. By 1986 they
formally organized and the sixteen members became the first iteration of NAPO. In 1987 they were able to have their services listed
in the California yellow pages consumer directory, and a year later
NAPO held its first conference.

Fast forward twenty-five years to 2013 and NAPO's silver anniversary celebration, which was held in New Orleans. They were a
festive—and orderly—bunch. There was a funny dichotomy between

the "Let the good times roll" essence of New Orleans and a ballroom full of people who keep things in line professionally.

The exhibition hall was full of products an organizer might use. Rubbermaid has a booth. Some are new vendors trying to make a go of it. The lady with the adorable and expensive paint can stickers to identify leftover paint might have those on her hands for a few years. The woman with the folders that say things like CRAP and NONE OF YOUR BUSINESS got a lot more traction. Fujitsu and Neat scanners are trying to encourage organizers to digitize clients' paper clutter. To make the point, there was a man dressed up as a giant paper monster covered with Post-Its running down the aisle as part of a presentation. Some organizers seem leery and worry that scanners will put them out of a job. One of the sales people made the argument that people who are disorganized in their terrestrial life will be disorganized in their digital life too. But what is striking is how many organizers there are from around the world. Twenty-two countries were represented, including almost half of the G20, a group of nations that control 85 percent of the world's gross product and 75 percent of global trade.[3] There were attendees from Australia, Brazil, Mexico, Canada, Germany, Guatemala, Israel, and Japan.

A doctor studying hoarding in Japan says people are often surprised by its existence. He has observed that "rampant consumption exists just as much as in Japan as in Western countries."[4] There is a very specific subculture of collector/hoarder in Japan devoted specifically to designer clothing. In a book called *Happy Victims*, photojournalist Kyoichi Tsuzuki published a series of pictures of Tokyo residents in tiny, tiny apartments packed with the clothes of one particular designer—Gucci, Nike, Agnes B. In the photos every inch—walls, floor space, furniture—is covered with these items.

The Japanese version of NAPO is called JALO, an acronym for Japan Association of Life Organizers. It was founded in 2008. Its goal is interesting and suggests a slightly different approach. JALO's motto is "For easier, more comfortable lives." Japan is home to probably the most popular professional organizer in the world. She has been the subject of a television drama in Japan and a comedy pilot for NBC in the United States. There is a three-month-long waiting list for her services. Marie Kondo's *The Life-Changing Magic of Tidying Up* sold more than two million copies and hit number 1 on the *New York Times Best Sellers* list in 2015. She does not believe in tips or suggestions about where to put things. She believes "Storage is a myth. . . . A booby trap lies within the term 'storage.' . . . Putting things away creates the illusion that the problem has been solved." She believes the problem is that people keep things because of an attachment to the past or a fear of the future. She asks her clients to take the control back by telling them to take each item they own, every single one, hold it and consider this: "'Does this spark joy?' It if does, keep it. If not, dispose of it. This is not only the simplest, but also the most accurate yardstick by which to judge."

In the United States, in an effort to further legitimize professional organizing, a nonprofit group was created to promote a national ethical standard in the field. The Board of Certification for Professional Organizers was founded in 2007. An organizer can earn the designation of certified professional organizer by passing a two-hour, 125-question test that is given three times a year. But before an organizer can even take the test he or she must have a minimum of a high school diploma or GED and have fifteen hundred hours of documented paid work experience in the last three years. Recertification is mandatory every three years.

Organizers often belong to or are affiliated with NAPO, BCPO, and ICD, or all three. ICD president Linda Samuels remembers that when she started her company, Oh So Organized, she needed to explain what she did for a living. "In the 1990s, it was 'Organizers? What's that?' In the next ten years, 'I could really use your help. I know someone who could use your help.'"

"Hmmmmm," was the first thing Samuels said when I asked her professional position on storage units. She chose her words carefully. "There's a place for them." Pause. "For someone in transition, it can be handy. As a long-term solution, it is incredibly expensive." Pause. "The pain of thinking about it and stress. It is also expensive on an emotional level. It is often things waiting for a life you are trying to live."

It was an opinion shared by other organizers. Storage facilities provide an opportunity to outsource the responsibility for your stuff. Sixty-five percent of all self-storage renters have a garage, 47 percent have an attic, and 33 percent have a basement, according to the Self Storage Association, a nonprofit trade group. Self-storage has its own association and lobbying group because it is big business, generating more than $24 billion in revenue in 2014. The United States is home to reportedly 48,500 to 52,000 self-storage units. That's about 2.3 billion square feet of storage. It is a business that has been called recession resistant by the *Wall Street Journal*. When the economy is bad and people are in transition because of eviction or downsizing, storage units provide a place to park their stuff until stability returns. The *New York Times* reported that in June 2009 Public Storage, the largest chain, had facilities that were 91 percent full, on average. At the time Public Storage had twenty-one hundred facilities. Conversely, when the economy is good, people buy more and need a place to put it. In 2015 Public Storage had twenty-two hundred facilities in thirty-eight states.

While locally owned and even national chains have a very basic, utilitarian look and feel, niche storage has arrived. Driving up to Westy's facility there are no chain-link fences, no garage-style units. There's a wrought iron gate and you must enter a code to get in. The building's white stone facade looks more like a fancy department store. Walking into the lobby you might think you've mistakenly popped into a four-star hotel. There are blazer-wearing concierges who greet you. The chrome is shiny and the floor is spotless. There are no garbage cans or Dumpsters. The interior of its Chatham, New Jersey, facility looks like the interior of the Frank Lloyd Wright–designed Guggenheim Museum in New York City. There are three levels, each with curved white balconies. On the walls hang framed posters of classic works by Roy Lichtenstein and Picasso. The units have shiny white metal doors. You can only access the facility during business hours and limited weekend hours. There will be no late-night shenanigans here.

In Westchester, New York, Katonah Self-Storage offers a place to put not only your skis, but also specific storage units for your wine. And your classic cars. In spring 2015 there were waiting lists for both.

For the door-to-door storage service there is PODS, Portable Storage On Demand. A giant contraption, a detachable lift system known as a "podzilla," will bring a storage unit–sized box to your home and deposit it in your driveway or on your lawn. You fill it, and then "podzilla" will return and make it go away until you are ready. Founded in Clearwater, Florida, in 1998, it was acquired almost a decade later by a Bahranian private equity firm for somewhere in the neighborhood of $430 to $450 million. In February 2015, PODS was sold to the Ontario Teachers' Pension Plan for more than $1 billion.

All the businesses that have grown out of American's relationship with junk have two things in common. The first is that the industries revolving around the axis of stuff caught on the in the 1980s. Second, they all became the subjects of television shows.

1980s

The iconic speech Gordon Gekko gave in *Wall Street* was not unlike an actual commencement address given on May 18, 1986, at the University of California, Berkeley. A year before he was sentenced to jail and after paying a $100 million fine for insider trading, Ivan Boesky captured the spirit of the free-range capitalism of the 1980s when speaking to a crowd of business school graduates. He told them, "Greed is all right, by the way. I want you to know that. I think greed is healthy. You can be greedy and still feel good about yourself."

One synonym for the word greed is *acquisitiveness*, which means the seeking of possessions. For a portion of the American population, 1980 to 1990 was a go-go decade of big hair, bigger houses, and the biggest appetites. Conspicuous consumption, a nearly century-old

concept, was emerging as an '80s cultural norm. As historian Doug
Rossinow wrote about this shift in his book *The Reagan Era*, "Capital-
ism, subjected to moral and cultural criticism in the 1960s and 1970s
by a generation longing for a simpler and more ethical life, received
a fresh blessing from the highest levels of American leadership in
the 1980s."[5] The Reagan era in Washington, one of "furs, jewels, and
limousines,"[6] was broadcast into the nation's homes. The country
watched as First Lady Nancy Reagan, who had elegant taste, spent
more then $800,000 in donated funds redecorating the White House
in the first nine months of her husband being in office.[7]

Despite economic downturns at the beginning and the tail end of
the decade, during the mid-'80s it was a full-on spend-a-thon for those
who could afford to, and even those who couldn't. This included the
government; the federal debt doubled during the decade. This was a
period when baby boomers, many of them yuppies, were coming into
their financial own, having learned at the hands of their parents that
it was important to spend. Their parents were told to conserve while
World War II raged, and then were encouraged to pump money into
the economy as part of the new postwar America. Historian Lizabeth
Cohen, author of *A Consumers' Republic: The Politics of Mass Consumption in Postwar America*, describes it this way: "The new postwar
order deemed, then, that the good customer devoted to 'more, newer,
and better' was in fact the good citizen, responsible for making the
United States a more desirable place for all its people."[8] The boomers,
the largest swath of population, learned to consume from an aging
population who were emotionally wired to save. That is a stuff tsunami.

In addition to this great audience of potential spenders and keep-
ers, the 1980s introduced new levels and ways to consume. In the
1970s the United States normalized relations with China after decades
of being cut off. A large, poorly paid (by US standards) workforce
led to inexpensive goods from China flooding the retail landscape.
In the 1980s Walmart was a dominant retailer in the United States.
Sam Walton, founder of the superstore, claimed that Chinese imports
accounted for only 6 percent of his sales in 1984. The investigative

news program *Frontline* found another source that put it "at around 40 percent from day one."[9]

Walmart is now the largest retailer in the United States, followed by Costco, which was founded in 1983. Although it has a radically different philosophy, Costco too played a part in the consumption culture of the 1980s. Fashioned after the French hypermarkets, these big locations with big inventory allowed people to buy at big discounts. Costco merged with Price Club, whose first location was actually in a converted airplane hanger. Think about that—a store the size of an airplane hanger. It was enormous, and it provided the average person the opportunity to buy in bulk. Of course, people have free will. These two retailers do not force people to come in and buy things—forty-eight rolls of toilet paper for example—but they do provide the opportunity to do so.

But what if you never even had to leave your house to buy something? The convenience and ease of QVC and HSN began in the 1980s as well. It started with cable television. Cable had been around since the early 1950s as a way to help geographically remote areas get some kind of reception. After a gradual loosening of the restrictions in 1984, there was seismic shift in the industry. The Cable Communications Act of 1984 sought to both regulate the industry with a national standard and give it enough freedom to grow. From 1984 through 1992, America was wired for cable. The industry spent a reported $15 billion doing so. It was considered one of the largest construction projects since World War II.[10]

A whole new kind of programming became available, things people had never seen before: rock stars lip-syncing their songs on music television, an entire network devoted to sports. Shopping would not be far behind. Home Shopping Club, renamed Home Shopping Network, was founded in 1982 and QVC (Quality, Value, Convenience) was founded in 1986. They feature comely hosts (and now celebrities) who chat like friends fawning over clothing, appliances, cosmetics, you name it, and they encourage the viewer to buy by simply calling in with their Amex or Visa at the ready. The channels play the scarcity card, broadcasing the dwindling number of items left.

Dr. Barbara Jo Dennison, who deals with patients who have hoarding issues, says, "QVC should be outlawed. It is like an alcoholic at a bar." Other professionals who deal with shopping addictions expressed the same sentiments about the relentless nature of television shopping. Unlike bartenders or casinos that can cut off those who overindulge, television shopping networks are not inclined to nor required to decline a credit card. Some people buy as entertainment and watch for companionship. The programming is there all the time. Hosts often greet callers by saying, "Hello, friend." One morning HSN was selling StoreSmart bags and compression totes, the kind you hook up to a vacuum cleaner to suck the air out of so your clothes or linens take up less room. The boyish, v-neck-sweater wearing, neat-as-a-pin host made a joke that you should get these bags so that you can make room for more things you buy on the Home Shopping Network.

Aside from giving cable television the opportunity to grow, that pivotal 1984 act listed as one of its goals, "to assure that cable communications provide and are encouraged to provide the widest possible diversity of information sources and services to the public."[11] I'm not sure conservative Arizona senator Barry Goldwater, who wrote the legislation, could have even forseen that the services to the public would include a show called *Hardcore Pawn.*

Show Business

On most Saturday mornings around 8:00 AM, Midtown Manhattan is quiet. The streets are empty in a borough that is home to 1.6 million people. The Friday weekend exodus to local beaches is complete. Anyone who stayed in New York City was likely sleeping off the night before. That's why it was unusual to see a stream of people walking west on Thirty-Fourth Street carrying bags, pulling loaded-up red Radio Flyer wagons, and juggling bubble-wrapped items. They were all headed toward the Javits Center, an enormous event space overlooking the Hudson River. The center normally hosts huge trade conventions like the international auto show or the boat show. This particular weekend it was host to *Antiques Roadshow.*

Antiques Roadshow was one of the first television programs whose content explored the relationship between an individual and object and value. The American version started broadcasting on PBS in 1997. The premise is simple: people bring an item to be appraised by professionals who will tell them what it is worth and why. The show travels across the country looking for participants. So far *Antiques Roadshow* has been filmed in forty-four states, the District of Columbia, and Canada. Tapings are ticketed events and winners are chosen by lottery. More than twenty thousand requests are made for the three thousand tickets available per season. Ticket holders are selected at random. Some people have a dream that their ticket could be like the golden one that got young Charlie Bucket into Willy Wonka's factory. You can see it on their faces.

Antiques Roadshow's nineteenth broadcast season kicked off in New York City. As people walk through the giant glass doors of the Javits Center, item in hand or on a wagon or what have you, they are warmly greeted by volunteers. Tickets are checked and directions given. The tickets are time stamped so that there is a steady and controlled flow. This is not only an event, it is a television show taping and there are cameramen, sets, and union rules to be considered. Section 3B on the first floor of the convention space has been turned into part television studio and preproduction staging.

Ticket holders are funneled into a maze much like the entry lines at a high-volume amusement park or TSA line. The first wave started lining up around 8:00 AM. There are people who look like they rolled out of bed and some who have arrived camera ready. There's a slim young man wearing shiny black vinyl pants and a gravity defying hairdo who just knows in his heart he is going to make it to television. (He doesn't.) My guide/minder for the day has been with the show for years. "We were in Chicago a couple of weeks ago. I heard this huge crash. I couldn't even look. Some of the ways things are transported. Some of the people are vulnerable—older or infirmed. They don't always anticipate how far they are going to have to go. Some of the things are ginormous." At that moment, as if on cue, a man walks by with a carved wooden horse on a dolly.

The people are waiting to enter an area that is called triage. It isn't life or death at these tables, but it is a fairly speedy and concise process. People present their objects and then are assigned to one of the twenty-four different categories of appraisal. The groups include glass, silver, sports memorabilia, decorative arts, jewelry, dolls, and folk art. The person is given a ticket to a table and off they go to meet one of the approximately seventy appraisers on site. My host explains, "No one gets turned away. It is like the ER. Here they determine which appraisal line you should get into. 'Yeah, that's vase but it goes to Asian art specialist. No, that's a folk art.' They really know. Here's where they help you define who's best."

Approaching a triage table is an auburn-haired woman of a certain age wearing a flowing floral tunic and a lot of costume jewelry. She's a bit panicked about what item to present. Ticket holders are allowed to bring two things. She turns to the two fellas behind her. "Does it look like an obvious piece of garbage?" she says, pointing to a beat-up painting of a street scene. She also has a piece of jewelry and a vase. "Well, you can always go to jewelry to get that appraised," offers the taller of the two gents.

"You're right, thank you." The triage specialist hands her two tickets and she just wants to confirm. "So I go to two different tables?" Once she gets a look at the tickets, one directing her to paintings and the other to glass, she seems satisfied. She turns to the man behind her. "Thank you for your patience and your help." She'll later find out the painting is worthless but that doesn't matter to her. She says she just loves it.

Next up at triage is a big man with a small dog brush. Not a brush for a little dog, but a clothing brush with a perfect ceramic canine figurine on top. It was in pristine shape and the puppy sculpture was really fine. He spied it at a secondhand store and stalked it for a while. "I saw it in the window. I bought it for five dollars. I've only seen one more like it online. It is just fantastic." Off he goes to collectibles.

Next is a curious group. It is a family, six people together, and they are very, very secretive. Everything is wrapped tightly and they are eyeing everyone around them, especially me with my recorder and notepad. They lean down to whisper to the assessor and start to unwrap what they have, all the while giving me the hairy eyeball. Their behavior is so odd and I have clearly spooked them, so I just close my notepad. Whatever they brought they believed was so special and so valuable that they didn't dare allow the media to know about it. Whatever it was, it didn't make the broadcast.

After triage, people line up to go the selected tables and have their pieces assessed by the official appraisers. This is real moment of truth for this group. Was that beer mug that your dad told you was an antique worth something? (No.) Was the story your mom told about the silk purse with the gold edges true? (Yes; it was worth between $15,000 and $20,000.) A tall, thin man in pink pants, wearing a giant Hermes belt buckle, presented a small lacquered box. The appraiser told him that there seemed to be a "condition issue with the lacquer" and that what he thought was amber was some sort of composite. After a polite thank-you he left the table and said "Darn it!" under his breath. Another appraiser is doing his best to be as professional as possible as someone presents him with a nutcracker, which could be rightly called a butt-cracker. The crushing part of this figurine is not the jaws.

A nice family from Connecticut hoped that a painting they found in their print shop would be something special. "I wasn't going to touch if it was worth $1,800, but since it is worth fifty bucks I'm gonna go for it." He's a little bit sad they didn't make it on the televised portion of the *Roadshow* because, as the husband noted, "I wore a clean shirt." Another lady said that her grandmother's grilled cheese maker was valued at "cool."[12]

The strangest thing I saw that day was an early 1900s breast pump made of a glass cup and two padded appendages resembling tongs.

The tongs would apparently press in on a new mother's breast and stimulate the milk that would then drain into the cup. A man found it in his grandfather's old saddlebags. His name was Dr. H. C. Walker, and he was a traveling doctor in Kansas City. This did not make it on the broadcast. While it is a good story, it makes some sense that a fairly tortuous-looking antique breast pump might not be the best subject for a well-established, respectable, high-brow television show. Remember, while people are milling about, having conversations, making new friends, and enjoying the event, the staff is there to produce a television show. That means they need not only interesting items to highlight, but also compelling characters to tell the story of the object.

When an appraiser sees something he or she thinks would make for a great spot on the show or meets someone who might make good TV, the appraiser pitches the story to the producers. We stumbled on that happening. The fellow was a bit disheveled, had a thick New York accent, sort of a salty dog type. He tells a good tale.

"I helped clean out someone's estate. It was like—ya know—three apartments worth. There was—ya know—a record collection like, five thousand records." One of the things he kept from the clean out was a lamp. The base looked like a genie lamp. "It's like if I rub it . . . like maybe a genie will pop out!" He'd clearly delivered that line before, but boy did he love delivering it. The reason the appraiser wants this fellow to be considered is that the lamp seems to be an atypical Tiffany lamp. The appraiser realized that the colorful owner doesn't know it is a signed Tiffany. As the appraiser talks to the producer, the owner starts talking to me. He's excited to be there and wants to share his story with me. As we are making conversation, the producer comes over and gets a little testy with me and my guide. I tell him it isn't her fault and that we were just chatting, but he huffs, *It can't happen.* We peel off as the producer starts to question the man himself.

My escort explains what happened. "If they are selected, they go to the green room, but also isolation. That's why the producer waved us off. Once a person has been selected then no one can talk to them and they don't want someone—we have to watch with social media and people will look it up and this thing is only worth two bucks." They are very serious about the no-contact rule. "This is reality TV for real. We want the reactions to be pure. So they don't want anyone polluting the experience."

I keep my distance and my mouth shut when we find another appraiser enthusiastically asking questions about a collection of sports memorabilia owned by an old-school Mets fan. He has two vintage figurines, one of Mr. Met and one he calls Miss Met. The girl bobble head has red hair in a kicky flip style and is wearing an orange bow tie and holding a Mets pennant. The bobble heads were part of the earliest mascot memorabilia for the Mets, a team founded in 1962. The appraiser knows these are the real thing and really old because Miss Met, who was called Lady Met at the time, was only part of the earliest team promotions.

"How did you get this stuff?" he asked the young guy. He told the appraiser that he was at a yard sale and the lady invited him in, "And she just gave 'em to me."

The fellow also had a souvenir ashtray from the opening day of Shea Stadium. That was April 17, 1964. The appraiser loved it. "It's very *Mad Men*," he says. He also realized that they were in good shape. Apparently the producers like this whole package because Mr. Met, Lady Met, and the ashtray all made it on one of the New York shows. The segment lasted one minute and fifteen seconds and went like this:

> Owner: It is a bobble head and I collect bobble heads and I went to get a bobble head from a yard sale and the woman who sold me the bobble head invited me in her house and she kept bringing out amazing thing after amazing thing. She had gotten them from her aunt that she said worked for the Mets and that's how she got the collection.
>
> Appraiser: And you are a Mets fan yourself?

Owner: Diehard Mets fan, born and raised in New York.

Appraiser: These are all dating from the 1960s—the very birth of the team. So which one of these is your favorite?

Owner: Lady Met because she doesn't exist anymore, which doesn't make a lot of sense to me because she is so cool.

Appraiser: These are obviously souvenir items dating from the 1960s. I think it says 1967 on the back. But not a lot of these were sold at the ballpark and not a lot of them are out in the wild. And when you do find them the hat is always gone, the pennant is always gone. You have a very early Mr. Met bobble head doll that predates that. You also have this wonderful ashtray from the dedication of Shea Stadium. Shea Stadium came into being in 1964. And what else is neat, there's a signed ball here and a pin from one of the hotdog vendors. Amazing collection. I wish you had more, but given what's on the table here, I'd insure it for $2,500.

Owner: Great.

While this baseball find was charming, it was not the sports memorabilia from the New York shows that made national news. That honor went to some Boston Red Stocking cards and handwritten letters from some of the earliest players. An older woman inherited them from her great-great-grandmother. The players often stayed at a boarding house she ran at the time, around 1871–72. The appraiser valued the whole collection at $1 million. The woman's reaction? "Holy smokes." If this show was on cable with a slightly different audience, the response likely could have been "Holy shit!" or worse.

Antiques Roadshow is the prim grand dame of this genre of television, but she has a group of unruly, rowdy, and thoroughly entertaining neighbors who have moved into town.

Reality television is a fun-house mirror of real life. You get a warped and weird image of what is actually true. The reality show industrial complex built around junk was undeniable by the early 2000s. The real tension that exists between the desire to buy and own, positioned against the stress created by the acquisitions, makes perfect

sense for nonscripted television. The deep dive into subcultures surrounding junk, plus the colorful personalities attracted to it, became
the engine for many, many cable television shows. Unless otherwise
noted, these shows were still broadcasting by the end of 2015 and I
gave myself the challenge of describing each in four words or less.

American Pickers, History Channel, 2010: Expert junk seekers
Auction Hunters, Spike TV, debuted 2010: Storage unit
bidders
Auction Kings, Discovery Channel, 2010–2013: Auction
house life
Barry'd Treasure, A&E, 2014: Outrageous collector seeking
junk
Buried Treasure, Fox, 2011: Antique dealers searching attics
Cajun Pawn Stars, History Channel, 2012–2013: Cajun
pawnshop life
Clean Sweep, TLC, 2003–2005: Organizing ambush
Clean House, Style, 2003–2011: Organizing and yard sales
Flea Market Flip, HGTV, 2012: Flea market upcycling
competition
Garage Gold, DIY, 2013: Removal runs for cash
Hard Core Pawn, TrueTV, 2010: Detroit pawn store drama
Hoarders, A&E/Lifetime, 2009–2013, 2016: Helping hoarders
Hoarding: Buried Alive, TLC, 2010: Ditto
I Brake for Yard Sales, Great American Country, 2013:
Upcycling junk
It's Worth What?, NBC, 2011–2011: Game show about junk
Junk Gypsies, HGTV/GAC, 2011: Decorating with junk
JUNKies, Science Channel, 2011–2011: Junkyard life
Junkyard Wars/MegaWars, TLC, 2001–2003: Engineers
upcycling junk
Mission Organization, HGTV, 2003–2011: Organization
makeover
Oddities, Discovery Channel, 2010–2014: Junk shop
operation
Pawnography, History Channel, 2014: Junk-based game show

Pawn Stars, History Channel, 2009: Vegas pawnshop life
Pawn Queens, TLC, 2010–2011: Female pawnshop owners
Picked Off, History Channel, 2012: Competitive antiquing
Picker Sisters, Lifetime, 2011: Lady junk pickers
Storage Wars, A&E, 2010: Auctioning repossessed storage units
Storage Wars Texas, A&E, 2011: Ditto, in Texas

While the stuff is the star, most shows rely on big personalities to make the viewers care. There is what's called and an A line and a B line. The A line might be about the junk that is being sold, bought, removed, or reordered. The B line will be about a conflict or a profile of the people involved.

The hosts of the show and the series regulars become like family to regular watchers. While eavesdropping at a yard sale in Franklin, Tennessee, I overheard two older gentlemen talking all about Mike. Mike this. Mike that. Mike found this old soda machine. One gent was actually a little peeved at Mike, something about overestimating the price of an object. It suddenly became clear the Mike they were talking about was Mike Wolfe, the star of *American Pickers*. It went like this:

"The Picker, Mike, he got that for $225 . . ."

"No, he sold it for that . . ."

"I like that show. That's some good, clean fun. No cussin' on that show."

"Yeah, but it done made all the prices go up. People think their stuff is worth way more than it is."

"Yeah. OK. Well, how much for your balls?" He was interested in some pool balls.

Mike Wolfe's boyish good looks and infectious enthusiasm for climbing around old barns while politely haggling over Americana has made him a star. He and his wife had to move because fans started showing up at their front door. He started out with a small shop, Antique Archaeology, in Le Claire, Iowa. It was full of cool things he "picked" on his travels. A second location in Nashville is now more gift store than thrift store. It is a sign of the success of the show. On a hot, hot Saturday in Nashville tour busses pulled up and out poured devotees of the show. They filed in slowly, one by one, waving their paper fans. Being Nashville, there was live music in the store. A brother and sister duo were picking at their guitars and trying to engage the crowd with an original song, but no one paid them much mind. There were a few cool "picked items" around, but mostly people wanted souvenirs from the shop and the show. There was a ton of merchandise for sale. Beer cozies. Lunch boxes. People streamed in and out all day, leaving with arms full of merch. One estimate says the store has more than two hundred thousand visitors a month.[13]

"*American Pickers* is great. It's about stuff. Half those people are hoarders but the show has a different tone." Matt Paxton should know. He is an extreme cleaning expert who is one of the popular contributors on the Emmy award–winning show *Hoarders*. "*Pickers* is produced differently and they celebrate stuff, as opposed to telling people to get rid of the stuff. I could do a totally different show with a person that is on *Pickers*."

When *Hoarders* first debuted it was something people watched with horrified fascination. Never before had the general public really seen what extreme hoarding looked like and how it affected lives. It was shot documentary style and it offered an unflinching look at what life is like for those who are gripped by a mental disorder that does not allow them to part with anything. It can be difficult to watch, but people did from the moment it went on the air. The debut episode was viewed by 2.5 million people, and at the time became the most-watched show in A&E network history. *Entertainment Weekly* television critic Ken Tucker called it "Exploitive, educational, gross, insightful, voyeuristic, and sometimes quite moving, *Hoarders* is the kind of TV that's difficult not to watch once you've started an episode."

There was one audience for whom the show meant more than even the producers could have imagined: adults who had lived in hoarding situations as children. This was the case for a pretty thirty-something mother named Nancy* who recalls the first time she saw the program. "I first realized that I was a child of a hoarder, my sister and I were talking and my sister was like, 'Hey did you see this TV show? These people are hoarders—and their house looks like ours did!' I said, 'No, I'll have to check it out.' I watched it. It was such a breakthrough. It was like freedom in a way . . . because you had a word to put with what was going on. It led to my research about COH."

Children of Hoarders (COH) is an advocacy group helping those who have suffered through a parent's extreme hoarding situation. Many of these adults, now in their forties and fifties, had no idea how to identify or contextualize how they grew up or that anyone else lived like they did. "The television show opened the door," is how a COH member named Tammy* described it. "Hearing the language saved my life. Knowing you aren't alone." She saw a *Hoarders* marathon that mentioned something about an online support group. She signed up. "It was normalizing. I find out it's not just me." The show was the first exposure many people had to what's called a "level-five hoard," which is how Tammy grew up. A level-five hoard has some of the following characteristics:

> Obvious structural damage, broken walls, disconnected electrical service, no water service, no working sewer or septic system. Standing water indoors, fire hazards and hazardous materials exceed local ordinances. Rodents in sight, mosquito or other insect infestation. Kitchen and bathroom unusable due to clutter. Rotting food and more than 15 aged canned goods with buckled surfaces inside the home.[14]

"I never want another child to grow up like we did and experience things like we have. It is unnecessary. It doesn't have to happen." Tammy likens it to child abuse.

A reed-thin woman with a cropped pixie haircut and perfectly applied makeup, Tammy loves her pristine 750-square-foot apartment and barely sees her mother, who still lives in the same hoarder house. "People are what's important. Stuff is not. If something is not useful, necessary, and loved, it is gone. I am very focused on what is important, and stuff just is not it."

To put it in historical context, the first true scientific studies of compulsive hoarding didn't start until the early 1990s when Dr. Randy Frost and his students at Smith College began working on the subject. If you are now a forty-five-year-old child of a hoarder, there wasn't any real information about what you were experiencing until you were well into your twenties. While the children of hoarders are often seen on the television program as the people seeking help for their parent, the adult children themselves have been through so much and are in need of assistance as well. While some people say a show that makes entertainment out of misery is deplorable, some COHs will quickly reveal that this very public exposure of hoarding provided a pathway out of isolation.

Nancy, Tammy, and two other adults, Jim* and Liz*, were part of a panel discussion that addressed some of the thorniest and saddest issues surrounding extreme hoarding. You could hear a pin drop as they told their tales.

"I was twenty-three years old before I realized you could throw away those Brillo pads before they rust." Jim went to an Ivy League school, is a successful blue blazer–wearing professional in his forties, and he grew up in the house of a hoarder. "The first time I realized something was different, that things were very different, [I was] as little as three years old and I could go into the house next door that had kids the same ages as me, but no one was ever allowed in our house." From that point on, he knew that nothing was normal about the way they lived. He learned that you change your underwear every day from being in the Boy Scouts. When he was little he rationalized what was going on and thought they hid it. As an adult he realized the home's peeling paint in an otherwise upscale community was a giveaway, and understood why his home was referred to as "the slum house." He also learned he couldn't outrun it, outearn it, out-educate himself from the pain and the history of his childhood. He described a shocking reunion with some friends: "Just a few years ago, through Facebook, we got together in a bar. I hadn't seen these guys in twenty-five years. A guy walks in and has his wife with him and says, 'There's the guy whose house we could never go in.' So twenty-five years later, that's what he remembers. That's how he had been describing me to his wife. That was like a punch to the gut."

"We were kind of the nasty family on the road." Nancy was well aware of the problems in her home. She made excuses by telling people there was always construction at the house. One day a clergy member tried to intervene. "I remember a preacher wanted to know, *Is everything OK at home?* My mom got very angry when someone wanted to question what went on inside." Nancy only bought her first suitcase in 2011. She was married and had a child by this time. "I never learned how to pack. And then I was scared to pack too much."

Many COHs worry about hoarding being inherited and fear one day it will kick in. Of the four speakers that day, three had siblings who began to hoard. Tammy had a half sister who had been given up for adoption who she met as an adult. That sister hoarded. Some science suggests there may be a genetic marker that leads some to collecting behaviors. The science suggests there is a predisposition to it in certain families and that modeling the behavior can be just as significant as genetics.[15]

Psychologist Dr. David Tolin, an expert in hoarding issues, says the genetic element is complex. "[What] we know definitively about genetics is one, there is a genetic link. Now, you know, genetics—they can never explain everything. And so when you have a genetic predisposition, that does not mean you're going to develop a disorder. And similarly, lots of people can develop a disorder without a genetic predisposition." He uses alcoholism as an example. "You can be genetically predisposed to alcoholism. And that doesn't necessarily mean that you will be an alcoholic. And similarly, there are lots of people who become alcoholics despite the fact that their genes are perfectly fine. So, the genes are just one of many potential vulnerability factors.

It's things like when we look at the genetic linkage across relatives, the thing that seems to be inherent is—it doesn't seem to be hoarding itself, although the behavior can certainly be elevated in relatives of hoarders. It seems like the best candidate for what's being inherited is a general difficulty with decision-making."

The COH support group helps adults who struggle with the heredity concerns, the issue of anger toward parents, the feeling that they should have been removed from the home, and in some cases estrangement from the parent. But one thing keeps coming up again and again during this emotional, riveting, and frank discussion—the television show *Hoarders*. After nearly eighty minutes of addressing the gathering, Jim says, unprompted, "I want to make a really quick shout out. I know sometimes the TV shows get some criticism for sensationalizing things, but people like Matt Paxton . . . seem to recognize that there are other people in the environment."

Paxton is a recognizable face to those in the hoarding community. He wrote *The Secret Life of Hoarders*, owns www.Cluttercleaner.com, and has cleaned out thousands of hoarders' homes. "I was proud of that group. They are the lowest on the totem pole. No one thinks about them—the adult children. They were born into this. It was thrown in their lap. I was proud to hear them verbally express their pain and then to find each other." He has become a fan favorite for his tough, no-nonsense approach on *Hoarders*, but he always tries to be compassionate. "I struggle with the fact that I am on a show that uses mental disability as entertainment, and that is what it is. It's hard. Am I doing good? Am I not? But we have helped people by finding out they are not alone. We definitely have made a difference."

The day we spoke, Paxton was preparing to head out to film a whole new season of a reincarnated version of the show. In 2013 A&E cancelled the program after six seasons. But after a special earned high ratings on its sister network, Lifetime, that network revived the series to relaunch in 2016. Fans on his Facebook page are thrilled to see the return of the show, and people often approach him on the street like an old friend. "The masses, 80 percent say, 'Man, I watch and [it] makes me clean. I clean my house so much.' It is the same thing, I watch *Biggest Loser*. I literally sit at home eating a bag of popcorn watching *Biggest Loser* and I think, *Maybe I'll go work out today*. That's 80 percent. The other 20 percent are hoarders. They say, *Man*, they say, *You let me know I'm not alone. You gave me hope. You let me know I wasn't crazy*."

9

TV JUNK

Q&A WITH BRENT MONTGOMERY, EXECUTIVE PRODUCER OF *PAWN STARS*

IN 2008 TELEVISION PRODUCER Brent Montgomery did what a lot of guys in their thirties do: he went to Vegas for a bachelor party. And if you go to Sin City, you will see a pawnshop or two because gamblers need cash fast.

Pawnshops are essentially moneylenders. A person brings in an item in exchange for a collateral loan with interest. The loan amount is made based on the value of the item. So let's say you want to play another round of blackjack and you are tapped out. You might head to a pawnshop and hand over your watch so you can get a little more dough to put down at a table at Caesar's Palace. Upon taking in the Vegas pawn scene (as a spectator, not a loan seeker), Brent's producer radar went up. He knew that the pawnshop culture would make good television.

He was right. A year later *Pawn Stars* debuted on the History Channel. It features three generations of the Harrison family, who have run the twenty-four-hour Gold & Silver Pawn Shop since 1988.

The concoction of people who bring in weird things to pawn, Rick Harrison's no-nonsense encyclopedic knowledge about random items, plus the behind-the-scenes family dynamic is reality show gold. The average audience at its height was 4.9 million viewers.

In a short amount of time, a lot of things changed for the Harrisons and for Brent. The business is now swamped with tourists. The wait can be a reported three hours to get inside, even though the store is open around the clock. In an effort to revitalize the area around the store and to accommodate his fans, Rick Harrison is investing $2 million of his own money to create a shopping and recreational center on the strip where his store is located called Pawn Plaza. In the spring of 2015 the first eateries open were Rick's Rollin Smoke Barbeque & Tavern, Rita's Italian Ice, and Smoke's Poutinerie.

Another thing that has changed: Rick Harrison *has* $2 million to put into a project like this. He and his family have done quite well as a result of *Pawn Stars*. So has Brent Montgomery, who is not only the executive producer of the show but also the owner and CEO of the company that produces it, Leftfield Pictures. In 2012 he was named one of the top fifty most-important people in reality TV by the *Hollywood Reporter*. The following year Leftfield acquired another company and became Leftfield Entertainment. The year after that, British network ITV bought 80 percent of Leftfield Entertainment for $360 million cash upfront, and Brent retained his position as CEO.

In 2014 Leftfield Entertainment had twenty-six series in production and thirty-one projects in development.[1] Not bad for a Texas boy who came to New York City to work as a production assistant in 1997. In his glass-and-brick loft office, Brent was happy to talk about the appeal of "trash to treasure" TV and the success of *Pawn Stars*. It all started with the task of finding that perfect Vegas pawn store back in 2008.

> Brent Montgomery: My sister-in-law calls every pawnshop in Las Vegas and comes back, and there's only two [pawnshops] that were family run, which was surprising.

Q: Oh, that's interesting.

Montgomery: Yeah. I was shocked. One was a Greek mother and daughter, and we had the idea that this would be more relatable to our audience if it were just old-fashioned American guys. It was the Harrisons and the patriarch, Richard, who we would call "The Old Man," his son, Rick, and his son and Richard's grandson, Corey. When we started talking to them we realized that every item had a story behind it. Some of the items have amazing stories, which don't create any value other than to the people who have experienced the story behind them, where others carry tremendous value. One of the hardest things they have to do is talk people off of sort of a ridiculous high amount because they have a personal attachment to an item. Other times, people might not have any personal attachment to it, and they're sitting on something that was unbelievably valuable. Walking around that shop before we ever started rolling, there were Picassos, Rembrandts, Super Bowl rings, gold medals. There were Olympic medals and then all kinds of other cool stuff. Where I sort of thought maybe there was a show here was when our main character, Rick, started telling me about this thing called the "Death Clock." That was sort of its street name.

Q: What is a Death Clock?

Montgomery: Yeah. I'd have to look up or find out for you that the real name of the clock is because I can't pronounce it. It starts with an A.

Q: I'll find it. *[It actually stars with an O: an Ormulu clock.]*

Montgomery: But it's a beautiful gold clock, and it has all of this history behind it. He starts telling me, 'You want to know why they call it the Death Clock?' I said, 'Sure.' He said, 'Because it was being made with mercury, and the guys who were working on it were dying.' He said, 'Do you know where the term 'Mad Hatter' comes from?' I said no and he said, 'Well, hatters back in the day used mercury in their hats and ended up getting it and going mad, so mad as a hatter.' So he starts sort of going off on a tangent, which was sort of a really cool and interesting way to absorb history. I think that's what people in everyday life really enjoy. I think when they're looking at these items they can either go look on Google and quickly find out on Wikipedia all sorts of stuff about this stuff, or they can hear firsthand from the person who owned it. Sometimes there is not all the information out there on something, which even leaves it sort of—leads it in a more interesting direction because it's sort of a little bit mix of guesswork and historical value.

Q: Were the Harrisons interested in being part of a television show, or did you have to do a little song and dance?

Montgomery: No, these guys wanted to be on TV more than just about anybody I'd ever met. They had already worked with three "Hollywood producers." They blamed those producers for not capturing the greatness that was them.

Q: Were they right?

Montgomery: They were. They were right to a degree.

Q: Yeah? What were the people missing? Something wasn't working.

Montgomery: I think the guys, left to their own devices, would tell the same jokes a hundred thousand times, which is not that uncommon for people or people who want to be on TV. The Harrisons, I think, in fact were right. They just needed somebody who could capture them in a way that didn't have them doing all the work and having, I think, the idea of really focusing on the items, which was more of a History Channel idea than our company's idea. It was sort of the missing ingredient. So I think us being able to get the guys to be themselves, the guys being so historically knowledgeable on such a wide variety of topics, specifically items, was also key. But really, the show is made by the cool, fun stuff that comes through the door, and that's the great thing about a pawnshop—you never know what's going to come through the door. They're not limited in what they buy and sell.

Your knowledge, whether it be a pawnshop broker, an estate sales person, or any person that moves and sells stuff, your profitability and your ability to sell a wide variety is based on how wide your knowledge is. So most pawnshops will only sell gold, silver, and electronics because you can basically hire a minimum wage person to weigh something and give the going price for that item. You can hire a minimum wage person to turn on and off a DVD player. You can't hire somebody for a low wage who can tell a fake painting from another.

Q: So that's what really made this family different, this business different?

Montgomery: Yeah. They were historians who had also, for three generations, been learning about stuff and passing that knowledge on to each other. And also, they can literally dissect a watch. You know? From top to bottom, and they would tell you, 'Look, a lot of the fake Rolexes, they're not twenty-five-dollar fakes. They've had $4,000 to $5,000 put into them to sell for $12,000 to $13,000.'

Q: Oh, that's interesting.

Montgomery: Yeah. And that first $4,000 will fool 99 percent of the people. So there is a real art to what they do, and there is a real knowledge that they've passed on from one to another. I think it goes back to—whether it's a garage sale or a high-end pawnshop like the Harrisons—it comes down to negotiation and how good you are at it and how much leverage you have. I think the reason why our show . . . is so popular was the fact that the economy was in the crapper in '08 and '09. The idea that people needed to save money, people were thinking, "Hey. If I lost my job, what is my true worth? What do I have in assets?" It's probably pretty easy to think about sort of the first-tier stuff that you have in your house, but really the place where most people go would be the garage or the backyard and try to figure out if they have anything that's valuable. Maybe they'd know and maybe they wouldn't know.

I think even when you were a kid, I remember going into my granddad's garage or attic and like looking for treasures. You know? I don't know what I was going to do with them. I guess, just take them to him and tell him, "You have something." But you would spend hours going through a ton of junk, and then you would find something that was cool enough to go and get the story from your grandparent for. So these guys, I think, you have to have a real love of stuff, a real love of history, and then that just—plus, these guys, specifically Rick, he was just a ferocious reader.

Q: You get this idea. Did you know to whom you were going to pitch it? Did you know you were going to History Channel? How did you decide where to pitch it and what was the elevator pitch?

Montgomery: It was interesting. We didn't know that we went to History as a practice pitch. You know? We thought it was pretty off-brand for them. We did not have the whole idea about it being so stuff related. We thought it would go on a channel like True or maybe A&E or a couple different places. Everything just sort of lined up. I heard that History was looking for a gun shop show, and there were a lot of weapons in the pawnshop as well: a lot of historical Samurai swords from the 1300s, rifles from the Western times, and all kinds of cool historical weapons. That was something that was most interesting to Rick and the shop. So I know most of these pawnshops can't carry weapons that are more recent than, I think, 1900. So it's not like we're talking about the typical gun shop that would scare a lot of people. So I heard that they were looking for that.

These guys, obviously, knew a lot about history, but we were very fortunate because we walked in right at the right time. The woman who runs the entire conglomerate now, but she was running the History Channel at the time, this woman Nancy Dubuc, she had been down in Florida and—I didn't know this until she told me a long time later—she had seen a news special or something on a pawnshop, because of the fact that pawnshops were becoming sort of busy places during that time.

Q: Yeah. A little more mainstream because of it.

Montgomery: Yeah, because of the recession. And so they had literally talked about a pawnshop like the day or two before we had gone in. So when we walked in, not really knowing that, there was an immediate reaction by the gentleman, this guy who we were pitching. He said, "Give me a day, and I think I can get you a pilot." He came back the next day with a pilot. So it was one of the smoother, easier processes. It was really a very organic start to the show. We just went out and shot a couple of scenes. We showed the network sort of how the guys could deliver information that was pithy. We kept on using the words "pithy" and "insightful" around what the guys were doing because we all thought back to college. When you go to college the focus rarely is on education first, but the stuff that most college kids remember are those professors who sort of went against the grain and told you stories. That's the reason why it's called history: his story. So we really liked what we were getting based on the fact that these guys were telling little pithy stories about stuff, and everybody could relate to stuff. Then to your point, sort of the game changer was the value. There's this great show, *Antiques Roadshow*, that's been on forever. It delves into stuff in a really fun [way], but it's pretty dry in comparison to *Pawn Stars* because it sort of stops right at the point where you put value on it and *Pawn Stars* has this nice, fun game show element to where you can really haggle back and forth, and I think a lot of people like to haggle. I think sometimes places just price stuff more for a higher price knowing that they're going to have to haggle, and the person would rather go away thinking they got a deal even though they paid the same amount that the shop wanted. They felt satisfied about getting a deal. It's very American. So yeah, that was the process. We typically would have kept shopping it around and would have tried to go with the highest bidder, but History had such a great reaction with that. We really believed in them, and they believed in us, and it worked out for both parties.

Q: When you were in the piloting process and you're looking at it, what worked, what didn't, how did you end up with the current configuration?

Montgomery: Well, we needed historical stuff. In the beginning, they had said that stuff would walk through the door every day. I think it did. It just didn't do it as much as we had hoped. So in the beginning, we had to just shoot a lot more in order to get the historical stuff. They had decades to accumulate what we were looking at in the shop. The first season you're shooting a show, nobody knows you're shooting a show. Nobody has heard of these guys outside of that community. After the show started airing, we had people from Michigan, Texas, driving in.

Q: Just showing up?

Montgomery: Just driving, showing up with their stuff, to get it first priced by the guys and then hoping that they could sell it or trade it on the show. And so it became more of an embarrassment of riches of the cool stuff that was coming through.

Q: Who comes to pawnshops? What have you learned about pawnshops from this?

Montgomery: It's a real cross section. The very interesting thing about pawnshops is they were banks before there were banks. I mean pawnshops go back to Babylonian times. I meant they go all the way back to Roman times. They are now banks for people who have trouble having credit. So you could be there. One sort of portion of the customers who go into pawnshops are guys who don't have credit. When I was there shooting the pilot, there was a guy who walked in and Rick was like—I can't remember the guy's name—but he said, "Our business is built off of guys like this." I said, "What's this guy?" He said, "He has his Xbox," and he's a grown man. "He has his Xbox and his rent check and some of his bills are due seven days ahead of when his paychecks hit his bank account. So he essentially pawns his Xbox once a month for a week and that money floats his lifestyle. He pays an amount of interest, but he can't go get a loan from the bank. He doesn't want to go to a loan shark or anything like that. He's probably borrowed from all of his friends, and he knows damn well he's coming back if he gives his Xbox because it's his most valuable possession," Rick said. "It's the same thing with construction guys who loan their tools. If a man loans his tools, he's coming back because that's how he makes his money."

Q: That's interesting.

Montgomery: So that's a portion of it. Certainly, there are derelicts that are going in there for money that God knows what they're going to use it for. But there is a large percentage of the clientele who go in there looking for a deal. I think that's what we try to highlight on the show. These are people who know the best place in the world to get a great watch or a great piece of jewelry is going to be a pawnshop. You're getting a diamond ring that should be as good as any other diamond ring out there, but for a discounted amount. That could be the same with tools. That could be the same with just a ton of stuff.

Q: It's something that sort of occurred to me as I watched a bunch in a row was that value is kind of the star of the show.

Montgomery: Yeah.

Q: It all revolves around the value of something and somebody's perceived value of it. You know?

Montgomery: I was a big baseball card collector and dealer when I was in like eighth, ninth, or tenth grade, and you'll see different industries or items having value at certain times. There was a minute where baseball cards were the hottest things. That kind of came and went, but there was nothing really behind it. Coins, there could be some value attributed to a coin just based on what was used to make it. But yeah, there is, I think, supply and demand. In a good time, a pawnshop is buying and selling, and other times it's pawning as opposed to buying and selling. When the economy hits the floor, people want to sell stuff. But a pawnshop, for instance, can't just accumulate all that stuff and take up space and not be selling it. So it's not that a pawnshop is adversely related to the economy, but it does have some spikes up and down when the rest of the economy might not.

Q: Why do you think people assign certain values to things? You sort of alluded to it in one of your answers about people think something is worth a lot of money when it's not.

Montgomery: I was there shooting at the pawnshop once when this nice couple came in with a piece of the Berlin Wall. I kind of was like them. I thought, *Wow. This is epic.* You know? *This is history. This is something that so many of us lived through and it was the first big political memories of our lives.* I'll never forget Rick was like, "You know, I'll give them five dollars just to be a nice guy." I go, "What do you mean?" He goes, "You know how big that wall was? You know how small that rock is?" He went into detail about how if it had graffiti on it that said something that was from a famous artist or something completely changes the value. But what he said to those people, he said, "You guys, even if I was going to give you $100 or $500 for it, you guys have a piece of the Berlin Wall that you guys got together when you were there that you're going to be able to pass down to your kids who pass it down to their kids." He goes, "Even if I was going to give you a lot of money, you wouldn't sell this. This is worth more as a piece of history."

That's not to say other pieces of history wouldn't have tremendous value, but it really, I think, is based on supply and demand. If there are millions and millions of pieces of the Berlin Wall, then it's not going to have a great value. If it was the flag that the fireman put up at Ground Zero, that's going to have a much different value than a piece of rock that was down there on the same wall.

Q: How did the success of the show change the show?

Montgomery: It's very funny. It's just hard to shoot the show [now].

Q: I figured that.

Montgomery: Because the guys went from having seventy people a day in the shop, seventy customers a day, to five thousand a day. The Harrisons' shop is in a top tourism destination, and it has become, I think, the number one or two tourist stop in Las Vegas. Certainly, during the daytime, there are cabs lined up around it. He's building a shopping center around it. He's bought a lot of land close by. The reason why it's hard to shoot the show, and it's kind of funny, is Rick. The Harrisons can't be selling and making as much money when we're shooting the show because we can't let everybody in. Literally—we tried it. People were getting in between the camera, the talent, distracting, screaming, and making out. So we allow a handful of people in while we're shooting, so we're always going against the guys who want to hurry, hurry, hurry so they can let more customers in. We need to take our time so we get the show done right, so we have a fun little back-and-forth.

But it is not the most exciting show to shoot. When you go see it, it's not like *American Idol* where there are these grand performances. It's just this quiet little engine. The tense moments are when the negotiation happens, but the rest is like listening to a little story being told by a fun professor off to the side about a piece of history. So the excitement level isn't sky-high. That's why our job in post is to make sure we pull out the most interesting moments and the most historical moments to highlight.

Q: Do you guys have any sort of limits on like, "We're not showing this kind of this thing"? Like, "I'm not touching that."

Montgomery: Yeah. People collect all kinds of stuff . . .

Q: Whenever I was in the South and I see the Mammy saltshakers, I just put them [face down]. It's just my little form of protest.

Montgomery: That's a good example. Yeah. There is shit like that.

Q: I know somebody is going to buy them, but it just makes me feel better for the moment.

Montgomery: There have been items that have been brought in. [Rick] made a very big point about it being—like, there was an elephant tusk and ivory and how that's not—sometimes, as you know, stuff is illegal in the States and legal elsewhere. Like there was a good example of some guy came in with a—I forget what you call the Russian police. I can't remember if it was some government authority, Russian, one of those very typical Russian hats. The guy came in and said to Corey, "I want to sell you this." He was like, "How did you get it?" He goes, "Oh, I stole it from a Russian cop." Corey was like, "I can't buy stolen merchandise. I'm going to actually have to ask you to leave right now."

There is a misconception that pawnshops want to buy hot stuff. What I've learned is it doesn't behoove them because once they buy something and it's hot, they not only have to give the money back for it, but they also have to hold the item in storage in perpetuity sometimes. So it becomes very expensive for them. The last thing they want to do is buy something that's hot. But for the most part, people are walking in with stuff that's on the up and up. There are those few items.

Q: How long does it take to shoot an average episode?

Montgomery: It's interesting because we don't shoot the show in a linear fashion. We might shoot pieces this week that go with an episode months down the road and vice versa. I would say it takes probably four to five days to get a full episode. That would be my guess. Because sometimes we shoot stuff that we think is a cool item and then sometimes it just doesn't end up being that great of a scene. We try to pick the very best. People get nervous. They come in and they kind of have the deer in the headlights look, and that doesn't make great TV. But yeah, I would say on average about four or five days.

Q: Are you doing a version for the UK and Australia? Is that right?

Montgomery: Yeah. We have *Pawn Stars UK* and *Pawn Stars Australia*, and so we're on our second season of the UK one and our first season, which hasn't aired yet, of the Australia one. I was over in London for New Year's Eve in 2012, and when you're in London or Paris or anywhere in that part of the world you just see history. In France, these buildings are twelfth, thirteenth century. They're being used very effectively today. So I thought if we have our own history in the US, being so relatively young and new, we're going back three hundred years, it would be really cool to see the British version with just historical stuff that goes back so far. It's been a lot of fun. You know?

Q: How is the stuff different?

Montgomery: Well, the stuff is different.

Q: Or are the people different about it?

Montgomery: The people are different. Brits are very different than Americans. I mean, we came from over there, a lot of us, and others from other places. But Brits don't say what they think at every moment. So British television hasn't had this same sort of runaway success with real-life people doing real-life stuff because it's very British to not go out and act like a fool on television.

Q: They're sort of more reserved?

Montgomery: Unless you're a football fan.

Q: Right!

Montgomery: Then it's par for the course. So we had to find people who would really be themselves, and we found some fun characters who absolutely acted just as transparently with the cameras rolling or not. Then I think the stuff was very cool. We've had books on there that were from the fourth century. It's been really cool to see just different stuff. On *Pawn Stars* we do have a lot of international items, but it's just not sort of at the same pace that you would have in the UK. Australia, they're just as young or younger than we are. So there's it's more about crazy, fun personalities and crazy, fun stuff to go with it.

Q: Can we talk about the genre sort of as a whole? The idea that there is *American Pickers, Storage Wars, Pawn Stars, Junk Gypsies, Garage Gold*, and they're also spread across all these different networks. I think that's interesting. Why do you think this is such a popular genre?

Montgomery: We call it trash-to-treasure or the hidden treasure genre. We do believe that it had never really been tapped into, and so when we sold *Pawn Stars* and then we sold *American Restoration* and several other shows in the same vein of the same genre, we thought it was more like food. You know? Forever there weren't that many food shows, and then there were only food shows on the Food Network. Then people realized there were ways to incorporate food, whether it be Anthony Bourdain traveling all over the world to make it a travel show, Fox to make it a business show like the Gordon Ramsey stuff. So we felt early on that it would be a wide genre because people, A) love stuff, and B) love the value of stuff and making a dollar. There's nothing more American dream than sort of creating something out of nothing. And so it was interesting after we sold a couple of them, there was sort of this, "Well, OK. That will be that." But then *Hardcore Pawn, Storage Wars, Storage Hunters, Auction Hunters*, and there's probably another thirty or forty of them.

Q: Yeah, just *Hoarders*. I mean the other extreme of it, yeah.

Montgomery: Yes. So it really tapped into something, I think, that was timely. What I always say about reality television is it exists because it's cheap, first and foremost, in comparison to scripted programming. But it also exists because it's very reactive. We can come up with *Pawn Stars* and shoot a pilot in March and have the show on in July. That was really reactive to the economy. Where scripted would wait until the economy was in the shitter and then say, "Hey, what works well in a bad economy?" It's comedy. And then it takes a year to find the right script and another year to find the right team to make it. So you're in a two- or three-year window versus a four- to six-month window. So that was part of why we thought there was a demand for it. Also, just seeing people in different environments. There's *Swamp Pawn*. There's all kinds of derivative stuff from it.

Q: Do you think it could sustain a whole network like HGTV or Food?

Montgomery: Yeah, I think if you were to take the best and put it all on one network, absolutely. That's a good idea actually.

Q: There you go. Note to self.

Montgomery: Yeah.

Q: How did *Pawn Stars* change your life?

Montgomery: Dramatically. It's amazing how much smarter you are after you have a show that rates well, when in actuality you haven't changed at all. [*Gets serious.*] But yeah, I think for us we made a show that resonated, and we did have some, I think, ESP with it. There was this way of drawing something interesting and pithy and knowledgeable out of characters and also making it fun. We kind of talk about these types of shows being laugh and learn. What female shows have continued to work well? Crime and drama, you know? Whenever there is drama in a ton of these female franchises, that tends to work. Then with men, it's usually action, information, or comedy.

Action had already been done, and done quite well, and was in our forte. Most of the people in my company came from making more female-skewing shows like the *Bachelor* and *Wife Swap* and *What Not to Wear*, and all this stuff.

So when we found this little formula of laugh and learn, that became something that was bigger than just one show. We went from a company having two or three shows [at] a time to a company now having thirty-five series going and being the largest independent production company in the country. And so we went from, when we started *Pawn Stars*, having twenty to thirty people to having eight to nine hundred people now. So it was definitely the foundation of building out a company. Like any other sort of sector of the entertainment world, you don't want to be a one-hit wonder. So for us, the focus becomes selling and making other styles of shows.

Q: But that have that sort of mission of laugh and learn?

Montgomery: Yes.

Q: Do you think this trash-to-treasure genre is saturated, or do you think there is still room?

Montgomery: I think it went through a point where it was, and I think it's coming back. I think that it's been thinned out a little bit. I think it'll just be the magic formula usually is finding the right characters with the right process and making sure that as the producer you can execute and make it as fun for the viewer as it would be for you being there at the shop. If you can do that, then I think there is plenty of room for more. The great thing is people are nostalgic. People always want to look back. But then there is also all this cool new stuff being created. This analog-versus-digital world is really interesting and topical because as a parent—you're a parent, I'm a parent—we're seeing [a change]. We played with toys. We played outside. We played with stuff. And now it's like a real fight to not just have the kids online the whole time. You know? Kids today are more apt to read about stuff than actually go and feel and see it and touch it with their own hands. I think cool stuff is a way to always sort of keep history alive.

IV

WHERE SHOULD IT GO?

10

ANNIE HAUL
PORTLAND, OREGON

Annie Hall: It's so clean out here . . . [in California]
Alvy Singer: That's because they don't throw their garbage away,
they turn it into television shows.

—*ANNIE HALL* (1977)

NOT IN LOS ANGELES, but 834 miles north in Portland, Oregon, the proprietor of the junk removal company Annie Haul bares no resemblance to Diane Keaton or the WASPy, flighty movie character from which her business takes its name. Feisty, strong, with steel-blue eyes, owner Kate O'Halloran could be played by a namesake and doppelganger, actress Kate Mulgrew circa *Star Trek: Voyager*.

"You know it's going to be a good day when you get to wear a wig and ride a bike!" That is exactly what Kate is doing during an early morning garage clean out. The homeowner was a working mom who dabbled in local theater and as a result had accumulated a lot of old costumes, plus normal kid stuff. This included the 1973 Schwinn that

Kate took for a little spin down the block while wearing the giant fake Afro. The woman confessed to having cleared out the garage in her mind many times and decided after ten years it was time to really do it. She read about Annie Haul online. "I thought the name was hilarious, and then saw it was woman-owned and local. That appealed to me."

The things on the outer perimeter were donateable, but the deeper the dive, the more useless the items became. There were a lot of old cat scratching posts that of course led to Kate singing a chorus of Ted Nugent's "Cat Scratch Fever." Kate and her crew worked diligently, pulling things out and making piles; donate, recycle, and no use to anyone. Kate looks at *everything* before it goes on the truck. As the back of the garage came into view the woman was making plans, "I was an artist in my former life. I can get to my paint now, I'm excited." The bad news was that in the formerly obstructed wall Kate discovered a bees' nest and evidence of rats.

Rats are a big problem in Portland. Apparently it is so bad that one man in the neighborhood told the local news, "They're like their own little gang. When I killed one . . . they pulled him back in there like it was like *Saving Private Ryan* or something."[1]

Nothing fazed Kate. Not the bees. Not the rodents. Her only comment looking around at the floor was the deadpan statement, "I just love me some rat shit."

Given all the shenanigans of the morning, Kate and her crew did the job in no time flat and on budget. The woman whose garage was being cleaned out was a little surprised but grateful. After paying Kate she added, "You are a rock star of junk."

"That's what we do," Kate responded.

After packing up their supplies, brooms, bags, and a blue wheelbarrow that has "Your mom wears army boots" spray-painted on it, Kate and her employees, Maurice and Ricky, caravan to the next location. Somehow the rides between jobs feel like road trips. Jokes fly around and stories are told. Kate often climbs up into the big cab and drives. "I like to have fun. And I've always said this about—I'm not working if I'm not having fun. And I want people to have fun at work, too. But I'm also—while I don't care about labor, spending time doing this and that and going through and donating, I'm also kind of like a speed freak. And it really doesn't have anything to do with the money. It's just I want to get the job done. I just like to be efficient. And so, I expect my employees to be efficient."

Right there is the paradox of Kate O'Halloran. She is the happy-go-lucky lady driving a bright yellow box truck, but she is also a savvy businesswoman with years of experience, in business and in life. One of seven children, Kate's roots are deep in Portland. Her father was a business agent and sometimes foreman for the Portland Iron Worker's Union Local #29. He was involved in building most of the city's high rises and it's iconic Fremont Bridge. She had her own landscape design business for fifteen years, until 2008. "I actually had some great years. I had a nice, big house, a decent loan, no weird crap going on. It was good. And then the economy changed, and then the phone stopped ringing. I mean, I used to hate my phone. It rang so much. I was a really good designer. I had a good reputation. I was mostly referral. And, the phone stopped. I remember this contractor called me one day and he goes, 'Can I ask you something?' And I said, 'Yeah, what?' He goes, 'Is your phone still ringing?' And I said, 'No, that's really weird.' He goes, 'OK.' And it took guys a while. They'd mumble around. 'Mine isn't ringing either.' And everybody thought we did something wrong. It's like, 'What did we do? Did we piss somebody off? Was I little too mean to that stupid doctor?' But it wasn't. It just stopped. And so, my money—I didn't have any money."

In her early fifties she was at a turning point when a chance encounter with a woman named Annie changed everything. She knew of Annie; everyone in town had seen her truck with the shamrock dotting the *i*. One day while snowboarding at Mount Hood, Kate noticed that Annie needed some help wrangling her two kids. Kate stepped in to lend a hand. It turned out Annie and her partner also needed some help with their junk removal business. Kate got involved again and the transition seemed natural. "They broached the subject with me over a couple of Guinnesses. 'Take it all over for us, Katie. You'll be grand at it, girl.' But I was like, 'Yeah, I don't know.' And truthfully I was a little bit concerned about the stigma of being a junk hauler."

In January 2014, Kate bought Annie Haul. She paid $12,000 for the truck and $18,000 for the business and received something price-less: a great reputation. "When I bought the business and I pull up and people would be, 'Oh, hey. Oh, you're not Annie.' I'm like, 'Well, we're shirttail cousins from Ireland.' You know, everybody loved Annie. She had that great Irish accent, and we're a lot alike as far as being very gregarious. And we just make friends. And so, I just kind of rode in on her coattails."

The business side needed work. It had been a mom-and-mom shop. Some of the client lists were handwritten. The website needed to be updated. The online profile had to be managed. And it was important to protect what the business had already built up, the goodwill. And then there's the fact that Annie herself was still very much a presence in Portland. At our first donation drop of the day a car pulls up next to the truck. It is Annie. She is wearing madras shorts, a T-shirt, and a porkpie hat. She has black, wavy hair flecked with gray and piercing eyes. Her Irish accent is thick and perfect. "My love," she says as she embraces Maurice, one of the hardest working fellows you will ever meet.

"This is the woman who saved my life," Maurice says. "I was homeless." He had lost everything in Hurricane Katrina. As a young African American man separated from his family, he wound up dis-placed and in a shelter in Portland. His story is long and complicated and, as Annie reminds him in the moment while glaring at me and my note pad, "is his to tell." She's protective of Maurice and clearly concerned for him. When Kate suggests that maybe I could inter-view Annie, she cocked her head toward me and said in a not-too-friendly manner, "She doesn't have enough time." Annie declined to be interviewed for this book.

Maurice, who worked with Annie for five years, was a great asset to Kate when she took over the business. He had certain institutional knowledge that, for all her business acumen, Kate simply couldn't have. She remembers one day that she made a rookie mistake: "I opened a cooler . . ." This cooler was at the center of a roommate war. The roommates left it closed up for nearly two years because they couldn't agree about who would clean it after a camping trip. Kate was the unlucky person to pop the top. "I opened the cooler, and I about fell over because of the stench. And it's toxic, the stuff that comes out of there. You can die if you smell that stuff in an enclosed area. That was my first mistake. I opened a cooler, and Maurice looks in and he goes, 'Miss Kate, you're going to know, never, ever, ever open a cooler. Don't do it.'" He insists on calling her Miss Kate.

In addition to the young, wiry African American man from New Orleans and Kate, the spunky Irish American owner, the third member of the crew is Ricky. Ricky is a white-haired, muscular, compact fellow in his early fifties. He has a fast mind and an endless capacity to discuss spirituality and life. While he is all about getting the job done, he does see deeper meaning in why people have made their homes into "warehouses," as he calls them. "There's an abundance out there, but if you come from the scarcity mindset, you will hold on to things. If you come from a place of love and abundance, you let go of things. It's a flow. If there's a blockage, people hang on to things. They feel they have to hang on. It's an illusion, and it's a story. You create a story and then you live it." He believes some people who can't part with their things are living a fear-based existence. "The more we have, the safer we feel. People are building a safety net. It is padding life with stuff. If I have enough stuff, I am OK." Ricky's relationship to Kate is interesting. Ricky is part of a farm community outside of the city where Kate lives along with their mutual friend, a woman named Jae. Ricky's late lover is the father of Jae's daughter.

Ricky, Kate, and Maurice didn't wear matching outfits and they don't really match one another, yet they get in a rhythm and have mutual respect that makes them extremely productive, both at junk removal and at donation/repurposing. This team that might not fit in somewhere else works perfectly in the People's Republic of Portland.

They each have their quirks, yet speak quite freely in front of one another about politics, sex, and religion. They always end the day saying to one another, "I appreciate you."

Annie Haul had three big, multiple-day jobs booked in one week with clientele as eclectic as its team. The first stop was a rundown home in an up-and-coming neighborhood. Any Realtor would be itching to get this house on the market. A woman had passed away and her son was trying to get it ready to sell after a year of not doing all that much. He was a big-bellied guy with a white beard and was wearing a ribbed sleeveless T-shirt under some dirty overalls. He'd gone to live up in the woods and was only in the city now trying to make sense of selling the house. Kate warned me that the late mom had a lot of figurines and a wet basement. It was a real mishmash of things. His mom had an artistic streak and a love of Birkenstock sandals. There were forty-two pairs of them in the closet of her arts and crafts room. There was also a gun.

There was an entire room that had become a closet. Someone had jury-rigged a length of pipe horizontally with two broom handles tied vertically at each end like a porch swing. The whole thing was suspended from the ceiling with rope to create a clothing bar the width of the room, which was probably ten feet. On the pipe hung an enormous selection of Quacker Factory clothing. Started by a spunky zaftig lady who liked a fun outfit, QVC favorite Quacker Factory lists itself as "one of America's leading brands of embellished clothing." Its top sellers include rhinestone capri pants, rhinestone dots button-down V-neck cardigans, and lady leopard animal-print sparkle cardigans. The room was filled with unworn glittering items. Kate often sees people who save up one kind of thing. "I think one is that people—we are taught to shop. This is what we do. We are taught as children to shop and to be workers and buy things. I think people self-soothe with eating and some self-soothe with shopping. I mean, you see so many shopping bags and so many things. So many jobs I go to, so many things have never been opened, never been used, never been touched. So I think there's a shopping epidemic. And then also there are people who just get overwhelmed."

This was a hard job for Kate because the son and his uncle were constantly picking through the piles of possessions, moving things out of the donate section and into some stack of their own. The elderly brother fished out an old Barbie doll. They both seemed put off that certain things were being categorized as worthless. Kate spent a lot of time talking to the men as she sized up the items. It is something she does in these situations. "I think it puts them at ease, honestly. It gets their mind off what we're doing. I get them to pay attention to me, although it's not all about me. I want to hear their stories. I truly do. I'm interested in it. And it just keeps their mind off it. Honestly, it sets them at ease with what I'm thinking. And they have things they want to say."

Practically, it helps her guys do the work and it is also something she sees as valuable. "We're sensitive. We're professional. We know that people are going through losses and stuff in their life that they can't tell me in ten or twenty or however many minutes we're there. But I know that there's something going on. So, just to be sensitive to that and their things." She asks about a sky-blue tackle box with CLARA painted on it. Clara was a little girl who lived across the street, and they all used to go fishing. Ricky believes Kate's relatability is the key to her success. "One thing Kate has a gift at is reading people and being the calm and creating the camaraderie that takes place in all this—it is her gift."

Once the guys have loaded the truck, it is clear they are going to have to come back for the next round—that was always the plan. Take the donateable stuff first and not contaminate it with the wet disgusting things from the basement. At the end of the day Kate goes to settle up with the fellow and he starts to barter with her. He tells her, "The clothes alone are $1,000!" His mom may have spent $1,000, but at this point they aren't worth that much. Kate gently points out the tax deduction is more valuable at this point, and that they had settled on a price earlier and that was it.

The haggling happened again the next day. It was a similar story. Bobby was all about getting everything out of her late sister's house. She and her husband were in from Alaska and under a time crunch. It was a beautiful home but Bobby wanted us to know it took her two weeks to get it to the point where it was now. The house had bags and bags of bottles that needed to be recycled and boxes and boxes of magazines that had to go. There was also a lot of really old canned food.

"All this stuff should have been thrown away!" the husband groused a bit. He was actually more interested in talking about fishing with Kate. Again there was a method to her chatty madness. "Bobby, she was real tight at first. And then I always put a big smile on. 'Hey, hi, everything is going to be OK'. And then, you know, next thing she's talking to Maurice like 'There's a song about you, Maurice.' And then she's cracking jokes, and her husband's out there telling me all about fishing in Alaska. And they just relaxed. But at first they're embarrassed, too. There's a huge amount of embarrassment." When it was time to leave the husband started in about how Kate packed the truck and that she could get more in for what she charged. In a firm and funny way she stuck to the original quote.

Of all the junk removal runs I observed and participated in for this book over the course of two years, the only person anyone haggled with was Kate. The things that completely distinguished Kate were her gender and her location. So was this a Portland thing, or a woman thing? "As far as being a woman, the only one that I see around out there. But I don't see any problem with it. In fact, I think it's a benefit. Because the customers feel more comfortable with me, I think, maybe."

Too comfortable perhaps, comfortable enough to question the price? What was her take on the hagglers?

"I don't let them win, do I?"

The Annie Haul mission statement is "Haulers with a conscience," and it is written across the truck. It is something Kate believes in, and Annie wouldn't sell her the business until she was sure of Kate's commitment. Kate will take extra time to sort out items that could be used by someone else and will make extra runs to make sure the donations happen. She only has one truck, so it isn't always in her best interest. "I waste labor doing that, but I don't care." She could load the truck differently and more effectively time wise, but that would impinge upon her donating ability. She sees it as playing the long game.

"We get so many references," she tells me as she hauls a chair with a broken leg over to an area across from the giant dump heap, "because they see that we take the time to go through and separate." She won't name names, but she says a lot of the haulers who say they donate just dump. "I want to go put my head on the pillow at night and know that I tried to do no harm. And I feel good about it. So, that is that. And then, yeah, if I tell people I'm going to donate, then that's just really important to me that I uphold that promise."

In a three-day period she makes three stops at Goodwill, a trip to the scrap metal yard, and a run to the hazardous waste chemical depot. She will only go to the dump after she has exhausted all other options. Even then she and her team take the time to pull out items that could be used by local artists. There's a special area to put those things.

The last donation stop Kate takes me to is a place where she frequently brings items she gets from clean outs that don't fit in any particular category. It is called Dignity Village. It is a city-sanctioned homeless encampment, a transitional campground. From afar it looks like a whimsical series of playhouses, but its history is rooted in a very serious issue.

Years ago a group of homeless people under the banner Dignity Village were setting up tent cities around Portland, and ultimately they took to living under the Fremont Bridge, the one Kate's father help build. But Portland had an anticamping ordinance. It was a crime to be in a sleeping bag, on bedding, or using a stove in the open while sitting or lying. A person could not sleep in a car, tent, or any makeshift structure. In 2000 a judge ruled it was basically unfair to punish someone displaced because he or she had to engage in acts of homelessness, especially if the city's shelters were full. His ruling read:

> The court finds it impossible to separate the fact of being homeless from the necessary "acts" that go with it, such as sleeping. The act of sleeping or eating in a shelter away from the elements cannot be considered intentional, avoidable conduct. This conduct is ordinary activity required to sustain life. Due to the fact that they are homeless, persons seek out shelter to perform these daily routines. Yet the City considers this location to be a campsite if the homeless person maintains any bedding. The homeless are being punished for behavior indistinguishable from the mere fact that they are homeless. Therefore, those without homes are being punished for the status of being homeless. . . . This court does not accept the notion

that the life decisions of an individual, albeit seemingly voluntary decisions, necessarily deprive that person of the status of being homeless.[2]

Judge Gallagher championed looking for alternatives.

The ruling opened the door for homeless advocates to push for
creative solutions. In August 2001, the Larson Legacy Foundation
negotiated a deal with the mayor of Portland to allow the Dignity
Village homeless group to develop its own campground community
on a 1.3-acre piece of land owned by the city. Dignity Village has
been on the site ever since.

Mark Lakeman was one the architects involved in the early planning of Dignity Village. He is a huge believer in creating these kinds
of spaces. "This is what we actually said to the city council. Legal-
ize this and within ten years—repeating the same settlement pattern cultural evolution that we've watched in the last ten thousand
years.—we will watch people go from being nomadic in shopping
carts, like they were before, looking for their promise land. These
people arrive at their place and they will generate a physical fabric
that reflects their needs and who they are. It will prove people are
hardwired place-makers."

It is located about seven miles outside of downtown Portland
within walking distance of one bus stop. The drive to the area known
as Sunderland is along the Columbia River. It feels like you are on
the road to nowhere. The area is open and flat and near the airport.
After cruising down an industrial stretch, the houses come into view
on the horizon. As we pull into a wide driveway we check in at the
security booth. They know Kate and why she is here. We are directed
to pull up to a shedlike structure to unload the donations. As she
opens the back of the truck, people suddenly appear and swarm the
trucks. There's a pregnant woman in a tight T-shirt interested in
some of the hair care products and an older woman with a few of
her original teeth interested in it all. Someone appears, voices are
slightly raised, and order is quickly restored by the manager who
will oversee the intake of the donations.

"Dignity Village, they'll take half-open bottles of shampoo. They'll take cat food. They'll take dog food. They'll take any kind of nontoxic household products—shampoo, soaps, candles, any kind of camping gear, propane. They'll resell wood if it's usable. They have a firewood business." She'll often put things aside during a clean out that she knows Dignity Village could use. Once the donations are accounted for, residents will be able to have access to things they need. Kate once brought plastic tiaras she found and they were a big hit.

A tall, slim, white-haired fellow named Mitch, a community leader, offers to show me around. If you took him out of his board shorts and floral shirt and put him in a cashmere sweater and jeans combo and presented him as the fraternal twin brother of Tim Cook, the CEO of Apple, I'd believe you. He explains the layout. "There are forty-two homes; about sixty people can be here." The homes are tiny structures built on platforms that are ten by twelve feet. "A local high school built this house," Mitch says, pointing to a newer looking structure. Local artists created beautiful murals on the exteriors of some of the original houses. They have nicknames like The Barn or The Castle. The small size of the structures and their colorful paint jobs make the place seem playful. It is a little cognitively confusing given the reason most of these people live here.

The houses are for sleeping and keeping a few personal items safe. Everything else is communal. Dignity Village is now a 501(c)(3) nonprofit with its own internal leadership and set of rules. It operates much like a cooperative apartment does in many cities. It has its own set of regulations:

> 1) No violence to yourself and others.
> 2) No theft.
> 3) No alcohol or drugs or drug paraphernalia on site or within a one-block radius.
> 4) No constant disruptive behavior.
> 5) Everyone must contribute to the operation and maintenance of the village.

Contributions include mandatory work hours and a membership fee, currently twenty-five dollars a month. Dignity Village has to pay for water and the little bit of electricity used in common areas. Security logs are kept and infractions are not tolerated. Breaking any of these rules means you have to go, and there's a waiting list of people who want in.

In helping design Dignity Village, the idea was to get down to the way humans interact with each other and their environments. Lakeman said in designing the village they kept in mind the goal of the project and the history of how functional communities evolve. "In more generative earlier societies people would create what they needed to meet their needs. They would create their physical infrastructure in a way that met not only their physical needs but their spiritual and their community needs. So not only would they create something that would facilitate gathering or storage of grains—it's not only storage for their grain; it would actually become symbolic because they did it together. That's what you see in Dignity. There's a design of an environment that is car-free. It's walkable. It is lined with places people live but also social edges, like porches. It is a very complete diagram of functional social commons, a full range of community infrastructure of commons from indoor meeting spaces to office spaces, workshops, creative spaces."

Mitch takes us to a room with three computers. It enables residents to look for jobs, apply for services, or keep in contact with family members. He points to a fairly discreet-looking shed and says, "Here's where we take showers." There are garden beds for decoration and produce. They also provide shade and cooling. The ground is blacktop, like a parking lot. Mitch points to big blue containers. "Those are rainwater barrels to collect water for the plants, although the mosquitoes are pretty bad." While the land is free, it is right by an area that will flood. Mitch shows us where the water will sometimes rush in after a storm. "Sometimes it floods up under the blocks. Also we have rat issues." The kind of serious rat issues that make the downtown Portland Private Ryan rats look like pets. The houses are all on eighteen-inch stilts for protection.

Because it is technically a campground, the zoning rules are different. The fire inspectors do show up, and at one point on a few houses the small porches had to be cut back and their wires contained for safety. Originally meant to be a temporary place for people to, as Mitch put it, "get it together," some people began to stay for years. In 2012, when Dignity Village renewed its contract with the city as it does every three years, a stipulation was included that no one can stay more than two years.

Mitch is nervous about the city or state intervening. There are citizens who are opposed to Dignity Village, citing the residents as non-taxpayers and freeloaders. And most recently there was a bit of bad publicity—four people who used Dignity Village as their residence were caught taking part in a luggage theft operation at the nearby Portland airport. But for all the people who have a roof over their heads and are able to hold a job, it is has been a godsend. Mitch says it is viable solution. "The system is broken. This works."

After we leave Dignity Village, Kate invites me up to her place on the farm for the evening. It is a beautiful drive into the lush, green forests of Oregon. The interesting thing is the little log cabin Kate calls home is not that much bigger than some of the Dignity Village houses. She has a small kitchen, a bed, and an overstuffed reading chair. It is maybe four hundred square feet. She likes it this way. It is enough room for her, her puppy, and her girlfriend to cozy up to the wood-burning fireplace that heats the place.

Kate is someone who doesn't want stuff in her life and tries to separate herself from all the things she sees and touches during the day. She follows a superstition when she works, always wearing a cap on the job. "One thing I learned is you keep a hat on. And you either wear a hat or you just keep your hat on because it protects you from—you just remember who you are all day. And you don't go down that road of sucking up their stuff, if that makes any sense." She doesn't buy anything. If she needs something she says it usually appears in one of the clean-outs. And she has basically decided at this point in her life she doesn't need that much. "What I find interesting about myself is that when I do come home, and you do say you can walk away from it, I do walk away from whatever happens. And I think that I'm not who I used to be either, because I've purged so much." She likes living free of stuff in a small house. And she is not alone.

11

ALL YOU NEED IS LESS

TINY HOUSES ARE BIG right now. The tiny house movement is made up of people who chose to live in homes that are sometimes as teeny as eighty square feet, while others call home a more manageable three-hundred-square-foot domicile. People who opt for this life want to lower their personal consumption to preserve natural resources and/or do not want to go into debt to own a home. It is a social, personal, and sometimes financial statement.

In 2002 the Small House Society was formed to support those who chose to live simply by simply living in miniscule spaces. One of the society's founders, Gregory Johnson of Iowa City, believes this lifestyle can improve one's existence: "It is the process of getting rid of things that aren't important to you. Most people say it is a better way of living because you are left with what matters."[1] He speaks from experience, having lived in a ten-by-seven-foot home from 2003 to 2009. There are some people in the tiny house movement who keep seasonal items or educational or hobby-related goods in storage so that they can achieve what Johnson calls "simple, uncluttered daily surroundings." However, Johnson says there are many people who "literally have everything they own and use inside of a tiny house."

A fellow society founder, Jay Shafer, shacked up in a bitty abode before getting married and having children. When his family expanded, he bumped it up to a spacious five-hundred-square-foot pad. He has become a tiny home designer and supplier of prebuilt small house units. He envisions and designs spaces where every inch is utilized. This can mean a clothes closet is adjacent to the kitchen and a ladder is how you reach your bed in a sleeping loft. Shafer describes the uberefficiency that can sometimes border on the nutty: "It's kind of like Lego meets Ikea and they make a porn movie together."[2]

The wacky nature of some of the homes has led to a good deal of skepticism and even parody. The television show *Portlandia* satirized small living by showing a couple sharing a twee, wee house where the tub/shower stall doubled as the TV room and the girlfriend had to use her boyfriend's back as a cutting board to slice some toast.

Some small-space advocates are trying to mainstream the movement with homes that look less like dollhouses and more like dream dorm rooms. Brian Levy doesn't refer to his house as a tiny house or small house. He calls his a minimhome. He stresses minimalism as opposed to shrunken functionality. He believes the best chance for acceptance is to aim for realistic living spaces, not the unconventional. "I think that some of the misconceptions are actually correct perceptions in some cases. That's one of the problems with the micro house movement, [it's] that people say these places are too small to live comfortably and I would say, *Yes, that is correct. Many are.* If you are a person living in one hundred square feet, that might be too small, but three hundred square feet per person is what Americans did before in the 1950s."

Brian is referring the National Association of Home Builders statistics that put today's average home around twenty-three hundred square feet. In the 1950s the average size of a home was 983 square feet.[3] For a family of three, that's just over three hundred square feet per person. He was amazed at how the scale has changed. "Now we are at nine hundred square feet per person. We've tripled in sixty years. I don't know if we've gotten three times as happy?" Brian asks rhetorically. "So what have we gotten? More space to clean. More to maintain. More to fill up with stuff."

Brian Levy owns a small piece of property at 21 Evarts Street in northeast Washington, DC. It is a triangular lot behind some row houses that once was littered with garbage, had pools of fetid water, and provided a home to an abandoned car. Now there are cherry trees in a garden area, an eight-hundred-gallon water cistern, and an elegant little house.

The house is just about eleven feet wide by twenty-two feet long. The interior is close to 210 square feet and the ceilings are nine feet eight inches high at the center. "It was sort of a New Year's resolution for 2012—I was going to build a tiny house." He purchased the land, made peace with the neighbors, and hired Will Couch of Foundry Architects to design the house he had in mind.

"I didn't want any lofts to climb up into; that's popular in the tiny house world. I wanted a little more functionality. I wanted to be able to have a dinner party for six, which I can do easily. I wanted a full-sized kitchen with a full-sized sink and full, big range. I wanted a little more closet space. I wanted a full audio-visual system, so I have a projector screen that doubles as a shade. I also wanted a full-sized keyboard for my computer. My architect rolled his eyes and said we aren't going to do all that. Yes, we are going to do all that."

When you walk in the front door, there you are. You are in the house and that's it. Brian gently asks that I remove my boots before entering. The wood floors are really nice and it is immediately noticeable that all the finishes are high end. There are stainless steel appliances and ceramic heating units. With a smaller space, Brian said he could spend more money on durable, high-quality materials. There are solar panels on the roof and foot pedals to pump water to the sinks.

The space is essentially a rectangle. As you enter the house, to your immediate right is a ten-foot full galley kitchen that spans the short end of the house. There's a small fridge, convection oven/microwave, and wall storage for food. Looking out the window above the sink you see a wood-burning oven in the yard. It was the one thing that couldn't fit in the kitchen. The top of a long sofa hinges open to reveal a space for water tanks. Across from the couch, on the other long side of the house, is a wall of windows. The other short end has a full bed, trundle style, which slides underneath a raised office area. Next to the office area is a five-foot closet, and on the other side is a tiny bathroom with a silver commode. "That's the incinerator toilet—a stainless steel shrine," jokes Brian. It is the only part of the house where his enthusiasm wanes when describing it. Incinerator toilets burn the waste and have a reputation for being stinky. "It's fine," he says, not that convincingly. "You have to baby it a little bit."

At six foot one, Brian is a lanky fellow with a beard and penetrating brown eyes, who speaks with conviction about the appeal of living with less—a lot less. "It is something that is culturally difficult. And sometimes it is a process. It can take years to pare down things. What I've learned is it is very doable. Humans are adaptable creatures. Psychologists have this thing called the adaptation principle. . . . We are amazingly flexible. We can reconfigure to adapt to situations. Most things, particularly the size space we live in, what kind of environment we live in. We adapt pretty well, generally."

Adaptation level theory suggests that a person's idea of what is normal slides and changes based on the conditions at the time. Psychologist Harry Helson suggested we base our "normal" position on what we have experienced in the past, and as our experience changes, so does our definition of neutral. You've heard of people who have moved from cold climates, say Minnesota, to hot ones, Arizona, who now need a sweater when it goes down to sixty degrees at night because that's the new norm. In his or her Minnesota days that person would have been running around in shorts if the temperature hit sixty.

Brian, like many small space converts, embraces this highly curated life. In his minimhome are books, family photos, and one box of important papers. He scans and digitizes everything he can. Laundry is done off-site. There's storage for just enough food. He knows this is not living for a family of five and concedes that downsizing was not simple. "Books were an issue. They are nice to look at and give some comfort, but I pared it down." He still has quite a few in the small space. "I had to pare down my alcohol collection. I have my six or seven drinks and I don't need thirty bottles of alcohol." That said, he does have a sweet bar setup.

Why would a thirtysomething man with a degree from Harvard's Kennedy School of Government who has a full-time job with an energy efficiency company spend his free time focused on small homes? For him it is about alternative urban planning. It is about infill and energizing unused space. It is about consuming less. It is also about a potential business.

He is getting into the small home design/build game. He has sold the plans for this house to at least forty people for $495 and is branching out to sell the actual completed units. He holds open houses regularly. He reports that they have become increasingly crowded, with empty nesters and millennials who see this as a real option, especially in places such as DC where housing costs are astronomical. "It is more diverse than you might think. I was surprised. I am surprised." The cost of his minimhome is, on the high end, $77,000 top to bottom. There are companies that offer teeny tiny design/build homes for as little as $18,000 if you are willing to build it yourself and to live in really collapsed space.

In some progressive cities there are areas being designated specifically for tiny house communities for people interested in collaborative living. The idea is that while your personal living space is small, you might share a larger open common space for socializing or for utilities. That's how Brian's house project started out, but it ended up with hurt feelings and two other tiny homeowners leaving Evarts Street on bad terms. Right now the law is working against Brian. He can't officially call the minimhouse his permanent residence because of a specific zoning law.[4] He is working with others to get some basic restrictions changed. So for now, he technically uses his minihome as a "showcase" house.

Like many organic grassroots movements, the people are far ahead of the policy. Building and zoning laws don't really apply to houses with this small of a footprint. In some places it isn't legal to live in a structure under a certain square footage. Many tiny homes are put on trailers but you can't park one indefinitely unless it is on land you already own. Certain RV parks won't accept tiny houses on trailers. A smart design build firm is going by the recreational vehicle book and makes tiny homes that are actually classified as RVs and recognized by zoning department codes as such because they have all the traditional utility hookups.

While there hasn't been a central spokesperson for "Tiny House Power," the news media has a fascination with people of means who make the choice to live small. They often get the *Lifestyles of the Rich and Famous* treatment in the reverse. News networks used words like "crazy" and "unbelievable" when describing the choice of a major league baseball player to make his tiny home in his van. At just twenty-one years old, pitcher Daniel Norris—then of the Toronto Blue Jays—earned a $2 million signing bonus and an endorsement deal with Nike. Instead of buying a McMansion or investing in a condo in Tulum, he lives in a 1978 Volkswagen camper van that he parks wherever he can. He has told reporters he keeps his personal life low stress so he can do his best on the field. The man pitches at ninety-two miles per hour. He performs at a high level while living low-fi.

On the other end, the pared down spectrum is the sleek, tricked-out micro apartment of Internet pioneer Graham Hill, who founded Treehuger.com in 2004, a website dedicated to sustainability. It was acquired by Discovery Communications four years later for $10 million. Hill now lives in a 420-square-foot apartment with over-the-top architectural wizardry, including moveable walls and beds that retract into shelving. Hill says he now owns six shirts and has digitized all the papers in his life. Hill speaks publicly about design and has started a site called Lifeedited.org. His TED talk titled "Less Stuff, More Happiness" has been viewed 2.6 million times on YouTube.

Hill is not an outlier. Major cities including Seattle and Boston have embraced building micro apartments, spaces three hundred square feet and smaller. In the summer of 2015, New York City welcomed its first prefabricated micro apartment complex of fifty-five units ranging in size from 260 square feet to 360 square feet.[5] While the individual spaces are small, there will be large common spaces and even storage available.

Tiny houses and minimalism are having a moment. Maybe these folks have hit on the one surefire way to keep stuff under control: to change your environment. In the last decades of the twentieth century, the adaptation level theory tilted toward humans' ability to obtain and keep more stuff in big houses and plentiful storage units. The first decades of the twenty-first century seem to be leaning the other way. One reason could be the generational influence hovering around the small space movement. Millenials don't have boxes of record albums, stacks of books, and photo albums. "It's all here. My address book. My music," said a young woman attending a tiny house meet up as she pointed to her phone.

Johnson of the Small House Society sees this shift as well. "I think everyone can relate to how technology is allowing us to live with less clutter because things that once filled up physical space now fill up a hard drive, such as movies, books, photos, magazines, music CDs, etc. People are needing less space now."

A 2015 article in the *Washington Post* titled, "Stuff It: Millenials Nix Their Parents' Treasures," found a stark contrast between how parents and their freshly adult children feel about things like old Christmas cards and grandma's rocking chair. A downsizing consultant interviewed for the article described it this way: "Eight times out of ten, kids don't want the parents' furniture or boxes of letters or scrapbooks. . . . It can create hurt feelings. But it's not that they don't love you. They don't love your furniture."

A 2014 Neilsen report, "Millenials: Breaking Myths," offers a few clues as to why tiny homes may be more than a passing fad due to cultural and demographic shifts. According to the report, "The American Dream no longer means a comfortable home in the suburbs. Millennials aspire to stay in the cities rather than moving to the suburbs or rural areas, presenting a potential problem for Boomers who will eventually want to downsize and sell their large suburban McMansions." More young Americans are moving to cities, forgoing the four-bedroom colonial and garage.[6] According to the report, 62 percent of millennials want to live in mixed-use communities and in urban centers, and 50 percent say when they next move, they want a smaller home. And if the market is determined by the demand, the numbers are on the side of millennials (1977–1995) and their successors, generation Z (1995–present). Together they make up 48 percent of the US population. And perhaps the true harbinger that living with little is here to stay? You can now watch the shows *Tiny House Nation* and *Tiny House Hunters*.

But for those who have been in the tiny trenches for years, they believe it's less about the design of it all, or the trendiness, or even the environmental aspect. Jay Shafer thinks, "If there's anything very constant about that movement, it's not the form of the houses, nay specific square footage, it's the lifestyle behind the tiny house idea. That you don't need a lot of stuff to be happy. In fact, a lot of stuff that you are not using that you're having to maintain and pay for initially? If it is not working for you it is working against you. If you can just streamline and get rid of all of that, it is easier to see where your happiness lies and follow that bliss. It's hard to know where your bliss is if you can't see it through all the crap."[7]

12

FREE JUNK
Q&A WITH DERON BEAL,
FOUNDER OF FREECYCLE

_____

"It is more blessed to give than to receive."

—Acts 20:35

T HE WORD FREECYCLE is a portmanteau. It is a linguistic blend of two words to create a new original term like infotainment, brunch, or shopaholic. The fusion of _free_ and _recycle_ led to a nonprofit group that helps connect people who would like to either find a specific item (free) or put that item out into the universe for another owner to reuse (recycle) rather than let the item end up in the trash.

It is called the Freecycle Network, and it can be found at Freecycle. org. It is so straightforward that it seems like there should be a catch. You join a user group in your neighborhood and you will receive daily emails showing what's available. Or you can post an item you would happily give away for free. It can be fun to lurk and see what people will put out there. For example, on a random Saturday the Metro Little Rock, Arkansas, freecycle.org page had these items up for grabs:

> OFFER: L Shaped Desk—Wooden office desk with 5 drawers and cabinet

> OFFER: Pilates Performer—This is an OLD piece of exercise equipment, not the new Reformer. That being said, it still has a LOT of life. Does need new two small rollers for ease but works as is. Let me know when you can pick up and why you want this equipment.
> Thanks for freecycling!!
> Dianna

> WANTED: Record Player—Would like to find a small record player with RCA audio inputs (red and white)

The process relies on an honor code that you actually have the item you claim and you will hand it over for free, or if you want an item that you will show up to get it. There's a pretty straightforward disclaimer that relieves the Freecycle Network from any liability. It is just a conduit. There are a few loose rules. When it comes to what you cannot offer, it is not a shocker that listings cannot include porn, booze, tobacco, drugs of any kind, or weapons.

What started as a small neighborhood posting in 2003 has grown to include 5,225 groups in 120 countries (and counting) with approximately 8.8 million members (and counting). So what's the catch? While its reach is big, its home base is small. There's not some huge staff in Silicon Valley controlling the Freecycle Network as it expands internationally. Local volunteers who moderate the different online groups support it almost entirely. According to its 2014 tax return, there are seven thousand volunteers who keep it alive. The only real central organization consists of a couple of individuals who maintain the website and keep the servers running, plus founder Deron Beal. They are the only people paid, not handsomely, to do this work. It is a nonprofit that relies on donations and grants.

The feeling of community and sense of volunteer ownership led to tensions between the founder and some of the more independent-minded operators. They didn't approve of some of the choices Beal made, including a few corporate alliances over the years and how he chose to maintain quality control of the groups. While the debate got a lot of traction online and at the grassroots level, it didn't destroy or hurt freecycle.org in any profound way. The harder hit came from a judge who ruled against Beal in his attempt to trademark the word freecycle. Instead, he had to settle for "The Freecycle Network." And on the TFN website there are very specific and detailed guidelines for moderators (and journalists) on what language to use. What detractors perceive as Beal's desire for control, his supporters characterize as his dedication to the organic nature of the premise.

Beal does not come across as some megalomaniac sitting in a boardroom counting corporate dollars. His office is a small, shared space at a renovated historic Y building in a college town. The complex is home to other environmental groups like the Sierra Club, a massage therapist, and a photographer.

Now in his mid-forties, his office attire consists of T-shirts, hiking shorts, and rugged soled sandals. He has a long face, sometimes scruff, and wears wire-frame glasses. At six foot four, he has to fold himself into a small chair behind his desk. On a nearby table sits a stack of books that clue you into his driving motivation. There's *Waste and Want*; *Go Green, Spend Less, Live Better*; *Trash*; *Garbology*; *The Overspent American*; *Gone Tomorrow: The Hidden Life of Garbage*.

He is a long way from his post-MBA life working for a Fortune 500 company in Europe. He enjoyed the finance work but did not find it fulfilling. He decided to move back to the United States and either teach German or get into environmental work. He moved to Tucson and started volunteering. He didn't suspect all this would happen when he started working for a local recycling company in Arizona that employed people who were transitioning from halfway houses to homes and who could use some free stuff to reboot their lives.

Deron Beal: I was the guy who kept the recycling program going. And so I did that for two and a half years. Like a year, year and a half in, we got known for taking just about anything. We also had an old beat-up pickup truck that we would drive around.

Q: You started changing to de facto junk removal?

Beal: Junk removal, yeah, exactly. That's what we did within that. So, these businesses were like, well, we have an old desk. We have an old computer. We just always said yes, because these guys are moving into apartments, right? And they could use most of that stuff. But we kept getting more stuff than I could give away. So, you can see where this is headed, right? So, well, we've got to figure out a way to get rid of this stuff. I filled up an old warehouse. So, I filled up, basically, a warehouse full of junk. And my boss said, *OK, figure out a way to get rid of this stuff.* So, I set up a Yahoo group.

Q: What in you made you say, yes, I can take this? Why didn't you just say, you know, we're recycling people?

Beal: Well, I lived for ten years in Germany. There's a strong recycling sort of impetus there, right? Everyone's totally into it. Then you come here. When I first moved here there was no recycling. And then they just had the little bins. I'm also the kind of person who, you find something on the sidewalk, you pick it up.

Q: You couldn't turn down a desk?

Beal: It's just a compulsion of mine. There are obsessive compulsives. I'm a, what would you say, an impulsive compulsive. No, an impulsive obsessive or something. . . . I see garbage, I just need to pick it up. And, yeah, so that's where the environmental bend of things [comes from].

Q: You just wouldn't, if somebody said, hey, I need you to take this filing cabinet, . . . have easily said no.

Beal: Well, yeah. No. It was just good stuff. . . . My house is the same way. It's got a used sofa. Someone gave me the table. And, these cabinets are used, and this is from someone else who was here before.

Q: Every junk guy's house is filled with stuff they've picked up. Every one I've been on, they all have it.

Beal: Yeah. And I'm not earning a lot of money, so there's also the impetus just to make do with what you can, right? So, why not? And neither my wife nor I are like, you know, we don't need the newest, latest, greatest stuff. It's like, OK, we'll just score a new sofa or whatever.

Q: So, you have this warehouse; you decide to start this Yahoo group. Why did you think that would work?

Beal: Well, I had been a member of the neighborhood association LISTSERV, and I knew it was easy enough to set up. And I knew it didn't take many people to succeed. There's, like, thirty or forty people chatting back and forth and communicating and stuff. And, I knew I had a ton of stuff to give away, so I knew that wouldn't be a problem. I knew plenty of people wanted the stuff because I'd been driving it around in our sort of Sanford & Son pickup truck before that going to nonprofit A, B, C, seeing who could take it. So, I knew that there was a demand. I knew there was an easy way of doing it. So, it seemed like a no-brainer just to set that up, and it truly was. And so, then I just decided do I want to call it—I was thinking FreeBay.

Q: FreeBay?

Beal: Or Freecycle. And Freecycle had the recycling in it. FreeBay was more consumption sounding. And plus I didn't want to get sued by eBay.

Q: The consumption thing, I want to talk about that . . .

Beal: Yeah, certainly there's a whole collaborative consumption aspect of it, too.

Q: It seems to me that this is as much about attitude; there are some people for whom this wouldn't work.

Beal: Yeah. It's a much broader base than I ever expected. When we first started off it was totally just the first few that you're

seeing popped up, like Portland and Seattle and San Francisco,
New York, Chicago, so sort of progressively minded, environmentally minded people, right?

And, Al Gore had just done his whole thing [*An Incon-
venient Truth*] and so that was sort of big. But then, later, we
slid into this recession, right? And we were getting written up
by the AARP magazine or *Parenting* magazine, just all sorts
of things we never would have thought of at all. And there
were people who had monetary needs, so it wasn't just the
environmentalists, or retirees who were downsizing, or kids
that are going off to college. So it was much broader than my
own personal environmental desire of keeping this stuff out
of landfills.

And so, it gives people that wouldn't necessarily be connected into the whole environmental movement an in. It's like
guilt-free. No one says, "you must" or "you shall." It's not government telling you anything either, right?

So, in our original volunteers that we had, just the Tucson
group, there was this libertarian guy who was totally like we
don't need government. We can reuse and recycle ourselves,
right? There was a former exotic dancer who is now a rancher
who's just into using stuff. There was me and the green, you
know, lefty.

**Q: With the business background so you know how to make
stuff run.**

Beal: Right, so I know how to make stuff run. And then, the other
guy was a prim and proper Republican who is still a member of
Rotary. He's a member of all these professional organizations.
He believes in having his tie straight and doing things right
and neat. And this totally fits into that, too. And so, we would
have potlucks where we'd get together. There's this disparate
group of people come together. And they're all equally into it
in their own way.

**Q: It's America! But yeah, the attitude, sort of the idea of, *We
don't have go out and buy something new, you can find it, you
can trade it, you can help somebody else out.* I think is very**

interesting for a place to start. And then you have the other part, people who just want to consume but not pay for it.

Beal: True. So, it works for both, right? But it's not just people wanting to consume. It's really, to me, if you were to—if we had these stats, you'd see these people are extremely low-income, right? And this is a way for them that don't have a couch to get a couch. So they're not saying, *Gee, I feel like I'm really doing this great thing for the environment.* It's like, *Gee, I need a couch and there's one there and this system works so I'll use it,* right? And that's, you know, whatever works for them, right?

Q: Do you have any sort of suggestions, or do the moderators suggest that people don't sell the stuff? Is that on your system?

Beal: We don't have any rules forbidding resale. We just do require that people let people know if they're picking up that they're going to resell it. And if someone's doing resale, it generally does come out because they probably do a lot of stuff. Otherwise it's not worth it.

Q: It's a pretty transparent system. You probably can tell.

Beal: Yeah. So, your junk comes out pretty quickly. And if they haven't told the person, then they just get removed from the group or they get told you have to tell people. But we're not against it. If it keeps it out of the landfill, whatever.

Q: That's your main goal, just keeping it out of the landfill? After standing in a landfill, I understand it.

Beal: Yeah, right, exactly.

Q: When did you know the whole Freecycle thing was going to work? What was the moment?

Beal: I got an article in the local newspaper, and we went from, like, thirty or forty—nope, maybe fifty or sixty members—to, like, eight hundred members overnight. And it was just cranking. People were just posting like crazy. And it was already working fine with thirty or forty members because I had tons of stuff to give away. And the warehouse we were in, there's a second half of a warehouse in the city, at least, to put—they moved their development office somewhere else. And so, there are probably thirty or forty desks and all these cubicle divider things and furniture. And they show up one day with a big semi and they said, "Or we're hauling it to the landfill." I'm like, "Give me thirty days. I'll clear out the rest of the stuff. You won't have to pay to throw it in a hole." They're like, "All right. We can come back in thirty days." And—

Q: Gone?

Beal: Pretty much everything. They didn't even have to bring a truck, so it was just like leftover bits, right? And we got at least one charter school totally outfitted. It's City High School downtown, which is a great program for underprivileged kids or kids with issues and stuff.

Q: Why hasn't someone done this before? Have you asked yourself that question? I mean, it's so simple. It's so direct.

Beal: Well, the short answer is it was done before. I was talking to a guy who moderated our local group in San Francisco. He said, *Yeah, back in the sixties in San Francisco, I was part of it. We set up a storefront for free stuff, free store. And it wasn't just us. It was us hippies in partnership with Hell's Angels.* Apparently all the drugs that the hippies were getting were run through the Hell's Angels. So, the Hell's Angels were pulling down good money, and that was kind of their—they were kind of giving back.

So, we're in over 110 countries. We have over five thousand local groups. It's actually 9.5 million members. And we have about seven thousand volunteers. So, all these homes you're in still probably won't cost any money, right? The top thirty leadership volunteers are like the management, and they head up all our groups or approving the groups or work with existing groups or tech teams, they're all doing like thirty-hour-a-week positions volunteer. Probably 95 percent are women, which is sort of interesting. And so, we have one contractor who's our engineer and me, and a guy that helps out a couple of hours a week, and that's it for the largest recycling user website on the planet with 9.5 million members. It's only possible because you have to pay virtually no one anything.

Q: Right, people are concerned with their volunteer work.

Beal: You get a grant here and there and we eke by doing this.

Q: Actually, it's funny. Somebody on one of my Facebook pages wanted to know why a guy with your background would use your talents like that. I think that is a compliment. So, why?

Beal: Well, I did the finance job with all the money and it wasn't any fun, so there you go. That was easy. And I realized I didn't need—the whole time I was doing the wealthy finance position that was like three years, I was earning good money. But I was also paying off all my student debt, so I wasn't living the big life. And, when the debt was paid off I'm like, *OK, well, the debt's paid off. I don't need any more money. And this is not fun.* So, what would inspire me so that when I retire at some point I say, *Well, I feel like I really did something that meant something.* And so, yeah, that's what I've done.

Q: I understand that. What are the global differences that you've noticed about the way people consume and trade?

Beal: Well, we're huge in the UK and virtually nonexistent in Mexico. But you go across the border and you travel in Mexico—like, where was this? This was somewhere on the Baja Peninsula. We went into a shop, and it was a bike shop, and there were all these shiny, new-looking bikes. And then you had a closer look, and they had taken old bikes, fixed them up again, put new tires on and repainted them. So, they had a new bike shop with totally reused bikes. And then you started realizing, well, that's because they're not throwing this out. They're already reusing all this stuff completely. Just because we need a new monitor, they're not going to throw away the monitor. They may give it to their aunt or a cousin.

Q: It's interesting . . . I was looking at the New York Freecycle, and it's funny what people want to trade. It's just sort of an interesting snapshot of a mindset.

Beal: Totally random.

Q: Random. Two Scrabble holders—and somebody put up a box of steel wool and it went.

Beal: Yeah, or one that says, "Just dyed my hair black tonight. Maybe it's your night tonight, too. I've got half a bottle left." It's like, OK.

Q: How did you decide what you wouldn't let people put up?

Beal: OK, so as a little nonprofit, we're just struggling to get by. We didn't have some lawyers to advise us properly of how to set up an organization and how to properly have legal structures in place for each local group. Franchising, legally it's franchising. We didn't do that. That's why we lost our trademark in the US, because we needed franchise agreements with each local volunteer.

Q: Because you don't have them, right?

Beal: Right. And so, then some guy went off and wanted to do his own thing with his little group and sell stuff, and we said, *No, you can't do that.* He said, *Yes I can.* We said, *No you can't. You're not a Freecycle group anymore.* And he sued us, and he won.

Q: Because . . .

Beal: We don't have a franchising. . . . You have to have thousands of dollars' worth of contracts with each local group, and you have to police each group, like McDonald's, where they come by and they see what kind of service it is and all that stuff. And, we didn't have any. There's no way we could have done any of that.

Q: Or it didn't seem like you'd even want to either.

Beal: We didn't want to, yeah. There's not interest, right? So, we still have a registered trademark in EU and Canada, Australia, New Zealand, all the English-speaking countries where we're biggest due to the limitations on the website.

Q: Well, it's hard for you because I think it started, Freecycle started to become like Band-Aid and Kleenex and Xerox. I'm making a Xerox. I need a Kleenex. And, that Band-Aid stinks. Well, that's not a Band-Aid. It's a Curad or whatever company. Is it hard for you to keep sort of the quality control?

Beal: So, just like Xerox, now we're trying to win back our trademark in the US.

Q: Funny things you've seen?

Beal: I don't remember what it was. So, there were some—so, we had one woman gave away her engagement ring. Apparently, she caught the guy cheating, so she gave it away. We had someone else give away a house. It was like a one-hundred-year-old house, but you had to move it. Still, you still see some double-wides and stuff like that. And, a number of cars.

Q: How do you decide what [to] allow and what to keep off?

Beal: So, our rules developed organically as we went on. Like, someone said, *Can you post a gun?* We're like, *No.* First we just had one rule: keep it free. Keep it free. That was our first rule. And then someone said, *Well, what about illegal substances?* I said, *OK, keep it free and legal.* And then we said, *Keep it free, legal, and appropriate for all ages.* So, that gave the moderators the power to say no if a guy posts—

Q: Porn or something?

Beal: Porn or whatever they're uncomfortable with, even though it's legal.

Q: Why is this different from Craigslist, posting something for free on Craigslist?

Beal: Well, a lot of people we talk to who use Freecycle can't stand Craigslist because there's so much spam crap on there. And so, that's the one side of it, the negative side, that we don't have a lot of spam crap on there generally, because we have the local volunteers who take care of the posts and approve members and all that stuff.

The other is that the sort of sense of community, like the first time I got it on, it was a George Foreman grill. It was actually like a year and a half in. I was so glad to get rid of all this crap, because I had to give away a house full of stuff. But it was a George Foreman grill. I said, *Yeah, I'd kind of like that.* And so, just on a whim I responded. He said, *Yeah, sure, come on over.* It turns out the guy lived a block away. I walked down to his house, and they keep chickens. I'm like, *How much do you have?* And he's like, *So you get to meet somebody.* He's like, *Here, have*—and he gave me six fresh eggs from his chickens

and a George Foreman grill. I was like, *How awesome is that?*
There's a new neighbor, have a nice walk, there's fresh eggs.

**Q: Have there been any Freecycle marriages, any Freecycle—do
you put that out there, hookups?**

Beal: Um, I think there were a couple. I just don't remember what
they were.

**Q: What about the no-show, the psychology of the no-show. Do
you have any insight on why people say they're going to come
and then they don't?**

Beal: Well, because it's lame and it doesn't cost anything not to.

**Q: Is there something about stuff being free that sort of alters
the brain chemistry?**

Beal: I totally think so.

Q: Tell me what you think.

Beal: Well, I think for some people who are just trying to score
a bunch of stuff, they just respond to everything. And they
might show up for half of them. And once something has a
value of—you know, if you're paying fifty cents for something,
you're still paying for it, so it has this extra meaning. I'm not
going to just throw away fifty cents.

But if you're getting it for free, oftentimes there's little to no
impetus for you to actually show up, outside of the respect for
the individual who's waiting for you. And, I avoid all that. . . .
I don't give them my address. I say just give me your mobile
phone number. I'll give you a call and give you directions. See,
if it's just an e-mail address, they've got nothing to lose. But
if I have their phone number and they don't show up, they're
going to have a problem.

**Q: That's a good one. I'm going to give that to a friend because
she uses it a lot and she's sort of getting frustrated by the
no-shows.**

Beal: I totally feel for her. I'm pushing hard. We don't want to have
people rate other people just because I don't like that because
all of a sudden you get a bunch of nasty kind of people rating
each other back and forth. No, thanks. But we do want to have a
checkbox for no-show, and so you can see . . . this is something

technical that you can track. The responder posts. You can check the no-show. And you can see how much stuff they're responding to, just count. Because if this guy's responded to ten, twenty items in the past week he's not really interested in mine. So, the number of items responded to in the past week and no-shows, count it. And that way you get it and say, *OK, this person has only responded to one thing in the past month, and they've always showed up.*

Q: Yeah, that's smart. You're going to try to do that, you think?

Beal: Well, I've been saying it for five years, but we don't have any money. So, I've got one engineer who's basically—right now two of our main servers are down, and so the other two main servers for our database are chugging along frantically trying to catch up. So, it's like get the water out of the boat.

Q: Do you have waves of activity?

Beal: Huge waves. The biggest wave is January first or second.

Q: Christmas stuff?

Beal: Because people slow down in the holidays. From Thanksgiving on through Christmas it's pretty [slow]. So it's, A, they got behind on all the other stuff they've been meaning to post, B, Santa ties.

Q: Really ugly sweaters and all that kind of stuff?

Beal: That's right, yeah. That's our biggest day each year, January second. And university towns, we see a lot of the hippie Christmas periods where usually when students leave there's a pile out on the sidewalk. Everyone comes by and says, *Oh look, ugly sweater.* Well, we're getting more schools involved in doing that. Over thirty-five thousand items a day are posted on Freecycle, thus kept out of the landfill. And, that's over one thousand tons a day, which is the equivalent of what a mid-sized landfill gets every day. So it's one landfill less on the planet. And in the meantime, it's over fifteen times the height of Mount Everest if you were to stack all that stuff in garbage trucks over the past year alone.

Q: And it's stuff. It's not even garbage because it's stuff that people would want. It's not trash.

Beal: One person's trash is another person's treasure, right?

Q: How do you feel about junk removal companies? Do you have any opinions about those? Like 1-800-GOT-JUNK where they come to your house and take your stuff.

Beal: I couldn't care less. If they want crap, take it. If they want good stuff, if they want to make some money off it, why not? Sure. I don't care.

Q: How long do you think you're going to do this? Is this you for the rest of your life?

Beal: Probably not. These things go in waves. This is—we've kind of settled in for the past three or four years at the same level.

Q: Does it still need you? Does it still need a human being?

Beal: Yeah.

Q: Why?

Beal: Well, the website, we're shoveling constantly. And so, this website is existing by a Damocles sword thread.

Q: It seems like it's such a healthy, vibrant thing.

Beal: No, it's just barely—we've got probably forty servers going at any given time and one engineer. Now, there's a startup doing something similar to what we're doing now. I'm drawing a blank on the name, but I just got an update from them. They have ten staff people, and they have venture capitalists, and I think it's a $2 million a year budget and four engineers full-time.

Q: Has any VC approached you, any angel dollars?

Beal: Well, we're a charity, so there's no money.

Q: So, they just have to give it to you?

Beal: So, in the beginning they approached us.

Q: I mean like a Bill Gates saying, "Here's money!"

Beal: Right, venture capital and social venture capital. And since we started, when I first started out, I'm like they need to have social venture capital that they track their investments and see how their return on investment is and growth and whatnot. That'd be a great thing. And some people started doing that now. There's a couple of organizations for social venture capital. Yeah, but I intentionally set it up as a charity because it's letting go of ownership, right? And so, the same guy that's two million bucks a year now, I think they're in their second or third year, they also just said, *Well, we're now up to thirty thousand*. Our goal was to reduce consumption overall of new stuff by 20 or 30 percent. Their total per year is thirty thousand items, which is what we do in a day. And that's $6 million later. That's more than we will ever spend in the whole existence of our organization. They burn through that in two or three years. That's why you don't want to go with venture because they want to grow fast and be big and bring in the bucks. Then they sell it. So we wouldn't be here anymore if we'd done that. But that's the beauty of what makes it work, is because people do it because they care.

V

HOW CAN YOU USE IT, FIX IT, OR LOVE IT?

13

JUNK RECYCLERS
REGENERATION STATION,
ASHEVILLE, NORTH CAROLINA

"**I**T'S FREE REMOVAL for this gentleman," Tommy tells Adam, who is driving the truck. Yes, he said free. It says so right on the vehicle, on the business cards, and on the website. Junk Recyclers of Asheville, North Carolina, has an interesting business model. Two uniformed guys will show up with a biodiesel box truck. If your stuff is just junk and not crap, they will take it off your hands and not charge you.

Phillip is a repeat customer. He used the guys before when someone gifted him a hot tub that he found he didn't use all that much. Those were better times and now his life is in transition. "I was married to a nurse and now I'm not, and I just can't afford to be here." His story sounds like a lyric from a country song. Phillip is soft-spoken and apologetic about some of the items because he knows the drill. He told them he has stuff worth taking away and now the Junk Recyclers team has to assess whether or not something is functional in some way. The guys in the field do their best not to appear judgmental, but it is part of the job. Tommy lays out the bottom line. "We'll see what items he has and the quality of it, and if it is something we can take for free. As long as it is not damaged, not covered with pet smells or stains or anything like that, then we can take items like that, try to find them a new home."

Junk removal is only part of the equation when it comes to this next generation junk removal company. The name Junk Recyclers is a tip-off. The company repairs, repurposes, and upcycles items it removes from homes and businesses. The removals become inventory for a retail co-business called the Regeneration Station. The store full of used goods is in a twenty-six-thousand-square-foot former pillow factory warehouse three miles from downtown Asheville.

So each removal job is a bit of a mystery. What will they find? Will it be salvageable? Can it be resold in the store? They've gotten really good at telling what has potential and what doesn't. They've heard some tall tales. "Maybe we'll get a 'limited edition' couch," recalls Adam with a laugh. It has become the company joke. One woman tried to convince the pick-up team that her couch was unique and of great value because it was a "limited edition" sofa. It was just a couch the lady paid a lot of money for and was now in sad shape. They see the endowment effect—people placing unreasonable value on their things—all the time. That is not the case on this job. Upon closer inspection Phillip realizes some of this furniture is in less than desirable condition. He just wants what is still in decent shape to go to someone who might need it. He chose Junk Recyclers because of its repurposing reputation. "There's something to be said for giving it away."

The final assessment from Tommy? "We were able to get a bookshelf, an old artillery crate, and a futon. The rest was too far gone. Too many chips." The artillery crate was really cool. It looked like a rustic wood version of a toolbox plus stenciled in the corner was a little bomb with flames shooting out of the top. For a creative interior designer it could be that showcase piece on a bookshelf or an ironic objet d'art in a modern home or maybe it would be the perfect surprise for the longtime NRA member who has everything. The guys on the trucks have a keen eye for potential value. The store depends on it. By the end of the day the crate was on the sales floor at the Regeneration Station with a tag describing it as an "ammo box" and it could be yours for twenty dollars.

Junk Recyclers offers to take away Phillip's busted chest of drawers and broken shelves for a small price. The material could be recycled or sold to local artists. Phillip opts for just the free removal and thanks the guys profusely. But he did have a question. "Every time you guys come it is a different guy—are you a cult or something?"

It isn't a cult but a growing business with seven guys and three trucks. This self-contained junk ecosystem was the brainchild of thirty-two-year-old Tyler Garrison, someone who thinks about life and business a bit differently than most entrepreneurs. Nine years ago, Tyler decided he wanted to go off the grid. He needed to figure out what he really wanted in life. On the surface he seemed to be living large, running a software franchise in his home state of Georgia. "I had the quote unquote American Dream. I lived in the suburbs. I had a ridiculous salary for a twenty-three-year-old. I was married, then went through a divorce." With his long hair, trucker hat, and scruffy goatee it is hard to imagine him as a nine-to-five kind of guy. "I made a fortune but I was just wasn't . . . I was kinda . . . I was existentially discontent. And so after the divorce I just had this awareness I should just give everything away and backpack. I packed a pack. Closed down my bank account. Turned off my cell phone. Gave it away. Gave away all my possessions. I spent three and a half years just backpacking across the country." He camped out. He took odd jobs. Hitchhiked. He says that when he needed something—food, a place to stay, a job—it always worked out. Objectively, he is hipster handsome, with the self-possession of someone who has had success, so his ability to make connections, grab a ride, and find places to stay is not that surprising.

The experience was Tyler's own version of the Aboriginal right of passage known as "the Walkabout" when young men at the dawn of adulthood wander alone into the wilderness to learn more about

themselves spiritually and their own drive to survive. "Doing something like that—it became the journey. Life is a deeply internal experience and we tend to ID with external." Material goods came to mean
nothing to him. He actually believed he might spend the rest of his life
as a "nomadic warrior," but a chance encounter in Florida changed
that. He went there to help out his then-girlfriend. Her grandma had
passed away and her home needed to be cleaned out. There he met
a guy he saw picking up trash on the sidewalks who would then sell
the stuff out of his house. The guy explained that because there were
so many snowbirds in the area often the items being discarded were
barely used. "This guy was sharp. Not what you think. He was *sharp*.
He told me he made 8K in a month. That's real money—no employees, no tax. The main thing seemed fun. Simple. Doing something
good for the Earth. All these wins." Given the combination of his
years living off his wits and his experience as a businessman Tyler
saw an opportunity to create a new junk removal paradigm.

Tyler moved to Asheville with a little cash in his pocket and a
pickup truck he bought from the girlfriend's dad. In 2010 he spent
it all to get the company up and running. "I had five hundred bucks.
Spent $70 on a storage unit and $430 dollars on an ad to run in the
Mountain Express. It *had* to work or I wouldn't pay rent that month."
He laughs now realizing that he hadn't really thought it through.

"For four months we had no company name. The first ad said
FREE REMOVAL and that was it. And my phone number." People
called. He took the stuff and within a month filled up a ten-by-
twenty-foot storage unit. Tyler advertised what he had for sale on
Craigslist and then sold things directly to people who responded to
the ad. It worked too well. By month number two he had to expand
to a twenty-by-forty-foot unit. By the third month he had four of
those units and by the end of the first quarter he had eight ten-by-
twenty-foot units and a steady flow of customers. When he found
himself digging through mountains of small appliances and climbing
over piles of furniture to retrieve an item someone showed up to
get he realized the truth. "I knew I needed another way to do this."

Another chance conversation led to an aha moment. "A seed is a funny thing to plant. A guy told me that Walmart gives away old buildings." The guy was off a bit. Given the timeline, what the man might have been referring to was a movement to rehabilitate and repurpose abandoned big box stores like Walmart and K-Mart. Published in 2008, the book *Big Box Reuse* by Oberlin professor Julia Christensen highlighted the creative uses for these kinds of giant spaces left standing empty. Giant former retail spaces have become churches, libraries, town halls, and one was even turned into an indoor speedway.

The conversation was a game-changing moment for Tyler in two ways. First, he knew he needed to find a large space for little money, perhaps some abandoned warehouse. Second, he also decided he wanted to build the Walmart of well-made used furniture. He watched as people spent a couple hundred dollars to buy pressboard dressers. He wanted to find a way for them to spend the same amount of money on gently used but beautifully crafted pieces of furniture that would last. "What a neat concept, to be able to have this mega reused repurpose salvage thrift store. The problem with most thrift stores is if you want to furnish a home you have to go to a million of them. Places may have a couple couches, maybe a lamp; it may or may not work. Why not do a big furniture store where you can have forty couches and you can have fifty beds and tons of lamps? I felt like people would come from miles around." He also tapped into the reality of the economy at the time. He started his company after the great crash of 2008. His point of reference is very different from other independents junk removal folks who got in early and had to adjust. He didn't scale his business to meet the new economic reality. An ambiguous economy was the norm for him and a lot of people his age.

"There are so many people who need to find ways to save money for their families. We've become so consumeristic. On one hand people don't want to buy this throwaway Chinese-made stuff; on the other hand, our economy is not exactly booming right now, and a lot of families can't afford to go buying a $3,000 living room set or a $6,000 bed." There's a little bit of unintentional Robin Hood in this model. He has inserted himself between the haves and the have-nots of the Asheville area. "The truth of the matter is the bread-and-butter of junk removal is really wealthy people. Is it only? No. Does everyone have junk? Of course. If you are on a fixed income or low income your first thought is you will load it in your Honda Civic and take it to the dump. I don't think it's the best choice, but if that's what you got to do, I get it. So the bread and butter is the wealthier, more affluent folks. Someone whose rate is $300-an-hour and just says, 'I just don't want to do it,' or 'I work hard so I don't have to.'"

Junk Recyclers has a geographic advantage. North Carolina is home to some of the finest furniture making in the country. The removal guys often pull out some exquisite furnishings from even modest houses. The end result is the Regeneration Station often has pieces made of teak or mahogany with dovetail grooves, the kind of furniture that pricewise would be out of the question for someone with limited means.

"There's a lot of value of these items," says Nikki Allen, the creative director of the Regeneration Station. She runs the retail side of the operation. "We wouldn't have one without the other. It started as just a junk removal company and the Regeneration Station was the outlet to sell what the guys got from the clean outs. Without them we wouldn't have the opportunity to recycle everything we can and do. It is a team effort." A petite brunette who looks more like a teenager than a woman in her mid-twenties, Nikki's gravity-defying ponytail swishes back and forth as she uses a push scooter to zip around the warehouse because it is so big. Her little dog, Bear, trails behind her. The enormous space is divided into sections with aisles that have street names. "I wanted to make this like a little town," Nikki says of the design. It also helps her direct people to the different booths. For example, when you walk in the door you can take a right onto Abbey Road, which leads to Shakedown Street. You can keep going and intersect with Electric Avenue or take a right on Love Street. The industrial look of the warehouse, the corrugated steel walls and exposed lighting, is offset by some urban funk. Nikki had two graffiti artists spend a night in the building painting a giant mural on the far end of the building. They are now spray-painting one of Junk Recyclers' trucks. Real vinyl records spin on an old player providing the background music for the store. It all goes to the vibe Nikki wants for the place. "I want it to be like a playground." A retro, hipster playground.

Booths are leased to likeminded local artists or upcyclers. You can find expensive pieces by people who are professional pickers, but most of the inventory is items from removals that have been upcycled by the team. Nikki is really good at reupholstering chairs. "We mainly try to keep things out of the landfills."

The term *upcycling* entered the mainstream in the 1990s. It means taking a used item and creating a new use for it, perhaps taking old shutters and refashioning them into a bed headboard, a table top made of old wood rulers, a bulletin board out of wine corks. There's even an upcycling blog devoted to the things you can do with dryer lint. Apparently you can make modeling clay out of it.

The credit for the term goes to a German engineer named Reiner Pilz who gave an interview in the mid-nineties where he criticized the way a certain business recycled. He said "Recycling. I call it downcycling. They smash bricks, they smash everything. What we need is upcycling, where old products are given more value not less."

Pilz would approve of the Regeneration Station's third outpost, the Regeneration Station Studio. It is a workshop where Tyler and Nikki send pieces that need some extra attention or refashioning before they go on the floor. Nikki gets excited when one of the pieces comes back from being fixed. "One thing about the older furniture is it is made well. It is solid! I mean, this is going to last through generations. People are now starting to see the value in it." North Carolina has been called the Furniture Capital of the World, and is home to some of the best woodworking from companies like Hickory and High Point. A former furniture pro who worked for several top shelf companies now runs the Regeneration

Station's shop. Nikki says Mike McCracken is the best. "He has been a woodworker for thirty-five years. He's great. He makes anything you want. We do a lot of barn tear downs, we make furniture . . . well, he makes them."

I can hear the machinery from the parking lot and sawdust tickles my nose as I approach the garage. Inside is Mike, who is building an industrial-looking oversized lawn chair out of some wood shipping pallets. "If someone walks in here and says, 'Can you do so and so?' I will tell them, 'I can build the Taj Mahal if you got the time and the money.'"

One listen to Mike McCracken's accent and you know his family has been in North Carolina since its founding, and he is proud of that fact. He's been in the furniture business—selling, teaching, overseeing quality control, designing—his whole life. "All my years of furniture . . . I've worked at the very high end. . . . I've made stuff for Reagan. . . . I've made stuff for Bush. I've made stuff for Dale Earnhardt Jr." He wants to show me a grand cabinet so he can explain how he determines the age and condition of a piece and, more important, how he is going to fix it. "Old furniture was big cases on little legs . . . you can tell by the style. This is definitely a [nineteen] forties or fifties cabinet. We're gonna strengthen it," he says, pointing to the areas that need help and makes two fists to show how strong it will be. He says he got it for nothing and he is ready to make it into something. "We fix it up. Repurpose it, make it presentable. Not going to be brand new now, but it will be functional and serve a purpose for someone looking for a bargain."

Even with all his years in the industry he does not turn his nose up at something that is broken or even something pulled out of a Dumpster. He likes the challenge, the creativity, and the freedom to do as he pleases with the material presented to him. Mike thinks the world is full of two kinds of people. "A guy walks into a room and sees it's full of horse shit. The guy says, 'Ooooh, wee, Oh Gawd, this room is nasty and terrible! I'm getting out of here.' The other guy looks around and starts cleaning and says, 'There's got to be a pony in there somewhere!' It is all how you look at things. I know I can make something out of it."

Asheville is an ideal location for a three-pronged business like this. It has a university and trailer parks nearby. It is a city that is a town. It is cosmopolitan and welcoming of tourists, but it is distinctly southern. You will drive down the Billy Graham Highway to get from one place to another. My rental car radio was preset to HIM radio, a contemporary Christian station. There are also neohippies grooving to drum circles in the revitalized downtown plaza. As Asheville's reputation as a livable city spreads, the more diverse the population becomes—and the needs are diverse as well. Nikki is a good example. "Asheville has a lot of transplants. People just come in their car. That's how I got here—I packed up a car from Indiana."

This business is run by millennials and it shows. Nikki and Tyler have a Regeneration Station podcast. Junk Recyclers/The Regeneration Station post videos on YouTube. They advertise on Craigslist. If an artist uses something he finds in the salvage area of the store and posts it on Facebook, the artist will get a discount the next time he comes in. They count their customer base as being a lot like them. "Ballin' on a budget!" is Nikki's battle cry, but she thinks it really goes deeper than just a good deal. "People in our generation are not so materialistic. They don't need the big houses, the material things. You'd rather just not have a bunch of debt. To have your own home under $30,000 now is actually more prevalent."

Asheville is an interesting mash up of the old and the new, the modern and the old school, the town and the gown. And it bubbles up among the staff from time to time. A couple of the junk removal guys are locals from just outside Asheville, and they have lived hard. One tells me of his time in jail for passing bad checks. He spent his life growing up in a trailer park near a meth lab. He is grateful to have this job and to be considered for promotions. Another hauler is a student at the university. He is studying sustainability. The clash of cultures is apparent one day when the subject turns to lunch. "The sandwich had gouda cheese . . . it was so good," says the student. The local dude, Nathan, a thin, reed of a guy, takes a drags of his cigarette and says, "I don't what the hell you are talkin' 'bout."

———————

"What is this?"

"Is this right?

"It said ask for Jonathan," says a skeptical twenty-three-year-old Nathan in a distinct North Carolina country drawl. They negotiate Junk Recyclers' truck into the small parking lot of an auto repair shop on an otherwise lonely strip of road about ten miles north of Asheville.

"No way," says Josh.

This is a first for the duo. They aren't exactly sure what it is they are going to haul out of this place. The are greeted by a soft-spoken middle-aged auto mechanic who happens to double as the new owner of this establishment.

"Are you Jonathan?" asks Nathan.

"Yes sir. Let me show you upstairs."

It starts to make sense when they hit the door. This must have been an old time garage for the locals in the Weaverville area. It has the distinct look of a place changing hands. While the garage itself is orderly and tidy, you can see in one of the corners a tangle mess of tools. Jonathan has only owned the place a month. Not so long ago the whole first floor looked like that corner, but now just the attic does. That's where the men were headed. They climbed up some brown, rickety wood stairs to what could generously be called a second floor. It was more like a crawl space. If you were just one hair over six feet you'd have to hunch over.

"I'm gonna be the first one to hit my head," says Josh. "It isn't a day at Junk Recyclers if someone doesn't get hurt." Nathan confesses he crushed his finger last week.

What the heck was up there? The ghosts of the previous auto shop including four ACs, water pumps, steering wheels, air filters, carburetors, more car parts, Carquest BF252 oil filter, and all of it was on industrial steel shelving. But to the trained eye, like Nathan's, there were nonautomotive items tucked away. Push aside a crushed old box and behind it was a blue tin of Laura Lynn coffee from a southern grocery chain. An old floral couch was covered up too. There was an old workout bench too. This wasn't just a storage space for parts. It appears someone and his cat bunked up there more than occasionally.

This is the moment of truth. What can they take for free? Nathan just wants to be certain he makes the right decision, so he calls Tyler to explain the situation. The issues are 1) this could be a daylong event, 2) the things they could remove for free, mostly metal, might not be worth anything. After a couple of minutes on the phone of listening and nodding, Nathan has an answer: "Well, if it is over five hundred pounds of metal we can take it for free. So there's definitely over five hundred pounds of metal. So it is worth *some* money." Tyler also suggests they look for any cool gears or any materials that Mike McCracken could use.

The client is polite, but isn't really interested in all that. He just wants to know what can go and if it can go today. Nathan tells him all the metal can go for free and anything else will be based on how much of the truck is filled, like all the other junk removal models. Jonathon considers this and hands them some disappointing news. "Well, take what you can for free and put the rest in the corner." Not the best answer for the financial bottom line. Hauling out the metal will be labor intensive, but not that lucrative at the scrap shop. It is going to be a long morning.

The next two hours are backbreaking and at moments a little scary. Taking all the car parts of the shelves and putting them into boxes makes a lot of noise in a room with low ceilings. The sound of metal on metal is frightening. Nothing good ever happens when metal crashes together. When they move the boxes from place to place it sounds like elephants clog dancing. Repeatedly they load up the dolly with the heavy boxes and slowly, very slowly, chug it down the steep narrow wood stairs one riser at a time. Ka-thunk-boom. Ka-thunk-boom. Ka-thunk-boom. "This one is going to be a backbreaker," says Josh, who was on the bottom-receiving end of one particularly enormous load. Nathan holds on to the top of the loaded dolly with all his might or else Josh will get a face full of gears. It was an extreme trust exercise.

When they finally get this particular load out to the truck, Nathan lets go of his end and Josh pops up into the air like the skinny kid on the end of a seesaw whose husky buddy decides to take a seat. It is a well-needed moment of levity. They notice that the wheels on the dolly look like they are going to pop and they pray the tires just hold out. After several hours they determine they can't do all the boxes of gears and the metal shelving in one run. They take what they can to the scrap yard and unload 860 pounds of metal from that job. It yields less than $100.

Tyler knows that free junk removal isn't going to pay the bills either. Keeping the store stocked is really what is important. "In the beginning I thought we could do *all* free removal. You can't." Now it is fairly balanced. He says in gross sales the store brings in about 60 to 70 percent of gross profits. He believes in this model and plans to expand to Florida. He thinks he's hit the financial and emotional sweet spot of what the customers want and need. "People fall in love with repurposing things and putting them in the home."

14

THE REPAIR CAFÉ

"Look! It's an actual typewriter." The woman placed the 1970s-era boxy machine with the familiar black keys and silver hammers on the table. She was enthusiastic about her recent purchase. "I bought it at a yard sale for five dollars! I just liked it. Now I need it to work."

Dimitri, a bald, sixty-something, retired mechanical engineer took off the top as the lady handed him the only new typewriter ribbon she could find. Dimitri quickly saw the issue. The existing ribbon uptake reel in the typewriter was much smaller than the new ribbon reel. Dimitri took the end of the new ribbon and fastened it to the empty smaller uptake reel. He then inserted the power drill into the center of that smaller reel. When he started the drill, an instant winch was created that automatically spooled in the ribbon from the big new wheel onto the smaller old one that fit in the typewriter. The MacGyver move drew a few oohs and ahhs from others who were taking part in this Repair Café in upstate New York.

"Repair Café is a free community meeting place to bring beloved but broken items to be repaired for free." That is John Wackman's elevator pitch at a Repair Café in New York's Hudson Valley. He organizes a regularly scheduled event where anyone can show up to the designated location with something to be fixed and volunteers will do their best to make it right. If you have a VCR that won't fast forward, a tinkerer at the electronics table might help you out. If the hem on your coat is loose, an altruistic seamstress will tack it right up.

Wackman sees a lot of worried looking people enter the room full of handy and neighborly folks. They aren't quite sure what to expect when they arrive with a busted object, but usually are quite happy when they leave. "People bring things they care about. It's broken [but] they'd like to keep it. They don't want to throw it away or buy a replacement. But where are they going to take it? That is what we address."

It is a common problem. For some broken items, especially older ones, the parts don't exist anymore, or the people who know how to fix these things don't exist anymore or have become increasingly hard to find. Or in some cases, a fix can cost as much as a new item. It is why so many nearly useable items are relegated to junk status.

This tendency to pitch instead of stitch really bothered Dutch journalist Martine Postma. She became concerned about the acceptance of the chuck-it culture. "It's a shame, because the things we throw away are usually not that broken. There are more and more people in the world, and we can't keep handling things the way we do. . . . I had the feeling I wanted to [do] something, not just write about it."[1] Her solution was simple: connect people with broken things with people who could and would fix them for free.

The first Repair Café was held on October 18, 2009, in the lobby of the Fijnhout Theatre in Amsterdam. Fast forward to 2015 and there are Repair Cafés in sixteen countries, including the United States. The small idea grew rapidly and the Repair Café soon morphed into the Repair Café Foundation, a nonprofit overseer of cafes that fall under its purview. The foundation stays alive through donations, including a six-figure grant from the Dutch government. To be affiliated with and replicate the Repair Café model, one must purchase a starter kit for forty-five euro, about fifty dollars. It includes a graphics package to use on promotional literature, a press kit, start-up advice, guidelines about safety, (e.g., "When in doubt, don't"), liability waivers, and language to use to describe a Repair Cafe. It asks that you use all of the logos and use the repaircafe.org site as your hub. It is a bit like a franchise without the commercial element.

The first official version of the Repair Café in the United States was held in Palo Alto, California, in October 2012, founded by Pete Skinner, who says he had no clue how successful the venture would be. "The community has been extremely responsive because people are kind of fed up with the whole buy-it-and-toss-it mentality. It just resonates with people. Whether it makes any economic sense or any sort of time management sense, the fact that they have an option to do something other [than] put it in their basement and never have it see the light of day or toss it out."

In May 2012 Pete was a CFO of a software company and read about the first Netherlands Repair Café in the *New York Times*. His own personal experience compelled him to make it happen in the states. "I fall in the category of the frustrated consumer who doesn't like to throw stuff out from both an environmental standpoint and bridling at our world of over-hyped consumerism. Also, I'm a cheap Midwesterner, so I just don't like throwing stuff out! What I am not is an expert fixer. When I read this article I had a basement full of stuff I wanted to try to fix, but didn't have the time or skills to tackle."

Within six months of reading the article, Pete found a location, secured the fixers, and started a 501(c)(3). He paid for the start-up costs out of pocket, about $1,000. Half of that went to establishing the nonprofit status. Pete found that big companies that wanted to donate services, like food for the workers or cases of water, wouldn't make donations without it being an official nonprofit. The Palo Alto Repair Café has been able to sustain itself and has no shortage of volunteers. Pete says thirty to forty show up at the quarterly events, and being in Silicon Valley you can imagine they are some skilled tinkerers. "We have a great collection of volunteers who are technically savvy and they are really comfortable tearing stuff apart and diving in. You might expect that in Palo Alto or any community with a big engineering population.... We see a lot of household electronics, stereos, receivers, CD players, toasters, microwave ovens, stuff that is—things that have printed circuit boards that require a special level of willingness to tackle complexity. The greatest volume—electronics."

Some of the Repair Cafés are more productive than others. In some cities it has been a one and done venture. It takes commitment to keep one up and running consistently. It requires a regular space, reliable volunteers, and good marketing. It is interesting that out of the approximately twenty Repair Cafes in the states, six of them—Kingston, Rosendale, Gardiner, New Paltz, Rhinebeck, and Poughkeepsie—are located in New York's Hudson Valley around the Catskill Mountains. It has allowed the Hudson Valley to have a fix-it event almost every weekend, hosted by a community entity like a church or a town hall. This part of New York state is a blend of progressives, hunters, college students, average income families, and senior citizens. The towns themselves are old. Rhinebeck was founded in 1686 and Kingston was the first capital of the state of New York. Maybe there's something in the DNA of the population in this area because, coincidentally, this the part of the "New World" settled by the Dutch. If there is an area that appreciates the old and how it can be new again, this is it.

At the Rhinebeck town hall a woman wandered in to see what the fuss was all about. The event has been advertised in the local paper and there's a big sign out front.

"Lamps are us!" a volunteer offers as she is greeted at the check-in desk.

"Well, I will run home and get my lamp!" says the lady.

"I think you should," says the volunteer.

"I think I will," says the lady.

And she does. She's back in twenty minutes with an old, black, three-pronged floor lamp. She explains, "It has been in the closet for five years. I took it to a lamp guy in town and he said it would be fifty dollars. I can't do that right now." Terry Nelson gets to work on it. Nelson is a skilled woodworker with her own shop in the area. The lamp lady doesn't know it, but someone who builds high-end furniture and has built an exhibit that appeared in a New York museum is fixing her old light. She often does small electrical work when she is installing her custom-made cabinets. "It is a bad switch. It is fairly simple, but you kinda have to know how to do it. You want to be safe with it. It *is* electricity."

Terry has volunteered at every Hudson Valley Repair Café so far. "I thought this is a fabulous idea because people are always asking me to fix anyway! I am always thinking, *What kind of donation or contribution can I make to help the community that's not paying money out to something?* I do it in real terms. That fits into that realm." Lamps and vacuums are the items seen most often at these cafés. She remembers the first one being exhausting and that she worked for four hours straight. "I've seen some nice antique lamps. It had a *Roadshow* feel. People come in and say *This was my grandmother's.*

You hear the story that *This was my great-grandmother's and it sat by her bed. And then it didn't work and it was in the attic for fifty years.* That's kind of fun."

The woman with the three-pronged lamp applauded when it lit up for the first time in years. She thanked Terry profusely and seemed at a loss for what to do. She seemed to want to pay Nelson or extend the interaction in some way. She was a bit discombobulated that she could just take her lamp and go home. She finally asked, "Can I do something for you?" Terry just smiled and said, "You can leave a tip." Small tip jars were on the table and it seemed to make people comfortable to stick a dollar or two in a jar for a job well done.

When John Wackman started the café in New Paltz, it was only the fourth in the country. He is a tall, thin man. His boyish face and thick, black-frame glasses give him a youthful look, despite a full head of white hair. As a former television producer he is well suited to bring together different types of people to work toward one goal. It was a good skill set when he had to go about finding the volunteers for this thing no one had ever heard of before. First, he went after the pros, like Terry Nelson. "Where do you find seamstresses, jewelry repair, digital? You reach out to the people who are already doing this, and then people would say, *Why would they want to volunteer and give away what they do?* The answer is, it is one Saturday every other month. There is no better way than to get out into community and let people know what they do. Although nobody talks about that. In fact, I have to remind these guys to *Bring your cards!*"

So many of the skills needed are only known by people of a certain age. Home economics and shop classes are relics of public school curriculums of the past. John went to the source to find folks who still knew how to fix things: retirees. "I became aware of the 'Retired men of New Paltz.' They meet for breakfast the first Monday of every month at the Plaza Diner. Every meeting they need a speaker. They invited me. I got immediately three or four guys."

"Gonna be a good day!" John said to no one in particular as he surveyed the room. His television production skills were on full display as he set the stage for the second anniversary of the New Paltz Repair Café. He prepared the basement of the United Methodist Church on Main Street by spreading out sunny tablecloths on card tables and placing small milk glass vases with bright yellow plastic flowers right in the middle. The muffled sound of the organist practicing in the chapel bled through the ceiling as he affixed posters to the walls and placed handmade magazine-collage-style posters on display easels at each station. They read, THINGS MADE OF WOOD, DIGITAL DEVICE RECONFIG., DOLLS & STUFFED ANIMALS, and CLOTHING AND TEXTILES.

He really wants the café and community aspects of the day to shine through. That means snacks would be offered; some volunteers have donated baked goods. In the kitchen area of the church, John was joined by four other fixers who debated about how to fix the coffee. They end up just dumping grounds into an industrial grade brewer and pressing start.

The finishing touches included posters with event-appropriate quotes to inspire or set the tone for the day. A line from the romantic English poet William Blake read, "Tools are Made," while another offered a deadpan humor provided by absurdist Steven Wright which read, "I couldn't fix your brakes, so I made your horn louder."

The sewing table sees the early action in the day. Lisa and Caroline are patient and full of advice. Lisa started as a kid creating accessories for her toys. "I made a sleeping bag for my Troll doll, with a zipper that went all the way around." Lisa will take care of work that needs a machine and Caroline will handle any hand stitching that comes their way. She unpacks colorful spools of threat and pieces of yarn. "The hardest thing is for me is the items go from the pragmatic to the sentinmental. . . . It is something like, either a zipper all the way to *My friend who died gave this to me and . . .* and the item is usually close to falling apart." Sometimes an item is too far gone and she's quick to tell people the truth, but if it can be saved Caroline will try and usually succeed. "I had a woman cry once. She was so excited."

Caroline met John at an Earth Day event and she had the thought, *I have skills!* When I asked her if she was ever a professional seamstress she hollers, "Oh, God no!" This is and has always been purely a hobby for the retired MBA (1972) turned environmental advocate.

She and Lisa often deal with poorly made clothing, and it is hard to tell someone that the item they brought in for a tweak is made of cheap material and the fix will be very temporary. Low-grade goods are something repairers deal with a lot. One of the woodworkers put it this way: "If it is something new, sometimes they are using materials that are not very strong that can't be glued. It can really only be patched."

"These would make really good garden stakes," jokes Rob. The seventy-five-year-old Repair Café regular was talking about some blinds that are behaving a bit wonky. At one point six men were standing in front of the blinds trying to figure out what to do with them. The gentleman who brought them in didn't exactly know what was wrong with the shades, just that his wife told him to bring them to get fixed, so he was following orders. Rob left the others to it and chatted with me for a bit before a big project arrived. He has been retired about twenty years and was one of the elders of New Paltz who heard John's presentation and liked the idea. "I spent my career as a biologist. My personal ethic is to try to fix things or reuse things, and not throw them out. Not always buying new stuff, because every time you buy something either it or its replacement is going to wind up in a landfill somewhere."

Rob would help tackle three projects that day: one that was just a tiny fix, one that involved glue and clamps, and something else that required the collaboration of two longtime fixers and a professional contractor. The first project was a wood rattle brought in by Repair Café regular Marybelle. "My cousin's husband made it and it lasted through Emma and we gave it to Simon and he was sitting in a high chair and they have a wooden floor." What happened next was pretty obvious: "And I'm thinkin', *I wonder what happens when he drops it on the floor?* And just as I was about to take it away from him . . ."

It was a lovely blond wood, smooth and filled with small hard beans that made a soothing chuck-a-chuck sound when shaken. The end had broken off. Rob sanded the edges, got out super epoxy, aligned the two round hemispheres to make a whole sphere. The catch was it needed time to dry, so Rob told Marybelle he'd bring it to her at church.

Then there are the strangers who walk in with big problems. A slight, middle-aged Asian man arrived with two terribly broken pieces of furniture. One was an older chair with a leg broken in half and the other a pedestal end table with one of the supports busted off. "Whaddya have a fight in your house last night?" joked Joe in a thick New York accent. He was up from Brooklyn to help. He is part of the Fixers Collective. They're a long-running local fixit group, and as someone who spends a lot time in the Hudson Valley, Joe likes to help out his upstate New York friends. "Is Patrick Murphy gonna be here?" wondered Rob.

This was a job that would require either a miracle or a professional. Enter Patrick Murphy, a master carpenter and contactor who owns his own firm, Building Logic. A friendly, soft-spoken fellow in his early fifties, he's happy to share his pro-level tools and industrial epoxies. He has all the good toys, like a pneumatic nail gun. "To me it is a no-brainer to do repair and fix things around my house, around my neighbor's house. It's the skill I possess." Once Patrick arrived it took all three men to figure out how to use a dowel and some rope—and I think a little bit of wizard magic—to get the legs back on that chair. The man left happy but never did answer the question about a fight.

Patrick likes being around the ladies and gentlemen who have lived a bit of life. They, like the items they fix, clearly have a lot of use left in them. "From my standpoint, the retired tinkers have time and patience, old work knowledge, everything used be repaired. I love all those guys and talking to them. I can bring the younger attitude and strength and tools and newer ways of fixing things. I am sucker for volunteering." It explains why a busy contractor who specialized in green design would spend his Saturdays helping to fix music boxes and mechanized Christmas trees. Patrick used to coach youth sports, and when his kid aged out he found himself looking for a way to contribute to his community. "I had no outlet for volunteerism." Like most volunteer opportunities he says he gets as much out of helping people as he gives. One of his most memorable days involved a woman's childhood memory. "A fifty-year-old woman brought in the piano stool she used when she was like eight years old, to learn to play the piano. It had been broken for decades." He worked on it for a bit and when the woman returned she didn't see the stool. She assumed it was too far gone and Patrick had just put it aside. When she asked about it, Patrick, who is a big, strong, blond guy, told her he was sitting on it and had been for a while. "I noticed that she didn't move. Then she just melted. She was crying."

The people who volunteer their time are a mix of tinkerers, former engineers, hobbyists, and environmentalists. Dimitri Galitzine is all four. He runs the Kingston café but also helps out at the others. He was the man who got the typewriter back in useable shape. He also fixed two vacuums and a turntable that day. He has an avuncular presence and the voice of Sean Connery. When he speaks he does so with authority. While he believes in keeping as much out of the waste stream as possible, he understands why people with limited means are almost forced to buy new. "When appliances break on you, are going to pay for the man just to come look at it, never mind fixing it? Which of course becomes noncompetitive in relation to the price of a new one. Which is why repairing seems to work only on a volunteer basis. And I think on that basis it is worth doing. And teaching people you can repair some things. Lamps are reparable. Textiles are easy to fix. The seamstresses fix dolls. And toys. In a great many toys, doesn't matter if it is perfect. It is still playable."

A middle-aged couple brought in a toaster that was only browning bread on one side. The man said he couldn't figure out how to remove the back of the machine. Dimitri showed him the one "safety" screw, sometimes called a one-way screw, that is used on many electronics to prevent tampering. It is slightly different and requires a special tool or some DIY ninja skills to unscrew it. Some tinkerers believe these screws are there to force the average person to abandon fixing things or are meant to discourage owners from opening up an item because it will void the warranty. Always floating around the edges of the fix-it coalitions is the theory of planned obsolescence, the idea that companies purposely engineer their products to fail.

Planned obsolescence was widely promoted by American economist Bernard London. In 1932, when the country was in the grip of the Great Depression, the idea of spending money on something, if you had the money to spend, was anathema. London argued this attitude had the country in an economic chokehold. He believed the way to breathe new life into the economy was to purposely truncate the life expectancy of a product so that people would be forced to buy.

He wrote a manifesto called *Ending the Depression Through Planned Obsolescence* which he published on October 1, 1932. In it he wrote the following:

People everywhere are today disobeying the law of obsolescence. . . . Worn-out automobiles, radios, and hundreds of other items which would long ago have been discarded and replaced in more normal times, are being made to last another season or two or three, because the public is afraid or has not the funds to buy now…. Furniture and clothing and other commodities should have a span of life, just as humans have. When used for their allotted time, they should be retired, and replaced by fresh merchandise. It should be the duty of the State as the regulator of business to see that the system functions smoothly, deciding matters for capital and labor and seeing that everybody is sufficiently employed.

This idea that companies purposely plan for products to konk out at a certain time certainly has anecdotal support. Who hasn't had a piece of equipment die just when the warranty runs out? There's a documentary called *The Lightbulb Conspiracy* that tells the story of the Phoebus cartel, which was a group of lightbulb manufacturers who allegedly got together in the 1920s to set a standard for lightbulbs worldwide. Part of this standard was for each company to pledge to never make a bulb that would last longer than one thousand hours.[2]

The twenty-first-century target for those who believe in planned obsolescence is big tech. In a piece for *Wired* magazine titled, "The New MacBook Pro: Unfixable, Unhackable, Untenable," writer and founder of the online repair manual hub ifixit.com Kyle Wiens lists all the ways that certain Apple products are made to expire. He notes that while the heavier professional laptops can be upgraded and fixed, the light ones aimed at consumers are not built to last. He notes how each iteration has become increasingly difficult to fiddle with or fix. In one version the battery is glued into the case. Yet, it has been a popular seller. Wiens wrote, "We voted with our wallets and purchased the device despite its built-in death clock."

The writer acknowledges that demand is high for these products so of course Apple keeps making them. But the 2012 MacBook Pro seemed to send him over the edge. He took issue with how unfixable it was. "Unlike the previous model, the display is fused to the glass, which means replacing the LCD requires buying an expensive display assembly. The RAM is now soldered to the logic board—making future memory upgrades impossible. And the battery is glued to the case, requiring customers to mail their laptop to Apple every so often for a $200 replacement."[3]

Wiens is part of the Right to Repair movement, an effort to pass strong legislation that would allow individual and independent repair shops to fix electronics. Many companies keep their manuals close to the vest and only allow them in the hands of dealers. A bizarre example has surfaced with farm tractors. Now there are John Deere tractors that are wildly computerized. If one of these tractors breaks down, a farmer can't really get in there and fix it himself. He has to have a Deere-approved repair person do it with certain parts and manuals only available to certain people. Deere and companies like it argue that they own the computer code in the tractors (or product) and they don't want anyone stealing it. If you want it fixed, someone they authorize has to do it with parts authorized by them.

The Fair Repair bill put forth in two states in 2015, New York and Minnesota, would empower the average person or repair person to have access to the information and parts to be able to fix smartphones, computers, and, yes, farm equipment. There is precedent for a law like this passing. Automotive repair folks won the right to repair in 2012. Now that cars are borderline spaceships, for a while independent mechanics and owners who were handy with a wrench were being turned down when they requested manuals and parts to fix cars, based on the proprietary argument. The first bill like this passed in Massachusetts with 86 percent of a vote and it will become a de facto national standard by 2018.

Where some see conspiracy, old hands like Dimitri see a business decision. "Apple computers are wonderful. Unfortunately, they are glued shut so they are very difficult to open and repair. It is almost impossible to get one of those open. . . . I am not sure that it is even malevolent planned obsolescence, but I am sure people will pay more for a lighter computer than a heavy one with screws. . . . There is a competition for making things smaller and lighter."

Unfortunately, Dimitri was not able to fix the toaster, safety screws and all. But the couple didn't mind. They just loved the idea that someone would try. John Wackman says there are occasional disappointments. "What we say is we cannot guarantee that the item you bring to Repair Café can be fixed. All we can say is that you will have an interesting time. People get that." There are disclaimers posted, and when people sign in they are acknowledging that, in the language of the foundation:

> Neither the organizers of the Repair Café nor the repair experts are liable for any loss that may result from advice or instructions concerning repairs, for the loss of items handed over for repair, for consequential loss or for any other kind of loss resulting from work performed in the Repair Café. Experts making repairs offer no guarantee for the repairs carried out with their help and are not liable if objects that are repaired in the Repair Café turn out not to work properly at home.

People seem to get it and are grateful, and they come back. One lady who brought in some curtains to be hemmed returned an hour later with a lamp. A woman who had the orange finger of a hand-knit glove fixed last month was back to have the red thumb patched now by the same expert knitter. Dimitri says sometimes he feels like a hero. "People get thrilled about the idea of fixing their mother's old clock. It is a good feeling. People like it. It is a good feeling."

15

FOR THE LOVE OF JUNK
Q&A WITH MARY RANDOLPH CARTER, AUTHOR OF *AMERICAN JUNK*, *GARDEN JUNK*, *KITCHEN JUNK*, AND *BIG CITY JUNK*, AMONG OTHERS

THERE IS A SMALL, framed picture of a cat whose body is made out of a human thumbprint, head, whiskers, and ears sketched in, perched on the aluminum soap dish above the kitchen sink in Mary Randolph Carter's Manhattan apartment. There are two more cat paintings above it, and in between them a turtle sculpture affixed to the wall and wrapped in palm fronds, the kind you get at church the Sunday before Easter. Below it all is a thin rack from which vintage white enamel ladles and spoons hang. To the left of the sink is a full-sized refrigerator whose doors are completely covered in a decoupage of pictures, photos, and random notes. An enormous old-school alarm clock teeters on top of the appliance.

Mary Randolph Carter knows junk. Mary Randolph Carter loves junk and lives junk. She is the author of the glossy, photo-heavy coffee table books *American Junk, Garden Junk, Kitchen Junk*, and *Big City Junk*. The titles of her more recent books, *A Perfectly Kept House Is the Sign of a Misspent Life* and *Never Stop to Think . . . Do I Have a Place for This?*, clearly state her position about stuff. She is for it! She does not want to dictate or lecturer people about why they should embrace junk, but she doesn't want to people to be bullied into thinking all junk is bad.

Carter's address is one that makes you think of ladies in Chanel suits carrying small dogs or investment bankers who are trustees on various boards. Entering the exquisite lobby of her Upper East Side doorman building, you would never expect that several floors up is a flat that can be described as homespun junk chic. The apartment is a beautiful concoction of found objects and personal obsessions that has been featured in the *New York Times*.

Carter is fabulous in her own right. She has spent the last twenty-five years working for and with Ralph Lauren, most recently as

creative director. She has an effortless style that is part southerner
(she grew up in Virginia), part free spirit, and part urbane design
icon. With long blonde hair and a clear completion, at nearly seventy
the way she looks in patched jeans and a chunky sweater would cause
a thirty-year-old woman to be jealous and a make a thirty-year-old
man look twice.

Carter brews great strong coffee which she serves in, of course,
unmatched cups at a pine kitchen table covered in Mexican oil cloth
because it is forty years old and has been repaired so many times.
She values old. She values worn. Perhaps it is because during her
lifetime her family had been the victim of not one but two house
fires that took not only all their belonging, but also their loved ones.

She raised her two boys in New York City with a patient and gen-
erous man who lives with all the crazy things in their home because
he loves her. He jokes that when they pass a yard sale on road trips
he always asks her, "Is your heart palpitating?" It probably is.

Conducting a traditional Q&A session with Carter is a bit like
trying to take in her apartment with a single glance. Just as your eyes
settle on one interesting thing (a giant owl lamp) you can't help but
notice something else (the nine-foot clock behind it). Our conversation veered right and left, taking detours, returning to original questions. After nearly two hours of talking, interviewing, and touring
her home, the joy and challenge of presenting this as a traditional
Q&A are both big. So I will say this isn't heavily edited, it is *curated*.
We started with her first days as a junk-o-phile.

> Mary Randolph Carter: So one day the junk thing happened. I
> attribute my conversion as junker to a little place called the
> Rummage Shop. It was a converted muffler shop. And there
> was like a big spider on the top of it that had been made out
> of old mufflers because the—I found out later the guy that ran
> it was like a frustrated artist and sculptor. And every Sunday
> this place was open. Didn't open until after all the churches
> were closed, so it opened like around 11:30, and there were

people lined up. I never went into that place. I wasn't really into thrift shops or junk, that kind of thing. I went to beautiful antique shows, I mean, looking for something special and unique and handmade. But the rummage thing and the thrift shop thing never. But for the last, let's say, five years I had been—everything got too expensive. The fun had gone out of it for me going to these shows, flea markets, whatever. So one day I just pulled in to the Rummage Shop, and that's where the conversion began. I mean, it was like a crowded—you had to make your way through all this stuff. And I just started picking up these things, and they were like—what's her name? Maureen that owned it, she just had these little old tags on there, 25¢, $2.00. I mean, it was kind of like the old five and dimes in a way. But I walked out of there with an armload of stuff for like $12.56 or something. And I had so much fun. And that was my junk conversion.

Q: What drove you to write your book *Never Stop to Think . . .* ***Do I Have a Place for This?***

Carter: I mean, I guess I wrote the book to give people—I mean, all my books are about the same thing. They're all about giving yourself permission to fall in love with the wackiest thing, and don't let other people deter you. Don't worry about other people's taste. Don't worry if it doesn't have a provenance. I don't think I ever bought, except for by accident, something that was of real value, but it had value to me. And that's what I always write about is giving yourself permission, liberating yourself to love what you want to love. And that could be people or things or whatever.

So this particular book, *Never Stop to Think . . . Do I Have a Place for This?*, I mean, I've met so many great collectors, and I was really curious like you in way. I mean, I featured other people's things in my book, but this was a deeper dive into the lives of people that really have a lot of stuff and live with it in different ways. I would go in and I'd say, *Well, why do you have this? And what does it mean to you? And what does your partner think, your children think?* And so it was definitely, I think, of all my books, the one that comes closest to really sort of investigative reporting about, you know. And all of them I said, *Never stop to think, 'Do I have a place for this?'* I mean, I would say, *Suppose you had to—you lost it all, what would you do?* Or, *Your house is on fire. What would you save?* And most of them just said, *If I lost it all, that's fine. I'll just start over again.*

Q: Start again?

Carter: Find something else that moves me. And for all of them. And for me it had to do with making them smile, making them happy. Then you can start talking about uniqueness and your personal style and money and space. I mean, there's so many issues. Why did I write that book? I've been writing this story. My first book was like 1988, *American Family Style*, and that was the most personal because it reflected the way I was brought up in a large family of nine, living through a couple of devastating fires, losing everything, starting over again, watching my mother and father recover from something like that.

Q: Can you tell me about the fire in the first house?

Carter: So that fire happened on February fifteenth, like '55, I think, so I was probably about ten years old. And that night my mother came up and got me, and she saved me, pulled me down. But my great-aunt and grandfather and aunt were all—all perished that night. So eventually we lived—we don't need to go into a lot of this, but—

Q: That's OK . . . .

Carter: We eventually—we actually lived in a convent. Right across the street was a beautiful old house that had been the convent where the nuns lived, and it wasn't any longer. But they owned the house, and they gave it to us to live in—until we figured things out. And then I think it was—it wasn't so long. I don't even think it was a year. My mother, she just—she was just very—the memories and it was just so hard. So she and my father just decided—we had this house down in White Stone that was our summer house. It had been a barn. We called it River Barn. And we packed up and moved down there. And I guess there were probably seven of us maybe at that point, or six. And we moved down there and started all over again. And then that house burned down.

Q: Did they lose everything again?

Carter: So five or six years had gone by . . . so the fire in White Stone—the house—everything was gone.

Q: Wow.

Carter: Everything was gone. It was an old wooden house.

Q: Oh, gosh.

Carter: They put the fire out. They thought they had. And I woke— we were sleeping on the floor of the next door neighbor's. And something woke me up, and I saw the fire, and it had started up again. The next morning when we walked over, there was nothing. It was like a sand pile of ashes. Everything was gone.

Q: Oh, my God.

Carter: Everything was gone. So for about another year maybe we were nomads trying to figure out—I was away at school. And then eventually my parents decided to build. And that's when they started—since we lost everything, they had to start over again. And so we didn't have the paintings of the aunts of our family. So Mother would find paintings of other people's families, and the ugly ones were my father's side of the family. And they started to collect. And maybe at this point they really—because it was an old house, and my father loved old— they both loved old houses. And they were in the real estate business, and their specialty was selling beautiful old houses. And so now, since they were in this seventeenth-century house, they started to try to find things that felt like they belonged in the house.

Q: The fire—did losing everything have an impact on you? Did the fires have an effect on your personal style, having all your things taken from you?

Carter: Of course. Of course. I mean, I think what you learn is everything is disposable, and what's important obviously are the people. That's what matters.

Q: Yes.

Carter: So people say to me, *Well, why do you have all this stuff?*
And I said, *Well, first of all, everything in our home has some
kind of meaning.* And I'm trying to build this comfortable—
not a refuge—but I wanted this home to be comfortable and
personal. My God. First of all, we've lived here for forty years,
so things do pile up. But my children come in here and they
say, *Mom, you know that little clipboard, the banana clipboard
and the shutter, that's been there since I was like six years old.* I
don't change things too often. I like things to stay. But—what
was your question?

Q: I was talking about—it was about the fire.

Carter: Oh, the fire. So the thing is, of course it did. But I think that
you lose everything, but you didn't lose your family. So there's
an optimism and a hope. And then you just go out, and you
need a table. So you find a table and new chairs to sit on and
beds. But I always loved country. I love painted. I love worn
and weathered things that had a history and a patina, whether
they had a provenance or not.

And that's what I—when I came to New York and had
my little—I lived on a five-floor walk-up. What did I bring
with me? I brought a couple of old patchwork quilts, a rocking chair. I didn't have a lot of space, but I wanted something
that connected me to where I'd come from. But I think as
time has gone by, my style has evolved, and I love finding just
the personal junk that has no—absolutely no value. But I love
the color. I love the texture. I love the contradiction of the way
a funny little elf will look next to an old primitive cupboard.
And this little pine table has been sitting here since we moved
into this apartment. I bought it down on Bleecker Street. And
it's so bad. It's falling apart. But we'd eaten every meal here and
[so have] our four children. And eventually there were nails
popping up. I had to put the oil cloth on it. But I would never
get rid of it. It's like an anchor.

**Q: One thing I noticed in your books, and I'd be interested since
you've interviewed so many people who have so many different ways of living with their junk, is many were European.**

Is there a difference between the way Americans look at the things in their homes and their lives and the way Europeans do?

Carter: I had a couple—I had a friend of mine, Nathalie Lete, in Paris, and Elena who's French but Russian, and her big family. That was the first time I had gone outside the borders. I wanted to see if there was a difference. Maybe a little bit in the style, but I don't think that the inclination to collect and live a cluttered, poetic life is that different. A flea market, you know, for me it was fun to go to the Paris flea markets because you're seeing different stuff and maybe a lot older.

Q: You mentioned your mom. I wanted to ask about that. And you told me here and I read it in your books that you learned a lot about your junk and things in life from your mom. What did she tell you? What did she teach you about the things that surround us?

Carter: Well, she never taught—I mean, lessons learned, of course, just by living with her and my dad. I guess she—I was talking about my mother the other day. She's ninety-three. My mother was like the most creative person, and she was so bold. She had no training. She wasn't a decorator. But she had an instinct for what she loved, and she—then we had beautiful American furniture and English furniture. She would find something kind of offbeat and just bring it in the house next to the beautiful French chandelier. So I guess the biggest lesson from my childhood and from my mother and my father was that they created a home. It wasn't a home of things. It was a home. It was comfortable and warm, and we were always—it was always about bringing people into our home and making them feel at home and being part of our family. And so sometimes if that meant we needed more chairs—like Thanksgiving, and we didn't have enough tables and chairs—so she brought the picnic table in. She said, *Bring the picnic table, that big old weathered picnic table.* So we brought in that and put it in the middle of this seventeenth-century kitchen. And it never left.

Q: Just stayed?

Carter: And she would put maybe pewter candlesticks on it. But it was kind of whatever you needed, you found it, and you made it part of it. But it wasn't about—there were no velvet ribbons over chairs. And we had some really beautiful—we still do have some beautiful furniture that was wrecked by people leaning back on the chairs and this and that. But she just felt, you should find things that you love, and then you should use them and make them part of your life. Use the silver every day. Let it get tarnished. But so I guess—and that's what—people always wanted to come to our house. First of all, it was an instant party because there were so many of us.

Q: There were nine of you?

Carter: Nine, yeah.

Q: Wow.

Carter: Seven girls and two boys. So there was always a lot of us there and friends. And so it was always some kind of activity, and people love that. But also there were—Mother, she loved candles and fireplaces, and she knew instinctively how to create a kind of feeling and warmth that made people just love it. And plus her personality, just everyone loved my mother. Sometimes you got jealous because all my boyfriends fell in love with her.

Q: Your husband has great energy

Carter: Oh, yeah. He's amazing—forty-four years we've been married.

Q: Does Howard get a lot of surprises?

Carter: Yes. But sometimes they're surprises that he doesn't even notice right away. *Where'd that come from?* We've been married forty-four years, so what do I need to say? But he has always just supported most of the time. All he wanted was one comfortable chair. He said, *Just give me one comfortable chair.* He's got an ugly black desk chair.

Q: That's his.

Carter: And I'm not allowed to touch that. But that's all he's cared about. Can we hang the TV up on the wall? And I get, *Don't touch my TV.* But other than that, it's like he loves it.

Q: Clearly he loves you. He loves you and this is you.

Carter: This is me, yeah. Absolutely.

Q: How much of being a southerner do you think is part of your full junk aesthetic?

Carter: Well, I would say certainly I have that thing about a tradition, a family, and the past. My father loved old—yeah, I think it's definitely in my blood, that sense of heritage and tradition. But as I've often said, there are things about my southern background that I'm not proud of. Not in my family. My family were, you know, whatever. But, yeah, definitely, coming from a place and living in old houses, and I certainly have an appreciation. I could have rejected it totally. But I didn't. I embraced it. I think particularly in the city, I'm always amazed that you walk into someone's apartment or home, and it doesn't feel personal. I'm just overboard on personal. Definitely. Definitely. I mean, I'm thinking about there's this hat rack that's been there for years that we're always tripping over, and it's falling over. And I'm thinking that, I don't know, maybe it's time to get rid of it. But it's hard for me.

Q: Do you curate what's in your home, and you move it around? Does it move around, or is it once it finds a spot, that is its home for eternity?

Carter: Well, let's walk in. I'll show you. Do I curate? I mean, we're actually getting this sofa recovered, so that's why it's sort of like this. But a lot of things have stayed in place and, as I said, I'll just add to them. I'll get a new painting and maybe move things around. But—

Q: Where is this post, this lattice from, this sort of—I don't know what to call it?

[Floor to ceiling wood posts made into a fence-like screen separating the room]

Carter: So one of the problems when we moved in here, I mean, I love cozy, small rooms, and the books are usually piled under this table that are out of control right now because we have been working on this sofa. I felt like this room was kind of like a bowling alley, and I wanted to break it up a little bit. But I didn't want to—I had to pay attention to the light because I didn't want to block the light.

Q: Right.

Carter: So these, this idea, when my mother—when we moved to the final house, the Cedar Point Farm, Mother used to collect—and this is a great story about her. She would see these. These are trap stakes that the fishermen use in the waters of Virginia to put their fish nets. They're long pine trees. Pine trees grow to these ridiculous heights. And so they take them, and they put them in the mud in the waters, and they attach their nets to them. And then when they turn to driftwood, and they're really no good anymore, they would just abandon them on the beaches. And Mother saw these things. She thought they were so beautiful. And so she started to get them and build beds out of them—

But I would say this dresser has always been here, and I always want to camouflage this. But the main pieces have kind of been here, and then I've just—actually, that piece, that dresser I got just a few years ago.

Q: Do you remember the story of every piece?

Carter: Just about. . . . This was a sampler that my friend Jan did for Howard and me when we got married. And recently my sister Carrie did these little watercolors.

And sometimes I do themes. Like here they're all like lots of—I think because the children lived here—I have sort of paintings with children and the childhood kinds of things. Yeah. So the one story I'll have to tell you, I have so many stories. I don't know. You have to ask me the questions.

Q: Found objects, objects you've just found at some shop that just you're so happy you have?

Carter: For me I guess I just love it all. Let me just think for a second. I just have to walk through. Well, I mean, I love this painting of the fried eggs. I got it in a thrift shop in Millerton for probably five dollars or something like that. I thought it was just so modern in a way. And then just so weird the way the perspective and everything is just like so totally wrong. I love the—I have a big collection of Infants of Prague, little baby Jesus. You saw a couple of them. Howard says I've got bedrooms turning into a religious shrine. I started collecting these because I think I'm a Catholic. And so I remember as a little girl always seeing the little baby Jesus dressed up like a king, and it was kind of fascinating. And when I had my junk conversion in Millerton at the Rummage Shop, the first thing I bought was this little Infant of Prague, little white Infant of Prague. And his head had been glued back on. And because his head had been glued back on, I loved him even more. I love things that have been chipped and tattered and repaired. I have things that I loved, and they've been broken, but then they're glued back together. Somehow you love them even more.

That's the thing about collecting. When you do land on one thing that you love, and for me a lot of it are these paintings, but things like the Infant of Prague, you start off, and every time you see one at a flea market, you have to have it. It's a little bit different from what you have. And then you start to get your eye—you get to be a little more discriminating. That one's not so great, so you leave that one behind.

But definitely, there is this obsession when you start to collect these things. Those Infants of Prague, I'm definitely a sentimental slob, so I know the things that mean the most to me connect me back to a person or a time in my life, my family.

Q: Does this help your creativity to have all your things around you?

Carter: Yes. Here's one of my Infants of Prague. And then this was a little statue when we had the junk shop, American Junk, and Dad came in one day and he—his office was around the corner, and he loved this little statue of George Washington. So we gave it to him, and it was on his desk. So after he died, I brought this back.

Let's sit here for a minute.

[We sit on a couch draped in textiles across from a table piled high with books and stacks underneath.]

Q: I wonder . . . you have such great style. I mean, it's your own style and personal style, but I'm imagining this is somebody else's house who doesn't have your style. It would look like a

crowded place where things don't [go]—or [work] in concert. But somehow it's all in concert. What advice would you give somebody who would aspire to be able to put it all into some sort of [order]?

Carter: I'm not so great at advice about how to do it. I guess it starts with, I mean, it starts with just learning. Listen, I'm almost seventy years old. OK. I've lived in this apartment for over forty years. So this didn't happen overnight. I look back at pictures of what this apartment looked like in the beginning, and it was much sparser. And so I filled it with things that I/ we love. So sometimes it's taking time, but I think the thing is I've never—it starts with, give yourself permission to fall in love with something. Yes, there are basics that you need—I bought a traditional sofa, but then I cover it with odd pillows and blankets. So I try to personalize it. So even though I want to have a comfortable sofa for my friends to sit on, there's a way to personalize it. I just think that you want to create some kind of your style, but it comes from you and your family and, oh, creating a certain kind of warmth. And I think eclectic is fun. I mean, I have a beautiful English bench in the hall, but then I have a junk shop pie safe that was falling apart, and I painted it green one day because it's not worth anything. And I've even thought of painting that old English bench, but I probably won't do that. . . .

I guess just in terms of the advice I would give is it's great to have a few big pieces that sort of anchor a space. Like this cupboard with all the pewter in it. I don't have a fireplace. I always wanted to have a fireplace in this apartment, but there are no fireplaces. So that's sort of my fireplace.

Q: Sure.

Carter: Because you walk in and there's like this big kind of piece to me that anchors the room, and then it's filled with pewter that my family gave us when we got married. And then I don't know. It's just an odd assortment of things that have meaning. And I love, I think, rugs. I love these kilims because I think that they have—I love the color and the pattern, and I love a mix of pattern and texture. Like this lamp next to you is this ugly owl lamp. We have this thing every Christmas called Nasty Christmas, and a lot of people play that. And everyone puts something in. And one of my nieces put that—I mean, and I didn't—when I opened it, I was so excited. And then I got this shade from Anthropologie, this funny bird shade. And then there's a beautiful old Swedish clock that doesn't work behind it. It's like such a mix of old and new. When I did my *Big City Junk* book, I was in Chicago, and I found that cityscape of Chicago, which I thought was just so gorgeous. And the tiger painting behind it I found someplace else. And the carved Native American I found in a shop down in—that was carved by this guy down in the Outer Banks. Everything is just—and when I get it, I just bring it in. Like last night I just brought some new things in. And it's so much fun to find a home for it.

Q: Do you understand at all the minimalist aesthetic?

Carter: It's hard for me. It's hard for me to understand.

Q: Do you relate at all?

Carter: Yeah, so about the same time I went to work for Ralph, so it was like over twenty-five years ago, and I thought we found another place, that I wanted to declutter this apartment because I was beginning to feel like it was just getting—I was beginning to feel like I was being possessed by my possessions, and I needed to purge. And I expressed this to some of my friends, and they just laughed. They looked at me and laughed. Are you kidding me? No, no. I'm not kidding. When we get that house in the country and I can just enjoy all my stuff up there, but I think I really want to clean out the apartment and make it—I walked into people's lofts, and there was just something really refreshing about the sparseness and how having fewer things made them maybe more important than having lots of things. And I said, *What I'd do is I'd clean everything out.* I'd leave that long table, so we'd have the dining room table. And the kids could—they were smaller then. They could ride their bikes through the house, and it would just be so much cleaner. And I think I would enjoy having two ways of living. I mean, I know I'm really fortunate because most people are lucky to have one way to live. So we got the house in the country, filled it up with more stuff, sometimes transferred, but more than likely it was like bringing stuff here. I guess I'm just—I appreciate and I walk into someone's—that lives more minimally than we do, and there's—the people have soul and character. It doesn't matter how much stuff you have. It shines through. It's just I'm not built like that. I have to have the stuff, but I appreciate and I've fantasized about living that way.

Q: You did say, and I think this is important, you don't believe in living in a mess.

Carter: No, I don't. Some people, you know, a mess is a mess is a mess, and clutter is defined in different ways. I call clutter the poetry of our lives because when I look around, I feel like—but mess is—

Q: You feel like it is . . . ?

Carter: I am very, like, every morning I have my rituals of like— you were coming. I said to Howard, *Get up. I want to make the bed.* I want the bed made, and I want the—oh, well, dishes. I don't like when there's disorder, particularly when you live with a lot of stuff. I think you have to have—you try to keep it in some kind of order. When I look around, I mean, I find—I see the stories, and I feel a kind of a poetry and memory, and I just—that's when I told you I started taking pictures of things because they speak to me. So I love having lots of things around me. They keep me sane and safe. When I come home at night, I feel like this is my home.

Q: When you find something in a store and you pick it up and you have it in your hands, is there something you should ask yourself before you buy it, or should you just go with your gut? Is it just a gut thing, or is it more than just, *Here's five dollars, I like it, I'm taking it home*?

Carter: I think it's gut. I mean, I believe when I see something that I love, sometimes maybe it's because I have that collection, so it might be tied to adding to something. But sometimes it just speaks to me, and if it's five dollars, I mean, come on—put it

in the bag. I do haggle, though, too. I think that's part of the
fun. But I would never insult someone. I try to—because I've
been in that situation myself as being a seller—I know that if
someone has put what they think is the right price, and you
kind of know, I wouldn't want to insult anyone by saying, can
you do better? . . . So sometimes it depends what the mission
is. If there's a utility and you're trying to find something, then
you have to ask some questions to be respectful of the person.
But for me when I go, I mean, what did I find yesterday?

Q: You're a hunter and a gatherer.

Carter: I am. I mean, I saw a little folding red metal chair yesterday
that was just—I love the color. I just had to have it.

**Q: Yeah. I have a milk crate from my parents' first apartment
on West Seventy-Fifth Street that is my favourite end table
in our house in Woodstock. It's always going to be there.**

Carter: Oh, that's so great. Yeah.

**Q: What's been a proud professional moment for you? We didn't
talk about your work very much.**

Carter: A proud professional moment?

**Q: People know about your professional life already, so I didn't
really want to talk about it too much. There's much to read
online. But I'm wondering if you have a proud professional
moment you think about and you're think, *Wow, I did a very
good job. That was a good thing.***

Carter: You mean like in my job at Ralph Lauren? I've been really—
I think that my work life, there are a lot of proud moments
because I've been working for a long time and for Ralph for
twenty-six years. I guess my proudest moment was the day that
I brought home the first copy of his fortieth anniversary book.
We printed it, and Lee and I had the first copy. And I was so
nervous because it was to celebrate forty years of his creativity. And though I had done it with him, I still had trepidation.
And I sat with him. Big book, 380 pages. I don't know. It's
big. And I sat with him in his office, and he just turned every
page, and I just sat there. And I think at the end, he'd written—we'd written something together about acknowledgments,

and there was something about his mother and father. And he just—Ralph's—he's a very emotional guy, and he just—he put his head down, and he's going, *Oh, my God.* And he lifted it up, and there were just like tears coming down. He knew it was a proud moment for me, too, because I think I—it was—I came to him. I always wanted to be a writer. I always liked doing books, and he allowed me in these last twenty-six years to continue to do my own books because he felt that was a part of who I was.

Q: That's great. Last question. This is the first question in my book, so hopefully this will be the last question. What is your definition of junk?

Carter: So for me junk—and not j-u-n-q-u-e or whatever, just j-u-n-k—it's a four-letter word. To me junk is—it's kind of—it's stuff. When you think of a junk store, you just think of random things that are detritus of people's lives that have been pulled together. They don't have any particular value. It's the things that when people have a yard sale, they're cleaning out. They want to get rid of this junk. I can't live with this junk anymore. But for me, to me junk is—yeah, it's the evidence of life. And some of it's—there's really bad, tacky junk, and then there's just meaningful junk. And I've always said, it's always—you give meaning. You give meaning and value to the things. So it is in the eye of the beholder for me. Junk to me is fun. It's color. It's whimsy. It doesn't cost a lot. But it's priceless.

EPILOGUE

A HUMAN BEING'S DESIRE to have his or her junk close by is nothing new. Ancient Egyptians were buried with their furniture, jewelry, and food because you never know what you might need in the afterlife.

About Need, want, and value are the pesky intangibles that lurk around the definition of junk. Need and want shape-shift depending on where perceived value decides to land. What you value may not be what the lady next door values, or even the open free market values, and that is why finding a modern universal definition of junk may not be possible. Although there will be those who try.

Just as I was wrapping up the second draft of this book I received a promotional e-mail from the behemoth junk removal chain 1-800-GOT JUNK. The subject line read, "Ways to know if it's junk or not," and the content of e-mail was a late night show–type top ten list. Initially it struck me as funny that I was getting junk e-mail from a junk removal company, and then I thought, "Well, this would have come in handy two years ago." But back before I'd taken a deep dive into American junk culture, I would not have seen the meaning in the list. It would have simply been funny and a good bit of advertising. The e-mail read:

"You know it's junk when . . . "
10. You've bought a newer version of it.
 9. You haven't used it in over a year.
 8. It's getting in the way.
 7. It's broken and can't be fixed.
 6. You're embarrassed by it.
 5. You can't remember what its purpose is.
 4. The cost of the space it takes up is more than its value to you.
 3. It has developed a strange smell, leak, or color.
 2. It is now home to woodland animals.
 1. The sight of it scares small children.

Number 1 is for comic relief, and junk can be funny, intentionally or not. Number 2 is a reality if you live in the pack rat territory. Numbers 3, 5, and 8 address the cognitive issues, such as "clutter blindness," that can come with being chronically disorganized. Numbers 4, 7, 9, and 10 speak to junk-related commercialism and the enabling of people to acquire more and more. The list codifies the way that junk has become a major influencer in the early twenty-first-century America.

While circling back to all the notes, books, articles, interviews, and events I experienced while researching this book, I realized my practical and cynical analyses of this country's relationship with stuff intersect. Because there is money to be made, junk is now a part of life, and as hard as minimalists try, I doubt the country can or will go cold turkey.

So what do we do about it? I came to a thoroughly nonprofessional, nonscientific conclusion based on what I had seen and experienced: mindfulness is the answer.

Saying the word *mindfulness* is risky. It can lead to eye rolling or slow nodding or mild confusion. But it is more than just a lofty message painted on a garden stone. Mindfulness is at the center of centuries-old religions and practices, yet it is quite useful in today's chaotic world where so much, well, *stuff* is coming at us.

I reached out to therapist Adrienne Glasser, who believes in the applicability of the practice in modern life. "The definition of mindfulness is remembering to come back to the present moment. This process is very helpful to increase awareness of habitual patterns because we can begin to see exactly how we get stuck. By seeing the true nature of our habitual patterns, we can start to become curious in the moment, about new options or new ways of being. Also being gentle with oneself with compassion is key to any change. Getting frustrated with ourselves and our 'junk' only creates internal conflict and feeling a sense of shame that can distract from what is actually possible in the moment."

Whether you have too much stuff because you don't have time to deal with it or you are extra sensitive to those who sell it or if your executive function doesn't work well, mindfulness as least gives you a chance. It also gives you a moment to stop and figure out if you really want to buy this thing or if you want to keep that object. The answer might be, *Hell yeah*, but mindfulness gives you the opportunity to say no.

Glasser thinks the original intention of mindfulness can apply directly to those who want to reassess their relationship with their stuff. She says, "Buddhist philosophy and the concept of impermanence are also very useful when it comes to the attachment we all have to our junk. If everything is temporary, then how important is it really? The over-attachment we have to our stuff is what causes so much suffering. Our appreciation of things in the moment can give us pleasure, but once we get hooked to expecting the same results from our things at a later date in the future, then we are caught. Appreciation in the moment and accepting all is impermanent allows us to feel the beauty of our things, and then gives us the ability to let them go."

I got up the courage to share my conclusion with a nationally recognized expert. Dr. David Tolin is an adjunct professor of psychiatry at Yale University School of Medicine. He was a principal investigator for the National Institute of Health. He is the author of more than 150 scientific articles. My original conversation with Dr. Tolin was about his experience with those challenged by disorganization. At the end of our straightforward interview I took my shot: I mentioned my thought that mindfulness might be the best salve for dealing with things. Dr. Tolin perked up at the idea. The exchange went like this:

> **Me: Something I've been thinking of since I've been writing this book is mindfulness. In terms of people who maybe aren't on the hoarding scale, who really aren't at that level of having some sort of mental illness, but who can't get a handle on things. Like people who have to diet their whole lives—it's about being mindful when you go to the buffet. So when it comes to buying stuff, it is being mindful when you go into Target, you know? It seems to me we've kind of lost our way when it comes to things.**
>
> Dr. Tolin: You and I are thinking along the same lines, because that's an area that I've been interested in as well. In the past one of the things that we used to spend a lot of time doing in our treatment was trying to change people's minds. . . . And you know, it's too early to make a definitive call, so I don't want to give it a clear thumbs up or thumbs down, but as the data are coming in about our treatments, I think we're seeing less and less reason to be optimistic about that particular angle. So increasingly we've been experimenting here with having people take somewhat more of a mindfulness-based approach, which is that, you know, look as you enter a situation where you have to sort and make decisions and discard objects. You're probably going to think a lot of things and you're going to feel a lot of things. Instead of struggling with those things, instead of freezing up and then trying to analyze your thoughts and decide if it's rational, and instead of trying to calm down, maybe what makes some sense would be for you to be mindful of it, recognize that you're having these thoughts and feelings and then sort of make a decision about, well, what do I want to do in the moment, not just what does this thought in my head

want me to do, or what does this emotion want me to do. And we sometimes refer to it as "being your own boss." You know, can I be my own boss rather than letting my thoughts and feelings be the boss here.

It is something I am facing as my own boss, now that this book is complete. I have a confession: as I packed up my boxes of research, I immediately put them in my basement. Yes, I put them in my basement. The last time I was down there I looked around and it looked a little full. A *lot* full. While it is nowhere near what my parents had acquired, I have a pretty impressive load down there.

So did I learn this behavior from my parents, or is it innate, or was I not mindful, or was I too busy to make decisions so I put stuff down there for later? Yes. The answer to all ove it is yes. And yes, I have junk. What will I do about it? I'm not sure. How about you?

ACKNOWLEDGMENTS

ABOUT A WEEK BEFORE Christmas 2014 I received an e-mail from Junk Busters USA Chief Junk Officer Steve Welhausen. We'd stayed in touch so initially I assumed it was a friendly holiday greeting. However the subject line read "Well that wasn't on the action list for the day . . ." Steve had cancer. Pancreatic cancer, the same disease that killed my dad and started me on this crazy journey. The e-mail was laced with humor and full of skeptical hope. But as I knew firsthand, pancreatic cancer leads to a painful decline and most people don't survive a year after this diagnosis. Steve passed away in August 2015 at age fifty-three. To tell you the kind of guy he was, during his illness he remembered my son was a Spurs fan. Through a friend he managed to get a signed basketball for my seven-year-old despite his own personal trials. That is a ball that will never be considered junk in our house. If you are inclined to continue Steve's goodwill, please think about making a donation to Pancreatic Cancer Action Network, www.pancan.org. It receives four stars, and a score of 96.84 out of 100, from the watchdog website Charity Navigator.

As always, I am grateful to my agent Jane Dystel, my editors Jerome Pohlen and Michelle Williams, and the folks at Chicago

Review Press. I'd also like to thank Silvia Peixoto, Lisa Stewart Crisp, and Scooter Alpert for their physical help and emotional support; Vicky Pasquantonio for her research skills; and my friend and three-time *Jeopardy* champion Tricia McKinney, a brilliant sounding board.

NOTES

Chapter 1: The 411 on Junk

1. Ronda Robinson, "Highway 411 Opens Up Charming, Peaceful Vistas," *Tennessee Home and Farm* website, February 15, 2011, www.tnhomeandfarm.com/travel/highway-411.

Chapter 2: Pack Rats (Human and Otherwise)

1. *The ICD Guide to Challenging Disorganization: For Professional Organizers* (St. Louis: Institute for Challenging Disorganization, 2012), 52.
2. Russell W. Belk, Melanie Wallendorf, John F. Sherry Jr., and Morris B. Holbrook, "Collecting in a Consumer Culture," *Highways and Buyways: Naturalistic Research from the Consumer Behavior Odyssey* (Provo, UT: Association for Consumer Research, 1991), 178–215.
3. "History of the wunderkammern (cabinet of curiosities)," Tate Museum, 2003, www.tate.org.uk/learn/online-resources/mark-dion-tate-thames-dig/wunderkammen.
4. Mary Beard, "Lord Elgin: Savior or Vandal?," www.bbc.co.uk, February 17, 2011.
5. Belk, *Highways and Buyways.*
6. PW Staff, "Geffen's Collection Tops in Value," *Private Weatlth*, June 6, 2013, www .Fa-mag.com.
7. Werner Muensterberger, *Collecting: An Unruly Passion* (Princeton, NJ: Princeton University Press, 1994), 3.
8. Lou Schuler, "Why Dwayne "The Rock" Johnson Is Technically Obese," *Men's Health*, April 16, 2015, www.menshealth.com/weight-loss/problem-bmi.
9. Henriette Kellum, LCSW, "Hoarding Behavior in the Elderly," Virginia Center for the Aging, Summer 2012, Volume 27, Number 3, 2.
10. Joyce Wadler, "Making Ends Meet in the Great Depression," *New York Times*, April 1, 2009, www.nytimes.com/2009/04/02/garden/02depression.html?fta=y&pagewanted=all&_r=0.
11. Dan Ariely, *Predictably Irrational: The Hidden Forces That Shape Our Decisions* (New York: Haper Perennial, 2010), 2.

12. Adam Waytz, Nicholas Epley, and John T. Cacioppo, "Social Cognition Unbound: Insights Into Anthropomorphism and Dehumanization," *Current directions in psychological science* 19.1 (2010): 58–62. PMC. Web. 26 Mar. 2015.
13. Kiara R. Timpano and Ashley M. Shaw, "Conferring humanness: The role of anthropomorphism in hoarding," *Personality and Individual Differences* 54.3 (2013): 383–388.
14. Ibid.
15. Kelly L. Haws, Rebecca Walker Naylor, Robin A. Colter, William O. Bearden, "Keeping it All Without Being Buried Alive: Understanding Product Retention Tendency," *Journal of Consumer Psychology,* Volume 22 Issue, 2 April 2012, 224–236.
16. Joshua Ackerman and Lawrence Williams, "Please Touch The Merchandise," *Harvard Business Review,* December 15, 2011, www.HBR.com.
17. Hal Arkes, Waleed Muhanna, James Wolff, "The power of touch: An examination of the effect of duration of physical contact on the valuation of objects," *Judgment and Decision Making,* Vol. 3, No. 6, August 2008, 476–482.
18. Roger Harrabin, "Magpies 'Don't Steal Shiny Objects,'" *BBC News,* August 16, 2014, www.BBC.com.
19. "Magpie steals woman's engagement ring and buries it in nest for three years," *Telegraph,* August 28, 2008, www.telegraph.co.uk/news/newstopics/howaboutthat/2637365/Magpie-steals-womans-engagement-ring-and-buries-it-in-nest-for-three-years.html.
20. Regina Macedo and Michael Mares, "Neotoma Albigula," *Mammalian Species Number 310,* American Society of Mammologists, June 30, 1998.
21. Brown calls the structure nests. Von Devender insists they be called dens or houses.
22. Elizabeth Svoboda, "For Clues on Climate, Seeing What Packrats Kept," *New York Times,* November 14, 2006.
23. Ibid.
24. Remy Melina, "Why Do Medical Researchers Use Mice?," *www.livescience.com,* November 16, 2010.

Chapter 4: From Austin to Akron

1. Sarah Coles, "First issue of *Playboy*—featuring Marilyn Monroe—set to sell for $2,700," http://money.aol.co.uk, May 1, 2015.
2. Juan Castillo, "Old story, new chapter: Austin leads U.S. in growth among biggest Metro Areas," *Austin American Statesmen,* March 15, 2013.
3. Colin Pope, "How many people move to Austin a day? Here's the official number," www.bizjournals.com, February 14, 2014.

Chapter 5: Defining Your Terms

1. The other definition of junk is the name of a Chinese flat-bottom boat.
2. Stephen Bleecker Luce, *Seamanship,* United States Naval Academy (New York: D. Van Nostrand, 1868), 50
3. Jeanne Fahnestock, *Rhetorical Style: The Uses of Language in Persuasion* (New York: Oxford University Press, 2011) 55.
4. Richard B. Kielbowwicz, "A History of Mail Classification and Its Underlying Policies and Purposes," Postal Rate Commission's Mail Reclassification Proceeding, MC95-1, July 17, 1995, 74.

5. C. P. Trussle, "Junk Mail Stirs the Ire of Congress," *New York Times*, December 27, 1954.
6. Ibid.
7. "Sanitation Department to Offer Anti Junk Mail Service," www.ny1.com, October 8, 2014.
8. Ray Everett-Church, "The Spam That Started It All," *Wired*, April 13,1999.
9. Philip Wolney, *The Truth About Heroin, Drugs and Consequences* (New York: Rosen Group Publishing, 2014), 9.
10. Ben Zimmer, "Junk," *New York Times*, December 30, 2010.

Chapter 6: Space Junk

1. "Space Debris and Human Spacecraft," www.NASA.gov, September 26, 2013.
2. *Collision Point: The Race to Clean Up Space* (Warner Brothers Films, 2014).
3. Tarik Malik, "Space Junk Forces Station Astronauts to Take Shelter in Lifeboats," *Space. com*, March 24, 2012.
4. "Limiting Future Collision Risk to Spacecraft: An Assessment ofNASA's Metreoroid and Orbital Debris Programs," The National Academies, Washington DC, 2011.
5. *Collision Point: The Race to Clean Up Space* (Warner Brothers Films, 2014).

Chapter 7: Junk Vets

1. Susannah Breslin, "How to Get People to Click on Your Links," *Forbes*, August 7, 2012, www.forbes.com/sites/susannahbreslin/2012/08/07/how-to-get-people-to-click-your-link.
2. Video interview with Jerry Flanagan, J Dog Franchise Official, www.youtube.com, April 22, 2013.
3. Scott Keller, *Marine Pride: A Salute to America's Elite Fighting Force* (New York: Kensington Publishing, 2004), 11.
4. Peter A. Gudmundsson, "The Hire More Veterans Act is misguided. There is no veteran's unemployment crisis," *Washington Post*, January 15, 2015.
5. Lilia Fernández, *Brown in the Windy City: Mexicans and Puerto Ricans in Postwar Chicago* (Chicago: University of Chicago Press, 2012), 2.
6. Louise Kerr, "The Mexicans in Chicago," *Illinois History Teacher-Volume 6*, (1991), 62–75.

Chapter 8: Business and Show Business

1. Ashley Lutz, "The Container Store Trains Workers to Ask This Question So You'll Spend More Money," www.BusinessInsider.com, February 19, 2015.
2. Gaile Robinson, "Store Founders Cannot Contain Zeal to Order Lives," *Fort Worth Telegram/Tuscaloosa News*, May 7, 2000.
3. Ben Doherty, "G20: As Brisbane prepares to host the 2014 summit, your questions answered," www.theguardian.com, November 10, 2014.
4. Eve Zaunbrecher, "Too Much Is Not Enough: Attitudes Toward Accumulation and Hoarding in Japan," Victoria and Albert Museum, www.vam.ac.uk, December 6, 2014.
5. Doug Rossinow, *The Reagan Era: A History of the 1980s* (New York: Columbia University Press, 2015), 125.
6. Ibid, 47.
7. Lynn Rosellini, "First Lady Tells Critics: 'I am Just Being Myself,'" *New York Times*, October 13, 1981.

8. Lizabeth Cohen, "A Consumers' Republic: The Politics of Mass Consumption in Post-war America," *Journal of Consumer Research*, Vol. 31, June 2004, dash.harvard.edu /bitstream/handle/1/4699747/cohen_conrepublic.pdf?sequence=2.
9. Sam Hornblower, "Walmart & China: A Joint Venture," *Frontline*, www.pbs.org, November 23, 2004.
10. California Cable and Telecommunications Association, "The History of Cable: 1980s," www.calcable.org/learn/history-of-cable.
11. The Cable Communications Act of 1984, Public Law 98-549, October 30, 1984.
12. From PBS Broadcast.
13. Erin Murray, "Exclusive Home Tour with Mike Wolfe," www.Nashvillelifestyles.com.
14. The NSGCD Clutter Hoarding Scale Official Organizational Assessment Tool, 2003, National Study Group on Chronic Disorganization, 6.
15. Jane Collingwood, "The Genetics of Compulsive Hoarding," www.psychcentral.com.

Chapter 10: Annie Haul

1. Hillary Lake, "Rats invade NE Portland street; neighbors fed up," www.Katu.com, April 10, 2014.
2. State of Oregon Plaintiff v. Norman D. Wicks, Sr. and Norman D. Wicks, Jr. Defendants, Case No. Z711742 & Z711743, Opinion and Order Granting Defendents' Motion to Hold Portland's Campng Ban Unconstitutional, September 27, 2000.

Chapter 11: All You Need Is Less

1. Tom Ashbrook, "Big Potential for Tiny Houses," *On Point*, WBUR/NPR, March 4, 2015, https://onpoint.wbur.org/2015/03/04/tiny-houses-micro-apartments.
2. Kirsten Dirksen, "Tiny House Pioneer Jay Shafer, Thinking Beyond Trailer Parks," January 2014, www.faircompanies.com/videos/view/tiny-house-pioneer-jay-shafer -thinking-beyond-trailer-parks.
3. Margot Adler, "Behind the Ever Expanding American Dream," *All Things Considered*, NPR, July 4, 2006, www.npr.org/templates/story/story.php?storyId=5525283.
4. Harriet Edelson, "Brian Levy Seeks to Spark a Revolution with His Innovative Micro House," *Washington Post*, December 4, 2014.
5. Natalie Shutler, "Home Shrunken Home," *New York Times*, February 20, 2015.
6. Sam Frizell, "The New American Dream Is Living in a City, Not Owning a House in the Suburbs," *Time*, April 25, 2104, http://time.com/72281/american-housing.
7. Kirsten Dirksen, "Tiny House Pioneer Jay Shafer, Thinking Beyond Trailer Parks," January 2014, www.faircompanies.com/videos/view/tiny-house-pioneer-jay-shafer -thinking-beyond-trailer-parks.

Chapter 14: The Repair Café

1. Sally McGrane, "An Effort to Bury a Throwaway Culture One Repair at a Time," *New York Times*, May 9, 2012.
2. Molly Scot Cato, "The Paradox of Green Keynesianism," in *The Post-Growth Project: How the End of Economic Growth Could Bring a Fairer and Happier Society*, ed. John Blewitt and Ray Cunningham (London: London Publishing, 2014).
3. Kyle Weins, "The New MacBook Pro: Unfixable, Unhackable, Untenable," *Wired*, June 14, 2012, www.wired.com/2012/06/opinion-apple-retina-displa.